Ultimate
MARTIAL ARTS
ENCYCLOPEDIA

ULTIMATE
MARTIAL ARTS
ENCYCLOPEDIA

THE BEST OF
INSIDE
KUNG-FU

Edited by
John R. Little and Curtis F. Wong

CB
CONTEMPORARY BOOKS

Library of Congress Cataloging-in-Publication Data

Ultimate martial arts encyclopedia : the best of Inside kung-fu / edited by
John R. Little and Curtis F. Wong.
        p.   cm. — (Inside kung-fu magazine)
        ISBN 0-8092-2835-1
        1. Martial arts.   2. Kung fu.   I. Little, John R., 1960–
II. Wong, Curtis.   III. Inside kung-fu magazine series.
GV1101.U58   2000
796.8—dc21   99-89715

Cover design by Todd Petersen
Cover and interior photographs courtesy of CFW Enterprises
Interior design by Amy Yu Ng

Published by Contemporary Books
A division of NTC/Contemporary Publishing Group, Inc.
4255 West Touhy Avenue, Lincolnwood (Chicago), Illinois 60712-1975 U.S.A.
Copyright © 2000 by John R. Little and Curtis Wong
Printed in the United States of America
International Standard Book Number: 0-8092-2835-1
00 01 02 03 04 VL 19 18 17 16 15 14 13 12 11 10 9 8 7 6 5 4 3 2 1

This book is dedicated to all those who seek the best within themselves and who realize that victory over others is never a substitute for victory over oneself.

Contents

PART TWO: TECHNIQUES

PART THREE: BEYOND THE FIST

ULTIMATE MARTIAL ARTS ENCYCLOPEDIA

PART ONE

Histories and Traditions

Dan Inosanto Remembers the History of Jeet Kune Do

Alan Sutton

Learn how an obscure hideaway on the outskirts of Los Angeles's Chinatown became the proving ground for Bruce Lee's martial-inspired philosophy.

In 1966 Bruce Lee had officially opened his third—and his last—martial arts *kwoon*. He chose to set up shop on the first floor of an innocuous two-story edifice adjacent to Los Angeles's Chinatown. Like its predecessors in Seattle and Oakland, the indifferent, gray brick structure bore no identifying marks or signs. To ensure anonymity, he saw to it that the windows were painted over with red enamel. The casual passerby sauntering down College Street noticed nothing out of the ordinary about number 628. The majority of traffic to and fro consisted of befuddled baseball fans who had lost their way to Dodger Stadium, a few blocks away.

Absolutely no visitors were allowed inside the Jun Fan Gung Fu Institute. He purposely limited enrollment to a select cadre of martial arts diehards and a few high rollers he knew in the entertainment industry. That was February. In May, satisfied that things were running smoothly, he transferred the teaching responsibilities to Dan Inosanto—the most unabashed diehard of them all.

"Most instructors don't have time for them-selves—that's why Bruce didn't want to teach in Chinatown," Inosanto explains, digging back through the years. "He started me off there, watching for the first three months to be sure that I was headed in the right direction. But after three months, he would come in once a week or so and check it out. He said that he didn't want to teach because, 'I'd cheat my own body. I could be using this time to develop my own body.'"

No, Bruce Lee wasn't selfish—just realistic. Although he was only 26, he had by then attained such an amazing level of proficiency that he was practically untouchable. There was simply no one around good enough to give him a meaningful workout. In lieu of a comparably matched opponent he was forced to train alone against a veritable army of mechanical devices and traditional boxing apparatuses, which completely overran his garage. He also kept abreast of all the up-to-the-minute breakthroughs in physical culture, including isometrics, isotonics, and nutri-tional hints. Aware that probably the best all-around collection of martial artists in the area could be found at the Jun Fan Institute, he dropped in regularly to maintain the keen edge of his already unrivaled skills. These visits also served a higher purpose; he was able to subject his most recent discoveries in the art of self-defense to the acid test—free sparring.

At the time he opened in Los Angeles, Lee was anticipating an acting career. The year before, he had returned to America following his father's funeral in Hong Kong. Accompanied by his wife Linda and their six-month-old son, Brandon, he came back to follow up on a part as Charlie Chan's son in an upcoming series to be called *Number One Son*. Soon after his arrival, he was informed that the series was definitely no go.

Another role was still in the offing; Inosanto, however, notes, "The *Green Hornet* series hadn't started yet, so he didn't have a job. Then he said, 'Let's get a

bunch of guys and work out.' I said, 'Can I get a bunch of my Kenpo buddies together?' That's how it started out. He was probably bored not doing anything. At first, it was mainly for fun. During that time we were training in Chinatown right behind Wayne Chan's Pharmacy—but not in a school. It was a room that is now a movie theater. Later on he decided it would be nice to bring in some money, so we opened the school."

For a time, when work was scarce, the unem-ployed thespian even considered a nationwide chain of Gung-fu schools. "In March of 1966 he was going to open up nationwide, starting with the Chinatown school in Los Angeles. But he only had that thought for a month. He came back in April and said, 'Nope, that's not it. That's not the way to bring out the art,' Inosanto remembers.

The scheme resurfaced later, fleetingly, as a means of exploiting his spiraling Kato fame. "More and more as the series progressed, he was approached by peo-ple to open up a string of 'Kato's Gung-Fu Schools.' But he didn't do it. He said, 'I'm going to continue with this Kato thing, but I'm not going to open up nationwide.' He told me, 'Don't do any advertising around the school,'" says Inosanto, adding, "He didn't feel that he could truly represent the art that way."

Truthfully, Lee never intended to make a living by teaching Gung fu. His unwavering belief in the individual and that each student deserved to be taught on a one-to-one basis would have meant that he was doomed to eternal poverty—something he *knew* wasn't meant for *him*.

"Bruce hated big classes. He felt that to maintain quality, teaching had to be one-on-one. And he was right. It's just like a boxing trainer: he can maybe train two or three at one time, but that's it. He has to know his fighter emotionally; he has to know his fighter's emotional hang-ups. 'Does he get scared before a fight? And if so, what can I do for him? How can I get him out of that state? Is he excitable? Is he calm? Is he lethargic?' In other words, you have to know the person inside and out," declares Inosanto, elaborating on why Lee ultimately rejected the "franchise" concept.

Bruce Lee began studying Gung fu as a teenager. At 22, he authored a unique text on the subject, which he titled *Chinese Gung Fu: The Philosophical Art of Self-Defense*, reflecting his preoccupation with spiritual as well as physical development. When the time came for him to pass his art along to others, he had no misgivings concerning his ability to do it better than anybody else. He was good and he knew it. Therefore, he gleefully thumbed his nose at tradition, cast the "book" out the window, and in the meantime revolutionized the martial arts—catapulting them into worldly prominence.

Understandably, the profile within the Chinatown school can be described as "loose." Like most young people, Bruce Lee was fond of music; he was not opposed to having the radio blaring or records spinning during class. The fact is, this superreal congregation of martial artists would warm up to the catchy theme from *Hawaii Five-O* (while also developing rhythm—a cornerstone in Lee's theory of martial arts). He was definitely an iconoclast. There was almost a Sawyer-esque aura surrounding the *kwoon*.

For instance, once class was under way, all doors were securely locked. "He once told me, 'If knowledge is power, let's pass it on discriminately,'" recalls Inosanto. After that, a tardy member who wished admittance had to give the secret knock before he could enter.

Nevertheless, the workouts themselves were far from fun and games. Revealing one of Lee's few compromises with the "classical mess," Inosanto states, "I never called him Bruce. In and out of class, I would always refer to him as *sifu*." Jerry Poteet, who still bears his original Jun Fan Institute membership card number 102, reveals why Lee put up with what he called such "pageantry." "He liked that because it showed that you meant business. He was the instructor, and you were going to go in there and get down to business. One time he got up in front of the class and said, 'I know that socially a lot of us in here are friends; and outside the school, I'm Bruce. But in here you call me sifu. Because of the informality, there has to be some discipline. If this school was in China, there would be a few people in here now missing their front teeth.'"

Yet there was another side of Bruce Lee that most people never glimpsed. "I remember one episode in class where we had this kicking set—not a kata, but a kicking exercise. We had a particularly clumsy guy doing it at the time; he looked really terrible. And one of the other students was laughing. Bruce just looked over and said, 'If you can do it better, come up here right now; or else wipe that smile off your face, and I want it silent from now on.' That was pretty good because although the guy was really clumsy, he was trying the best he could—and the other guy was laughing. Bruce didn't like that. As talented as he was, he respected you for your ability. He hated what he called BSing; that he couldn't stand. But he always respected his students. He realized our capabilities and shortcomings," Inosanto praises. Poteet adds, "One time I was short of money and I felt badly because I could not pay. Then he wrote me a letter saying, 'Come on in; forget all about it until you can.' He said, 'You're sincere, that's what counts.'"

"The emphasis," Inosanto goes on to say, "was on physical fitness. I think that's what weeded out a lot of people. In other words, you had no business being in a martial art if you weren't physically fit. He used to say that if you didn't have the basic requirements—if you couldn't do at least thirty sit-ups and if you couldn't run a mile without stopping—you had no business being in this class. Of course, he'd slack off in certain areas. For example, if you didn't have the flexibility, he'd say, 'OK. You work on it.' The thing that we liked about him was that everything was individual. Everyone had his own program. He took the time for everyone. That's why he didn't like big classes."

Lee was a stickler for conditioning because of an unforgettable incident that occurred in Oakland, California, a number of years earlier. There was a challenge that Lee accepted, and the outcome, as it was originally reported, could be characterized as a "draw" at best. Although his mediocre showing was due in a large measure to his thick-headed adherence to his particular style at the time, Wing Chun, which was ill-suited to his opponent's Choy Li Fut techniques, Lee confessed to Inosanto afterward: "I was tired, Dan. I was so tired I could not even punch him." Shortly thereafter, Lee scrapped the traditional Wing Chun style he had been addicted to in favor of his own pulverizingly modified system.

In attempting to get his point across, Lee was not above resorting to such Machiavellian ploys as "reverse" psychology. "Our training was both physical and psychological. He taught us how to be mentally prepared for combat. That was his big thing—the mental attitude. We formed a high opinion of ourselves; that's what he wanted. And then he would tear us down so we wouldn't get too cocky. It was a constant flow of yin and yang," Inosanto muses.

"I'm very passive," Inosanto smiles, "at least I was until I ran into Bruce. I wasn't aggressive; I'd seldom speak up in a crowd. He changed my personality. To cite a case, once when we were side-kicking he said, 'Dan, throw a side kick.' I threw a side kick, and he said, 'No! No! You're just posing. Throw me another,

like you mean it.' So I kicked again—this time he was holding a bag. He said, 'No, Dan, kick it *hard*. Think of something you hate.' I kicked it without thinking of something I hated. Then he nonchalantly walked over and—*whap*—right across my face, he slapped me! For a second I forgot he was Bruce Lee, and I came toward him. He laughed, 'OK, *now* kick the bag. That's what I want!' And I kicked it, and he was right."

Most classical Gung-fu systems insist that the beginning student spend anywhere from the first six months to a year poised in the rudimentary stances or "horses." This is required in order to build strength, instill patience, and check the student's sincerity. Beyond this, their practical application is a topic of much debate. Bruce Lee termed such ancient rituals "exercises in futility." He took nothing for granted.

Whereas the majority of practitioners sheepishly imbibe their instructor's words as if they were ambrosia spilled from heaven, Lee scrutinized whatever he was asked to do and then demanded, "How come?" Predictably, the reply was, "That's how it's been done for the past thousand years." Not good enough for Lee.

Still smarting from the drudgery he himself had endured for many years, Lee was determined to make things more utilitarian as well as stimulating for his followers. Showcasing his typically wry sense of humor, Lee once quipped, "If you were to teach basketball like they teach Gung fu, students wouldn't have a basketball in their hands for one year."

"You see," Inosanto begins, "people look at a man and say, 'Gee, look at his form—he's a good martial artist.' But Bruce didn't measure that way. The only thing that counted with Bruce was, Is it workable? Can it be used? Bruce was the kind of person who questions everything. That's why he grew—because he questioned." Picking up the ball, Poteet concludes, "He admired that quality in other people. And when you started pushing him to answer, that's when he excelled. He loved it when you asked questions, because it made *him* think, it made *him* do problem solving. That's why he called Jeet Kune Do problem solving."

Another basic tenet of Jeet Kune Do was *self-knowledge*, which Lee equated with creativity and, ultimately, enlightenment. In short, he encouraged his students to question so that they would discover new ways of training, learning, and, ideally, living. Interestingly, Lee arrived at the above axiom partly as a result of attending acting classes, which came with the long-awaited Kato role in the autumn of 1966. According to Inosanto, "He said, 'If you want to improve at this, Dan, you have to be creative. You have to constantly break tradition.' I think he got this from the Stanislavsky philosophy of method acting. 'Look at this guy [Stanislavsky],' Bruce said. 'If he would have been a martial artist, he would have been fantastic. Here's a guy who says something that I believe in: you constantly break tradition to improve it.' In other words, it's a continual process of revision. He also gave me *The Book of Changes, I-Ching*. In the book, he underlined a whole chapter on creativity. It goes something like: 'If you don't get it from yourself, where can you get it?'"

Lee never limited himself to martial arts handbooks; he drew from every available source at his disposal. "Erudite" would be a fitting epithet, as anyone who has read his books (along with the already noted text, he coauthored a Wing Chun book with his close friend, James Lee, in order to raise money for expensive cobalt treatments that the latter was undergoing at the time) will attest.

"The school opened in February of 1966, but the term *Jeet Kune Do* was not developed until 1967,"

Inosanto continues. "By this, I mean the *term Jeet Kune Do*—the principle behind it. I know it was 1967 when he came up with the term, but he was already JKD by the end of 1966, November or December. All the students could tell that something was going on inside of him. He forsook his modified form of Wing Chun, which we felt was a really good technique. I still think that it was very good because it had a lot of truth in it. But you could see that he was progressing. He went on this thing with the body. 'Don't look for secret moves,' he used to tell me. 'Don't look for secret movements. If you're always hunting for secret techniques, you're going to miss it.' He said, 'It's you, Dan; it's your body that's the key.'

"A lot of people think that JKD is something metaphysical, but it's not. It's really quite simple. Basically, I think this is what it is: JKD is Bruce Lee's philosophy, based on things he observed to be true."

Today, 628 College Street houses a sewing factory. The windows are no longer covered by red paint, and the interior is clearly visible—with nary a trace remaining of its former tenants. Gone is the imitation tombstone that once greeted students with the famous inscription: "In memory of a once fluid man crammed and distorted by the classical mess."

This material originally appeared in the August 1988 issue of Inside Kung-Fu Presents.

The Five Major Styles
of Tai Chi Chuan

Dr. Paul Lam

What is tai chi? Tai chi is the most popular Chinese internal martial art style. Internal styles place emphasis on breathing and the mental component of their training. Execution of the movements is generally soft.

Many other martial arts concentrate on the external form and feature vigorous body movements, dynamic kicks, and harsh punching actions. In contrast, tai chi consists of fluid, gentle, graceful, circular movements. The deep and slow breathing aids visual and mental concentration, relaxes the body, and allows the life force or *chi* (a life energy inside the body) to flow unimpeded throughout the body. These techniques help integrate the mind and body and allow the achievement of total harmony of the inner and outer selves. A person living in harmony is more likely to be happy, fulfilled, and healthy.

The Different Styles

What kind of benefits will you gain from knowing the martial arts origins and the intrinsic intention of tai chi? It is helpful to think of it this way: if you are learning tai chi and your teacher only shows you the movements (e.g., put your left foot to the left and bring your left hand up, in the case of ward-off Yang style), you are simply following the movements. Subsequently, you will only learn the movements. This is good in the sense that as you are moving your body, you are exercising and being active.

However, if you learn how to keep your body upright, maintain balance, transfer weight from the left to the right leg, step to the left, then transfer weight as you ward off, this training becomes more internal. Plus, you will understand the movements better and learn them more quickly. Given that you spend the same amount of time, you will benefit more.

Your understanding and interest in the art will grow if your teacher explains when and how you incorporate your breathing, how to control the flow of chi, how to deliver internal force, and how to discover the meaning behind martial art movement. You will also build a solid foundation and enhance your potential for progress.

To learn the internal component of the movements, you need to understand the intrinsic martial art intention. This does not mean you need to apply tai chi for self-defense, but understanding the internal component is an essential step in the evolution process. In fact, discovering the magical health benefits of tai chi depends on how well you practice it. Understanding the general characteristics and historical backgrounds of different styles will help you understand the inner meaning of tai chi.

Knowing Different Styles

It is widely accepted that all tai chi styles follow similar essential principles. Knowing the characteristics of different styles, however, can be useful because

- All styles have unique characteristics. Certain styles are more appropriate for certain people. Choose the most suitable style so that you can

Dr. Paul Lam and Master Peter Wu practicing sparring using Chen style. Wu is a disciple of the late Grand Master Hong Junsheng.

Dr. Paul Lam performs "falling lotus" from Chen style during the Chinese National Competition Forms.

Professor Kan Gui Xiang from Beijing University of Physical Education, creator of Chen Style Chinese National Competition Forms, performing "leisurely tying coat, Chen style," which is closer to a combat posture.

progress more quickly. For example, Chen style can be more interesting to an advanced martial artist.

- Different styles have different approaches to the same forms. Learn to use the different approaches to solve a difficult problem. Like looking at a problem from a different angle, using a different approach can give you a better and sometimes quicker solution. Also, it can give you a more complete understanding of a problem. For example, the "single whip" of Sun style appears simple compared with the Wu version. This can help students appreciate how to mobilize the inner force by eliminating confusion.

- Knowing different styles broadens your horizon. Learning different skills from different styles, which are based on similar principles, can give you more depth and increase your level of skill.

The Five Major Styles

Outlined below are the five major styles in chronological order as accepted by most practitioners. It must be emphasized that being the oldest style does not imply it is the best. In fact, older things are not necessarily better. Tai chi was certainly not created by an incredibly wise person who designed a perfect set of forms like a square box that does not change.

Rather, tai chi is a vast reservoir of knowledge accumulated throughout the centuries by many dedicated individuals. The reservoir is so vast that no one can learn it all and no one can really say he or she is the best. Different styles have different characteristics and are unique and valuable in their own ways.

Chen Style

In the 1670s, Chen Wangting, a retired army general of the Chen village in Henan province, developed several tai chi routines, which included the old frame

Master Kam Lau Fung, gold-medal winner of the 1997 United World Kung-Fu/Wushu Championship in Orlando, Florida, and the Fourth International Tai Chi Competition in Beijing in 1997. He is performing "cover with hand and punch with fist."

Yang style tai chi swordplay as shown by the author.

form still practiced today. He assimilated into ancient martial art routines the ancient philosophical techniques of *daoyin* and *tuna*, together with the use of clarity of consciousness as developed in the practice of Taoism.

Daoyin is the concentrated exertion of inner force, while tuna is a set of deep-breathing exercises that in more recent times have been developed into the popular *chi kung* deep-breathing exercises. By combining the martial art exercises with the practice of daoyin and tuna, tai chi became a complete system of exercise in which the practitioner's mental concentration, breathing, and actions were closely connected. This paved the way for its use as an ideal form of exercise for all aspects of health care.

Chen style was kept almost exclusively within the village. It is said the clan only taught daughters-in-law and not their daughters. Divorce didn't exist in those days, so masters knew their secrets were safe. In the early nineteenth century, the highly acclaimed and respected Chen Fake began teaching tai chi in Beijing. He was universally well liked, made no enemies, and taught in Beijing until his death in 1957.

Chen style is characterized by an emphasis of spiral force, and its movements are close to those of the martial arts. Every move, no matter how small or innocent in appearance, has an effective application. Slow movements intermix with fast, and hard movements complement soft. It is also characterized by explosive power and a low stance. Chen style's prac-

Master Peter Wu performing "leisurely tying coat" from the Hoa style, which indicates the closer-to-the-body positions.

tical and effective techniques make it more enticing to younger people.

Yang Style

Yang is the most popular tai chi style. Yang Lu Chan (1799–1872) created it in the early nineteenth century. Legend has it that Yang was so eager to learn the art, he pretended to be a beggar and fainted at the front door of the village elder. He was rescued and accepted as a servant in the Chen household. Yang learned the art by peering through a crack in a wall while others practiced late at night. He soon became a highly skilled practitioner. When he was discovered, the village elder was so impressed with his skill that he

formally accepted him as a student. Yang later developed his own style, which he taught to a great number of people, including members of the imperial court. Yang's movements are gentle, graceful, effective for health promotion, easy to learn, and suitable for almost all ages and physical conditions.

Wu Style (a.k.a. Hoa Style)

This is different from the next Wu style in Chinese characters, so to avoid confusion I will call it by its other name—Hoa style. It was created by Wu Yuxiang (1812–1880) and passed to Hoa Weizheng (1849–1920), who significantly contributed to its creation.

Hoa is not a well-known style. Its creators studied both the Yang and Chen styles. The style is characterized by slow and loose, close-knit movements. Great emphasis is placed on the internal force, or internal power, and correct positioning. The external movements and the transference of substantial and insubstantial are completely controlled by internal power. The style also features fullness of substance.

When looking at a high-level practitioner, the style appears larger and more rounded, as though its inner power has extended further than the outward physical shape. Hoa style has very stringent requirements; it is usually harder to learn and progress in this style. The advantages are that it is challenging, deep, powerful, and effective in martial arts.

Wu Style

Wu Yuxiang (1812–1880) created this Wu style, characterized by softness and with an emphasis on redirecting incoming force. Its movements are relaxed, natural, closer to the trunk of the body, and nimble. It is full of hand techniques, especially for push-hands (a gentle two-person exercise used as an alternative to sparring) exercises. Wu style tends to have a slightly forward-leaning posture.

This Wu style is easier to learn, pleasant to look at, and does not necessarily require strong lower limbs. It is suitable for almost anyone; even people who have a leg disability can learn it. In fact, one famous Wu style master had a limp from a congenital disability. And since little space is needed, the style is ideal for city dwellers.

Sun Style

Sun style is the youngest of the major styles. It was created by Sun Lu Tang (1861–1932), whose daughter Sun Jian Yun is still living in Beijing. Sun was a well-known exponent of the *xingyiquan* and *baguazhang* (two famous internal martial art styles) before he learned tai chi. In 1912 Sun ran into Hoa Weizheng (see Hoa style), who was sick. Without knowing who Hoa was, Sun kindly took care of Hoa by finding him a hotel to rest at and a good doctor to treat him. After Hoa recovered from his illness, he stayed in Sun's house and taught him tai chi.

It was said that Sun only spent a short time learning from Hoa and subsequently incorporated his expertise in xingyiquan and baguazhang into his new style. Therefore, Sun style may not resemble other tai chi styles, although some movements could be mistaken for the older Hoa style.

Sun style is characterized by lively steps. Whenever one foot moves forward or backward, the other

foot follows. Its movements flow smoothly like water or clouds. Whenever you turn, there is an opening and closing movement, which is a powerful chi kung exercise. Sun style also features a high stance.

On the positive side, Sun style contains plenty of chi kung, which is effective for relaxation and healing. The higher stance makes it more suitable for older people to learn. Interestingly, from an outward appearance Sun style is not like Chen style. But when you reach a high level, you can appreciate the many similarities of the styles' inner components.

Conclusion

Although this overview contains the five major styles of tai chi, many lesser-known internal arts are being practiced around the world. The numerous styles and forms in tai chi can be overwhelming to stylists of all ages. You should view this choice as an opportunity to expand your repertoire, rather than as a daunting task that will lead to confusion.

Studying tai chi can be simpler and easier if you define your aims and objectives, investigate what each style has to offer, find a qualified teacher, and do everything you can to get the most out of the experience.

Dr. Paul Lam is a tai chi teacher and physician based in Sydney, Australia. His students have competed successfully at the international level. Dr. Lam was the first person from a Western country to win a gold medal in the International Competition Forms (42 steps) in China. This information originally appeared in the September 1999 issue of Inside Kung-Fu.

Aikido
The Way of Harmony

John Stevens

*A*iki, the first half of the word *Aikido*, consists of the two Chinese characters *ai*, meaning "to come together, to blend, to join, to harmonize," and *ki*, a word with manifold meanings that include (as in this case) "spirit" and "disposition." Aiki has always been a central theme of Asian philosophy, but Morihei Ueshiba, founder of Aikido, declared: "My interpretation of aiki is much broader than those of the past." Ueshiba defined aiki in the following ways:

- Aiki is the universal principle that brings all things together; it is the optimal process of unification and harmonization that operates in all realms, from the vastness of space to the tiniest atoms.

- Aiki reflects the grand design of the cosmos; it is the life force, an irresistible power that binds the material and spiritual aspects of creation. Aiki is the flow of nature.

- Aiki signifies the union of body and spirit and is a manifestation of that truth. Further, aiki enables us to harmonize heaven, earth, and humankind as one.
- Aiki means "to live together in harmony," in a state of mutual accord. Aiki is the ultimate social virtue. It is the power of reconciliation—the power of love.

Ueshiba's vision of aiki closely corresponds to the notions of *integritas* (wholeness) and *consonantia* (harmony) in Western philosophy. Integration—between body and spirit, self and other, humankind and nature, truth and beauty—is a condition that all people should strive for; and integrity is a moral state as well: those who are whole can act in the best and fairest manner.

Consonantia (*harmonia* in Greek) is "a fitting together." The wise ones of the West, too, perceived the harmony of the spheres and the process in which all elements orchestrate themselves into the greater whole. As Hippocrates wrote, "All things are in sympathy." In present-day physics this is stated as, The amount of positive energy in the universe is exactly equal to the amount of negative energy; the universe is, and always has been, a perfectly balanced energy system.

The intuition that "all things are in sympathy" was a common belief in both the East and West. Tragically, modern civilization has been poisoned by the misguided contention of some that life is nothing more than an intense rivalry between species and only the fittest can survive. Life is always a trial, and people need to be physically and mentally fit to get along. This is one of the reasons why people practice aikido, but the pernicious view that existence is a constant battle against foes who must be totally subjugated or annihilated has directly caused much of the exploitation and destruction of both humankind and the environment that has violently surfaced in the nineteenth and twentieth centuries.

The emphasis on being the "victor," whatever the means and whatever the cost, has largely obliterated the noble ideal of "sportsmanship" in contemporary athletics. Ueshiba wrote, "Sports nowadays are only good for physical exercise; they do not train the whole person. The practice of aiki, on the other hand, fosters valor, sincerity, fidelity, goodness, and beauty, as well as making the body strong and healthy." In traditional aikido there are no formal contests, and thus no winners and no losers. This position is very difficult for certain people to accept, and even some of Ueshiba's closest disciples disagreed with the master on this point; they insisted on establishing some sort of competition, either in the form of judo-style matches or Olympic-style point-system contests.

Ueshiba, though, maintained to the end that aiki is cooperation. In each aikido exercise, partners take turns being the attacker and the defender, the winner and the loser. In this manner, a trainee learns much from experiencing both sides of the aikido equation. Onlookers (and sometimes students themselves) often remark, "Aikido techniques only work if your partner cooperates." That is exactly the point. Rinjiro Shirata

Sensei used to explain aiki thus: "Living in harmony, let us join hands and reach the finish line together."

Aiki, as a healing agent, connotes resuscitation and revitalization. The best doctors in any culture understand that a proper diagnosis largely depends on being in tune with the patient in order to sense what really ails him or her. Then an appropriate remedy can be suggested. (In the old days in Japan, a type of aiki was used to resuscitate people knocked unconscious in accidents or in comas from illnesses.) Ueshiba often spoke of the health-giving, restorative properties of aiki training: "After a good workout, you should have more energy than you began with!"

There is another meaning of aiki that is central to true harmony: the consummate union of a man and a woman—a blissful state of complete physical and spiritual intimacy. (In Chinese sex manuals, aiki was the term used for the ultimate sexual experience.) The natural and pure integration of male and female principles is at the heart of all creation. Libido should not be mistaken for mere concupiscence but rather should be understood as a sincere yearning for integration and fulfillment. Male and female remain barren until

united; the desire to cleave together as one, to restore the primordial unity, is a key goal of aikido (and all other arts).

Similarly, there is a kind of aiki embryology: the ideal child is conceived when both parents are in total harmony, truly as one in body and soul. If the parents remain in accord during the pregnancy, the fetus is nurtured with aiki, a quality that beats in the mother's heart and flows in her blood. Technically, aiki is "perfect timing." In the dojo one attempts to blend smoothly with the attacking force, applying just the right amount of movement, balance, and power. In everyday existence, one tries similarly to fit right in, responding to the various challenges of life with a keen aiki sense.

Do, the second half of the word aikido, symbolizes both a particular "path" that one treads and a universal "way" of philosophical principles. Those who walk the path of aikido wear a special type of outfit, meditate in a certain manner, and practice distinctive forms. This is the cultural path of aikido, the context of practice based on the ideals and classical techniques of the founder, Morihei Ueshiba. The way of aikido involves the broader spectrum of life—how people interact with other human beings outside the narrow world of the dojo, relate to society as a whole, and deal with nature.

In this sense, aikido is tantra, a knitting together of the macro- and microcosms. The basic truth of tantra is, "All that exists in the universe exists within one's own body. What is here is there; what is not here is nowhere." In Western gnosticism this is expressed as, "When you make the above like the below, and when you make the male and female as one, you will enter the Kingdom" (Gospel of Thomas), or more succinctly, "As above, so below." In Ueshiba's idiom this is stated as *ware soku ucha*, "I am (we are) the universe!" By cultivating their individual bodies and souls through aikido practice, by acquiring true perception and creating real acts, people learn to live cosmically.

Aikido is also yoga, a "yoke" that unifies, conjoins, and harnesses people to higher principles. The eight limbs of classical yoga parallel the teachings of Ueshiba's classical aikido:

1. *Yama* means "ethics," the primary of which is *ahimsa*, "nonviolence." In Ueshiba's words, "Those who seek competition are making a grave mistake. To smash, injure, or destroy is the worst sin a human being can commit."

2. *Niyama*, "discipline," in aikido is termed *tanren*, "forging." "The purpose of training is to tighten up the slack, toughen the body, and polish the spirit."

3. *Asana* refers to "graceful postures." Sometimes it is helpful for trainees to think of aikido movements not as lethal martial art techniques but as asana, physical postures that link the practitioner to higher truths. Like asana, aikido techniques are painful and difficult in the beginning, but eventually they become easier, more stable, and agreeable. Indeed it is said in yoga that "the asana is perfect when the effort to attain it disappears," and "one who masters the asana conquers the three worlds." Ueshiba taught, "Functioning harmoniously together, right and left give birth to all techniques. The four limbs of the body are the four pillars of heaven."

4. *Prjanayama*, "breath control," is necessary to partake of the breath of the universe. "Breathe out and let yourself soar to the ends of the universe; breathe in and bring the cosmos back inside. Next, breathe up all the fecundity of earth. Finally, blend the breath of heaven and the breath of earth with your own, becoming the Breath of Life itself."

5. *Pratyahara* connotes "freedom from bewilderment," a withdrawal from the distraction of the senses—a mind that is steadfast and imperturbable. Regarding this, Ueshiba instructed, "Do not stare into the eyes of your opponent; he may mesmerize you. Do not fix your gaze on his sword; he may intimidate you. Do not focus on your opponent at all; he may absorb your energy."

6. *Dharana*, "fixing the mind," is also known as *ekagrata*, "keeping the one point," a well-known concept in aikido circles. "If you are centered, you can move freely. The physical center is your belly; if your mind is set there as well, you are assured of victory in any endeavor."

7. *Dhyana*, "meditation," is a state of penetrating insight and clear vision. "Cast off limiting thoughts and return to true emptiness. Stand in the midst of the Great Void."

8. *Samadhi*, "total absorption," goes even further. In samadhi, the distinction between knower and known dissolves, a transfiguration that Ueshiba expressed as, "I am the universe!" Ueshiba's supernatural powers originated in his all-absorbing samadhi, and his eccentric behavior likewise was characteristic of the highest levels of yoga, a kind of divine madness that transcended time and space. "If you do not blend with the emptiness of the Pure Void, you will not find the path of aiki."

Ueshiba's teaching was summed up in the phrase "*Takemusu aiki.*" *Take* stands for "valor and bravery"; it represents the irrepressible and indomitable courage to live. *Musu* typifies birth, growth, accomplishment, fulfillment. It is the creative force of the cosmos, responsible for the production of all that nourishes life. Takemusu aiki is code for "the boldest and most creative existence!"

The Other Aikido

Dr. William Durbin

Everyone knows the most famous branch of aikido was created by Morihei Ueshiba, the founder of the *Aikikai* and the person to originate the term aikido. For a long time, aikido was considered the martial art of Ueshiba, with the Aikikai seeming to be the only legitimate branch of the art. Even after some of Morihei Ueshiba's direct students began to develop offshoots of aikido, in the United States many people still thought of Aikikai as the only true aikido.

Eventually, students of *Tomiki-ryu* aikido and *Yoshinkai* aikido brought their branches and interpretations of the art to the States, and martial arts students became aware of aikido's other branches. Currently, there are many branches of the art as established by Morihei Ueshiba, most of them directly connected to the main lineage by the teachings of Ueshiba's students. The main styles, which continue to use the term *aikido*, derived from the Aikikai are *Shin-*

shin Toitsu aikido, *Nishio-ryu*, *Tendo-ryu*, and the aforementioned Tomiki-ryu and Yoshinkai.

There are two theories as to the development of the *ryu*. First of all, it is known that Chijiro Yokoto studied under Ryuho Okuyama, back in the days when Okuyama taught *Daito-ryu* and before he founded *Hakko-ryu*. It is also known that Yokoto studied *Yoshin-ryu*, though it is not known who his teacher was.

It is also recorded in family tradition that the Yokoto family trained in martial arts for years, being of the *shizoku* (warrior) lineage. One theory holds that the Yokoto family had an ancient connection to the Yoshin-ryu and that many generations ago the style *DaiYoshin-ryu* was founded by one of the feudal Yokoto warriors, who then passed the art down through the family until the time of Chijiro.

The other theory is that the family trained in the main branch of Yoshin-ryu, originally founded by

Yoshitoki Shirobei Akiyama, throughout the feudal era. Thus Chijiro learned the Yoshin-ryu from his father and then furthered his training under Okuyama, who had studied under Matsuda Hosaku, a direct student of Sokaku Takeda, the great Soke of Daito-ryu.

Some believed that Chijiro Yokoto coined the term *Dai Yoshin* at that time to represent the combination of Daito-ryu and Yoshin-ryu. He then taught the combined system, teaching a full range of *aiki-jutsu* martial arts and *bu-jutsu*, representing the full magnitude of combat skills, including *kempo*, *ken-jutsu*, *jo-jutsu*, and many other weapons skills.

Regardless of whether the skill was passed down over many generations or founded by Chijiro himself, Dai Yoshin-ryu is a complete and comprehensive fighting system. The primary art was aiki-jutsu; as a combat art it was devastating and inexorable. It combined the royal grappling skills, especially those designed to be used in armor, with the powerful striking art of kempo, designed for those times when fighting out of armor was needed.

Yet Yokoto was a man of his time, and he realized that the combat art of aiki-jutsu was extreme for modern times. The combat art was brutal, designed to destroy the joints of a sword-wielding opponent. It was designed for the feudal battlefield, not self-defense in a civilized country. While he wanted to preserve his martial art in the traditional, combat manner, he also wanted something more refined and gentle for modern self-defense.

Chijiro Yokoto looked at the development of modern martial arts and saw in the three newly developing arts of aikido, judo, and *karatedo* a new concept, the development of gentleness in response, that mirrored his own budding concepts. It was especially in the aikido developments of Morihei Ueshiba, whom Yokoto viewed as a brother in Daito-ryu, that he saw the most intelligent and spiritually advanced ideas.

Thus Yokoto developed a modern self-defense art that he called aikido, to teach along with his traditional bu-jutsu. Yokoto spent a number of years in the United States, where he taught a man by the name of Albert C. Church. When Church first studied under

Yokoto, he was taught the Daito-ryu aiki-jutsu system. Later, after Yokoto had returned to Japan and when Church was stationed there due to business considerations, Yokoto taught him the actual Dai Yoshin-ryu systems, including aiki-jutsu and the modified self-defense form of aikido.

Dr. Rod Sacharnoski had the opportunity to study under both Chijiro Yokoto and Albert Church. When Yokoto died he had been in ill health and never had the opportunity to pass his martial art on to his family, as was the usual tradition, or any Japanese students. Church had already died, and so it fell to Sacharnoski to continue the tradition. After having his claim to Dai Yoshin-ryu registered in Japan, Sacharnoski has worked hard to promote the ancient tradition of the system's bu-jutsu and also the self-defense method of aikido.

While there are many excellent teachers of Aikikai aikido and its numerous derivatives, one of the biggest complaints registered against aikido is that many teachers practice the art as a form of gentle exercise, or cooperative ballet, without any regard to actual combat effectiveness. This trend was already becoming evident before Chijiro Yokoto died; therefore he emphasized that while aikido was to be a more spiritually advanced and gentle form of self-defense, it was to always be effective.

Sacharnoski observed, as many of Morihei Ueshiba's contemporaries did, that O-Sensei's (Ueshiba's) skills were immaculate and extremely potent. As Ueshiba aged, his skill reached a new high level. His movement became so superb that while he seemed to perform his aikido without *atemi* (strikes) the opposite was actually true. O-Sensei himself taught that one blow in aikido kills. The idea was to try and reach such a high level of skill that strikes were not necessary in self-defense. But Ueshiba was a realistic martial artist, and while he strove for the ideal, he developed the reality. Those who understood combat saw the many subtle atemi that permeated the techniques of the aikido master.

Following this example, Chijiro Yokoto taught his aikido in a similar manner. While he emphasized that aikido should be capable of being performed without strikes, he taught his students to keep their eyes open and be able to deliver atemi wherever and whenever appropriate to the situation.

In the traditional art of Dai Yoshin-ryu aiki-jutsu, the techniques are taught in the manner of Daito-ryu, with an emphasis on striking the opponent. The strikes used in the art were designed to be devastating; if a strike landed perfectly, no other technique would be needed. Yet in real combat, exactly what one wants to occur seldom does, so each strike is viewed as a pre-liminary movement into any of the myriad techniques of the art. All *jujitsu* skills of the past taught truly effective striking techniques that were lethal when used against a person not wearing armor.

There is also a set of stunning blows for less than life-and-death situations, so that a person can be stunned by a strike, which then allows an *aikidoka* to blend into a throw, takedown, or other control technique.

The ending pinning techniques are not empha-sized because Yokoto considered the flow of actual combat to be more fluid than that. He seldom used the pinning techniques of Daito-ryu, preferring to use the typical hold-downs associated with aikido, which leave the practitioner in a less precarious situation.

Since many of the techniques of Aikikai aikido and Dai Yoshin-ryu aikido are derived from and named after the Daito-ryu aiki-jutsu techniques, many of the skills have the same designations. But just as Ueshiba coined certain special names for some of his skills, this is also the case in Yokoto's art.

Some of the techniques, while possessing the same name—such as *shiho nage*, *kote gaeshi*, etc.—are performed slightly differently. It is believed that this is due to the teaching methods of Sokaku Takeda. Takeda supposedly had an incredible wealth of knowledge, not only to the point of knowing literally thousands of techniques, but also in having numerous variations of each technique. Thus he would often show techniques to different students using the same name but empha-sizing different principles and concepts.

While the techniques are basically the same, they differ just enough so that those who think of a tech-nique as having only one form endlessly debate over which one is right and which one is wrong. Those who understand that any given technique can have multi-ple forms emphasize the principle known as *henka*, which means "variation." The similarities of techniques in Aikikai aikido and Dai Yoshin-ryu aikido truly show their common roots, while the differences show the unique perspectives of the individual instructors.

This material originally appeared in the April 1999 issue of Inside Karate.

Kempo
The Source

Dr. William Durbin

Kempo, as popularly known in the United States, derives from a conglomeration of arts melded together to form an excellent method of self-defense. But in the Orient, kempo is considered much different. We will consider the views in reverse historical order.

During the modern era in Japan, the Okinawan martial arts were introduced to the island first as kempo, with karate being a secondary designation. Many of the Japanese martial artists really liked the effectiveness of the Okinawan arts but preferred to maintain their own heritage by practicing jujitsu and *kendo*. During this time, several masters combined the kempo karate of Okinawa with forms of jujitsu, or judo, as well as the footwork of kendo in some cases and created new forms of self-defense systems, which were generally termed *kempo*. Two particular systems derived in this manner are Nippon (or Japanese) Kempo and *goshindo*.

Another modern kempo system that is a blend of other martial arts is the *Shorinji* Kempo, founded by Michiomi Nakano So Doshin. In the case of this art there is no Okinawan influence. Rather, it is a blend of an old form of *Shaolin Quan*, which Nakano studied while acting as a spy for the Japanese government in China during the Pacific War, with jujitsu, which he learned from his grandfather before going to China and from Ryuho Okuyama following his return to Japan after the war. It is believed that he studied Daito-ryu aiki-jutsu from Okuyama, before the master founded his own system of Hakko-ryu.

The second form of kempo were the temple martial arts, dating from as early as the tenth century and present even in modern times. The Buddhist temples of Japan were started either by Chinese monks visiting Japan in order to spread their religion or by Japanese monks who had traveled to China to train in their new faith. In many situations, as the Buddhist adherents trained in their religions, they also learned the martial arts connected to the faith.

In the Japanese temples the martial arts which were taught were a combination of the Chinese kempo (*Chuan fa*), brought from the continent, along with the indigenous arts, including jujitsu-based skills and the weapon arts. The weapon arts used a variety of weaponry, from the typical *katana* (sword) to the full range of combat weapons, specifically the *yari* (spear) and *naginata* (halberd), but also included some very specialized weapons, ranging from the *kusari fundo* (weighted chain) to the *kusarigama* (chain and sickle).

Today the empty-hand martial arts of some of the temples in Japan call their art Jikempo, temple fist law. This art contains not only exceptional striking skills, but also the typical throwing techniques of jujitsu, including the joint locks of aiki. Jikempo practitioners claim that the modern form is taught in the exact manner as in ancient times. In this art, as in many of the Japanese jujitsu systems, strikes are delivered in a manner that sets up the throws and joint locks of the art. The main difference between Jikempo and most forms of jujitsu is that the strikes delivered in Jikempo are often struck with the fist, and when applied to the vital points, the blows can finish an opponent. Thus the punches of Jikempo are designed to defeat an opponent, rather than just set up a throw, but in the situation where a blow does not take out an aggressor, the Jikempoka learns how to flow into a grappling skill.

The oldest form of kempo is the original *Shaolinssu Quan*, referred to in Japanese as Shorinji Kempo. When the martial arts first spread from China during the dissemination of Buddhism throughout the Orient, they were known by their local names in the countries they entered. In Japan, this was kempo. The ancient art of Shorinji Kempo was primarily a fist-and-palm art, not yet extensive in the use of other hand formations, but highly effective nonetheless.

Later the five animal forms of Shorinji Kempo were introduced to Okinawa, but by the time they developed, Japan had closed its borders to outside influences. This is why the animal forms did not really influence the development of Japanese jujitsu until Okinawan karate brought the influence over in modern times.

For the most part, martial arts historians see Chinese kempo as the foundation of both the Japanese and Okinawan martial arts. In the commonly accepted tradition, the Japanese took Chinese kempo and adapted it to their environment and social conditions, merging it with the indigenous arts to create Japanese kempo. This style was designed for fighting in heavy winter clothing and armor, thus dictating an emphasis on grappling. The Okinawans took the Chinese kempo, also merging it with their indigenous art, and adapted it to their own warmer climate, thus emphasizing striking. Since they wore less clothing, grappling would have been harder to perform; blows are more effective against uncovered or lightly covered skin.

Thus kempo can be looked at from three perspectives in Oriental history. First there is the original Shorinji Kempo, as the Chinese art was called in Japan. Second is the *Jikempo* of the temples, which began with Chinese kempo and mixed with the indigenous martial arts of Japan, developing into unique Japanese forms of kempo. Two good examples of this are the *Kosho-ryu* kempo taught by the Mitose family and the *Sato-ryu* kempo taught by Seiko Fujita. The third form of kempo is the modern martial art that is a blend of Okinawan karate and Japanese jujitsu; the one exception being the Shorinji Kempo, which is a blend of Chinese kempo and Japanese jujitsu.

While the names are different, the similarities of the footwork between Okinawan karate and Japanese jujitsu help us see the kempo link between the separate developments of the two countries' arts. In jujitsu the six main stances are *shizentai* (natural body), *hidlari shizen dachi* (left natural stance), *migi shizen dachi* (right natural stance), *jigotai* (self-protect body), *hidlari jigo dachi* (left self-protect stance), and *migi jigo dachi* (right self-protect stance).

These six jujitsu stances correspond to the following karate stances: *soto hachiji dachi* (outer figure-eight stance), *hidari renoji dachi* (left V-shape stance), *migi renoji dachi* (right V-shape stance), *kiba* or *shiko dachi* (horse or square stance), *hidari kakuto kiba dachi* or *hidari shiko dachi* (left fighting horse stance or left square stance), and *migi kakuto kiba dachi* or *migi shiko dachi* (right fighting horse stance or right square stance).

Since the ancient style of kempo uses these six stances, and they are found in the Japanese jujitsu systems and the karate systems of Okinawa, it is safe to assume that they mostly derived from a single parent art. Though it is true that only so many stances can be taken in any given fighting form, the stance connection seems strong evidence for a common source.

Kempo, as it was originally practiced in China, Japan, and Okinawa, was a complete and total system, using throws, joint locks, and strikes. The arts developed differently in Japan and Okinawa, due to differences in climate and culture. Japan's severe winters dictated the wearing of many layers of clothing, robbing strikes of much of their power. Also, armor was worn in battle, negating the effectiveness of empty-hand strikes. Thus the Japanese arts tended to emphasize grappling skills.

On the other hand, Okinawa's much warmer climate allowed for less clothing to be worn. Thus, especially when a person was hot and sweaty, grappling techniques were much harder to apply, but strikes were highly effective. Also, since the Okinawan *bushi* were much more like police officers than soldiers, and the common man did not wear armor as part of his daily garb, that barrier did not exist to negate the punches of the island's martial artists.

The original art of kempo differs greatly from the composite arts that purport to be kempo. This difference might be referred to as "the unified nature of boxing," as opposed to an eclectic conglomeration of techniques. For example, some modern kempo styles teach karate strikes, judo throws, aikido locks, and tae kwon do kicks. Whenever they perform a technique from a given art, they have to take that art's stance, which obviously differs from the stances used for performing other techniques in their eclectic style. The biggest problem that martial artists of this nature have is remembering each of the techniques they "steal" or "absorb" from the many arts that make up their kempo.

Original kempo is a unified blend of movements that have many interpretations. Techniques in true kempo are used only to teach proper movements, not specific skills for dealing with specific attacks. Real kempo is a study of motion that gives its practitioners an understanding of purposeful action. No motion is undertaken without meaning, any move can have a large number of interpretations, and multiple stances can be used in the performance of strikes, throws, or joint locks.

This is the main difference between original kempo and composite martial arts. The stances of original kempo are merely the mobility for all techniques, whereas eclectic arts are combinations of techniques gleaned from other arts. The combined arts have no unified principle of motion; this is the very foundation of true martial arts.

Kempo, in its original form, possessed all the techniques and principles that formed the foundation of the arts of jujitsu, karate, and the many arts these gave birth to, including aikido, tae kwon do, judo, Hapkido, and many others. Practitioners of these other arts can look to the old form of kempo to see the unification of stance, technique, and motion.

This material originally appeared in the October 1997 issue of Inside Karate.

Classical Jujitsu and Its Modern Forms

Dr. Tom Corizzi

Jujitsu is the empty-handed fighting style that developed in Japan during the thirteenth century. It can be translated as *Ju*, meaning "gentle," and *jitsu*, meaning "art." It is also known as the "art of suppleness." There is no one individual style of jujitsu. Similar to the many styles of kung fu, there are many styles of jujitsu. Classical styles of jujitsu include Daito-ryu, Kito-ryu, Tenshin-ryu, and many more. Forms of aiki-jutsu are all systems of jujitsu. Through the years some of these systems have coalesced. Techniques from one style were added to another to make a better fighting system. Jujitsu techniques include methods of striking, kicking, throwing, choking, and most particularly, joint locking. Students learn to move from one technique to another depending on the resistance and movement of the opponent.

Besides classical styles, many new systems have arisen. Due to practicality or philosophy, some styles such as judo and aikido have become do, or "the Way." Though not necessarily jujitsu systems, these styles still use modified jujitsu techniques.

Though it would be almost impossible to list all of the classical styles of jujitsu or the newer systems that have arisen from them, the following are the most significant.

Classical Styles

Though the empty-handed techniques of jujitsu mark this style of martial art, other aspects were taught to the samurai depending on their rank and status. These aspects included strategy, history, first aid, medicine, and of course, weapons. Weapons training would include the sword, spear, and knife but could also include the *yawara* sticks, throwing weapons such as *shuriken*, spikes, and archery. What was taught to a samurai depended on his fighting abilities and his "job" on the battlefield.

Remember that jujitsu training was battlefield training. The styles of classical jujitsu still being taught today exist for one of two reasons. They were either strong enough to survive the battlefield and centuries of feudal warfare or were kept alive because they were popular among the officials of the Japanese courts.

Daito-Ryu Aiki-Jutsu

Daito-ryu is one of the strongest and best known of the classical forms. It was founded by Minamoto no Shinra Saburo Yoshimitsu (1045–1127), the last grandson of Emperor Seiwa. Yoshimitsu taught *so-jutsu* (spear), *toho* (sword methods), and *tai-jutsu* (body arts). He was noted for having dissected the cadavers of executed criminals and slain enemy soldiers. Through this study of the human body, he mastered Gyakute and Ichigeki Hissatsu (techniques of killing with one blow). Yoshimitsu is considered the one who originally developed the techniques of Daito-ryu by adding to the previously secret techniques of the Minamoto clan. Modern systems that have developed from Daito-ryu are aikido, Hakko-ryu, and Hapkido.

Probably the best known practitioner of Daito-ryu is Sokaku Takeda (1858–1942). He was instructor to Morihei Ueshiba, the founder of aikido, and Ryuho Okuyama, founder of Hakko-ryu jujitsu. He also instructed Horikawa Kodo (1894–1980), who received, among other titles, the "Order of Eternal Mastership"—the highest title in *budo* society.

Though there are Daito-ryu schools throughout the world, very few teach or even know much of the complete curriculum still kept alive by the Takeda family in Japan.

Judo

Judo, "the Gentle Way," was developed by Jigoro Kano in 1882. Judo is a form of self-defense as well as a sport. Sensei Kano was a jujitsu practitioner whose training included classical styles of Kito-ryu and Tenshin-ryu jujitsu. Kano developed judo as a form of exercise to be used in the public schools of Japan. Jujitsu competitions often resulted in severe injuries as well as some deaths. To reduce injuries during competition, all strikes and the majority of joint-locking techniques were removed. Kano advocated that judo's purpose was not to win competitions, but to perfect one's mind and body for the mutual benefit and welfare of all mankind. It was first known as Kano Jujitsu and then Kano Judo. Eventually Kano adopted the name Kodokan, after a famous Shinto temple. The name *Judo* was not new. It was actually the name of a traditional style of jujitsu that had been practiced for several hundred years. Kano may have felt that the name *Judo*, "the Gentle Way," best expressed his philosophy toward his art.

Techniques in judo include *ukemi* (falling techniques), *nage waza* (throwing techniques), *ne waza* (ground techniques), and *atemi waza* (vital-point techniques). The last incorporates striking techniques that are illegal in competition and taught only to advanced ranks. They were taught to Kano by Gichin Funakoshi, the father of Shotokan karate.

Judo / Daito Connection

Shiro Saigo (1863–1922), a member of the Daito clan, trained in Daito-ryu aiki-jutsu and was recruited by Kano to join the Kodokan. His judo skills combined with his previous Daito training enabled him to win many contests held between the Kodokan and other jujitsu schools. His prowess tremendously helped judo's attainment of notoriety.

Aikido

Aikido means "the way of harmony," or "the way of spirit." It is an unarmed method of self-defense founded in 1942 by Morihei Ueshiba. He was a religious man and combined his martial skill with his religious beliefs and Zen meditation. Aikido is based on the principle of harmony and nonresistance to one's opponent and is essentially noncombative and noncompetitive. Its primary purpose is to develop a healthy mind and body together with a wholesome spirit.

As mentioned before, the founder of aikido, Morihei Ueshiba, trained in Daito-ryu jujitsu. He did not learn the entire curriculum, only the first one hundred techniques, which he combined with techniques from other schools to create aikido.

There are many branches of aikido. It can be practiced gently for exercise, health, or its religious aspects. It can also be taught as a hard style stressing the aiki aspect of Daito (the striking and bone-breaking techniques).

Judo/Aikido Connection

By the choice of Kano and Ueshiba, neither judo nor aikido contained all the elements of true jujitsu. Both had chosen the techniques they wanted to teach according to the philosophies of their founders. In order to increase their abilities, many students cross-trained between the *Kodokan* and the *hombu*. Judo students would train in aikido, which emphasized momentum and ki. Aikido students would train in judo to strengthen their hip throws and ukemi (falling techniques).

Some modern systems taught today combine judo and aikido, looking to join the best elements of both styles. One such system is *Miama-ryu* Combat Jujitsu, founded by Antonio Pereira. Pereira first learned a style of jujitsu called Combato during World War II. In 1961, Pereira traveled to Japan to train. Training eight hours a day for six months, Pereira attained a *nidan* in judo and received a teaching certificate in aikido signed by Kisshomaru Ueshiba, the son of the founder. Miama-ryu combines the original techniques of Combato with judo and aikido.

Danzan-Ryu

The Chinese characters for *Danzan-ryu* denote the Hawaiian Islands. The founder of Danzan-ryu was Seisho Okazaki, born in 1890. Okazaki and his family moved from Japan to Hawaii in 1906. In 1909 he was diagnosed to have "incurable tuberculosis." In defiance of his condition, Okazaki started training in jujitsu with Yoshimatsu Tanaka. Whether due to the power of martial arts training or a miracle, Okazaki's tuberculosis healed. He decided to devote his life to teaching and promoting jujitsu. His training included Yoshin-ryu, *Iwaga-ryu*, and *Kasagabe-ryu* jujitsu. Combining these techniques with karate strikes and kicks, knife techniques from the Philippines, and the Hawaiian killing art of *Lau*, Okazaki developed Danzan-ryu jujitsu. He also thought it important to teach restoration techniques from his studies of the Japanese arts *Kappo* and *Seifuku Jutsu*.

One of the best known students of Danzan-ryu was Professor Wally Jay.

Hakko-Ryu Jujitsu

Hakko-ryu is a style of jujitsu founded in 1941 by Ryuho Okuyama in Japan. Okuyama, having studied Daito-ryu jujitsu and being a shiatsu (a form of Japanese massage) practitioner, put his medical and martial art knowledge together to form his system. Hakko-ryu, "the school of the eighth light," is designed to handle attacks by applying pressure on the body's meridians to cause intense, but nondamaging, pain, reducing the attacker's will to continue. The techniques employ minimal strength, yet generate maximum efficiency.

Hapkido

Hapkido was founded by Yong Shul Choi, who from 1919 to the beginning of World War II, studied Daito-ryu aiki-jutsu. Choi combined jujitsu with *Hwarangdo* and *Tae kyon*, Korean martial art forms. This combination became a strong defensive style against the Korean styles. Its teachings include the most practical weapon for street defense, the cane.

Kenpo Karate

This modern form of karate was originally known as *Kenpo* jujitsu. It was introduced in Hawaii by James Mitose in December of 1941 at the beginning of World War II. Emphasizing the attack of vital points similar to Japanese atemi waza, it employs throws, locks, and takedowns. Kenpo was Americanized by a friend of Mitose, William K. S. Chow. Ed Parker was a disciple of Chow who adapted the system to what he considered a more modern combination. It was probably these changes in the system that led Kenpo to become more of a karate style than its original jujitsu counterpart.

Goshin-jutsu

Goshin-jutsu means "the art of self-defense." It is a form of jujitsu developed by Tatsu Tanaka, who opened his dojo in Tokyo in 1952. Finding classical jujitsu unsuited for his tastes, he decided to eliminate injurious techniques. He removed kicking and striking techniques and placed emphasis on locking and throwing techniques. Goshin-jutsu has twenty-one techniques against a knife, a stick, a gun, a grab, or a strike.

Small Circle Jujitsu

Small Circle jujitsu was founded by Professor Wally Jay, one of the best known jujitsu practitioners of the United States. Jay started his martial training at the age of 11 with boxing. At the age of 18 he started training in jujitsu while continuing his boxing. Five years later, Jay started training in Danzan-ryu jujitsu under Juan Gomez, a student of the founder, Seisho Okazaki.

The fundamental principle of Small Circle jujitsu is "two-way" wrist action. Jay credits Ken Kawachi, his judo instructor, for teaching him this.

Besides coaching a championship judo team, Wally Jay has also been the instructor for many well-known martial artists, including a young Bruce Lee, who was looking to add grappling to his own martial arts style.

Gracie Jujitsu

This is a popular style of jujitsu due to its impressive ground-fighting techniques that have been displayed in contests such as the Ultimate Fighting Championship. Gracie jujitsu was founded by Carlos Gracie. Carlos trained as a teenager under the great Japanese jujitsu champion, Mitsui Maeclakama. Carlos was interested in street fighting. Combining his boxing experience with the classical jujitsu and then modifying the combination into a style for the Brazilian streets, Carlos constantly worked to make it more effective. To do this he fought anyone who was willing, regardless of size, weight, or fighting style. The tradition of open challenge continues today.

Events such as the Ultimate Fighting Championship have not only been profitable for the Gracie family, but have shown the effectiveness of the Gracie style in one-on-one competition.

Kamekan Jujitsu

The word *Kamekan* is Japanese for "Turtle Hall." It is not the name of a new system of jujitsu; rather, it is the name I gave to the original dojo where I teach. Kamekan is a combination of different styles that includes elements of classical and modern jujitsu such as goshin-jutsu, judo, aikido, and Hakko-ryu jujitsu. Most of these techniques were taught to me by Sensei

Harry Glackin, who studied several systems including *Yoshitsune* under Michael Depasquale, Sr.; Miama-ryu under Antonio Pereira; and Hakko-ryu under Azo Ninamiya to put together his system called Goshindo Martial Arts.

Besides Goshindo Martial Arts, I have also studied White Dragon kung fu, aikido, and Daito-ryu jujitsu. My goal has always been to learn as much as I can and adapt the techniques I teach for combat situations.

The Future

There are many "new" styles of jujitsu appearing today. Most are combination styles like my Kamekan jujitsu. These new styles attempt to regain all of the fighting elements of jujitsu that have been discarded for one reason or another by the founders of the modern systems and return these styles to their original combat efficiency. In this way jujitsu is completing the circle. Jujitsu started out as a combat fighting style. Individuals such as Kano, Ueshiba, and Tanaka changed the systems to make them safer to learn but gave up some of their street effectiveness. This return to complete fighting systems is a positive step. The "founders" of these new systems should realize, however, that they are not creating anything new, but simply returning to something very old.

Dr. Tom Corizzi is a chiropractor and instructor of Kamekan jujitsu. This material originally appeared in the November 1997 issue of Inside Karate.

Pankration

The Ancient Greek Martial Art of "All-Powers" Combat

Norm Leff

In 648 B.C. *pankration*, a dynamic art that combined boxing, kicking, and submission wrestling, was introduced to the Olympic Games. With time, pankration became the ultimate fighting art of the ancient Greek warriors. They used it on the battlefield with great success. During the conquests of Alexander the Great, who invaded India in 326 B.C., the Greek soldiers used this fighting art against their enemies, and they also put on public exhibitions of their awesome fighting skills for their vanquished foes.

Many credible martial art historians believe that ancient Greek pankration preceded Chinese boxing, Okinawan karate, Japanese jujitsu, and other Asian martial arts. The late grand master of Japanese karate, Mas Oyama, believed this to be true. Jim Arvanitis, grand master of modern day pankration, has this same belief.

Is there a link between ancient Greek pankration and other Asian martial arts? Other martial art historians dispute this belief. But the fact is, many techniques of pankration are similar to Chinese boxing, karate, and jujitsu. Authentic martial art historians must assiduously research this controversy before a definite conclusion can be determined as to whether there was indeed a link between these fighting arts. Classical ancient Greek pankration was a bloody and brutal fighting art, and often the matches ended in death for one of the fighters.

Legend says that the great sports hero, Theseus, was the founder of pankration. Theseus was a skillful wrestler, boxer, and kicker. He used these techniques to defeat the ferocious monster Minotaur.

Pankration was an all-out combat sport that allowed bare-knuckle punching, striking, kicking, and submission grappling. The only so-called prohibitions were biting and gouging. Besides these two prohibitions, everything else was fair game. In many instances, the officials turned a blind eye to these so-called fouls. Pankration was not a combative sport for men who lacked courage.

After several years of such contests, the pankratiast's family and friends and even his dog could not recognize his face. That is how savage, violent, and bloody the matches were. Such was the average pankratiast's future, provided he was not killed while fighting. His face was beaten beyond recognition; many of the fighters suffered from crippling injuries, and in addition to these injuries, they were also afflicted by pugilistic dementia. (*Pugilistic dementia* is the correct term for being punch drunk.)

Pankration champions, however, were worshiped as heroes by the public. Glory, fame, and fortune were their rewards. These popular sport heroes were adored by the masses and glorified by the poets. All the world loves a winner, and as long as they were victorious in their matches, they were proclaimed as demigods!

These champions received pensions and lands for life. Therefore, a young, strong, and well-built athletic man had great incentive and motivation to try his luck in pankration competition.

Some wrestling historians describe pankratiasts as wrestlers who could fight with their fists and kick with their feet. They were also considered pugilists who were able to wrestle. All were depicted as men who could kick like donkeys. One pankration champion was portrayed as a man who is as brave as a lion, is as cunning as a fox, and attacks like an eagle. Another famous champion in pankration is described as "a fighter with a bull's neck, the powerful shoulders of Atlas, the beard of Hercules, and the big eyes of a lion. The way he defeats his opponents even Zeus the lord of Olympus would feel awe and respect for him."

The Techniques of Pankration

What did their techniques consist of? According to Jim Arvanitis, who has researched Greek martial arts

for the last thirty years, they delivered powerful hook punches, open-palm strikes, spear-hand thrusts, backfist strikes, hammer-fist blows, downward chops, right or left crosses, straight punches, sledge-hammer uppercuts, and vicious elbow strikes with power and accuracy to the vital areas of the body. Low kicks to the shins, knees, groin, and stomach were delivered with speed and power to destroy their opponent's legs and balance. (If the opponent's knee was broken, the fight was over because he could not stand and the pain of the broken knee would make him submit. They would try to break their opponent's knees and legs with these savage kicks.) The kicks were generally delivered below the waist. Front kicks, however, were aimed at the stomach.

Sweeping and reaping techniques were used to knock the pankratiast off his feet. Once the fighter was off his feet, his adversary would then deliver a series of blows and kicks to the head, face, body, etc. The adversary would then move in to grapple with the fighter and finish him off with submission grappling techniques. The submission techniques included arm locks, joint locks, leg locks, body locks, neck locks, and a variety of strangling techniques.

Fighters used other techniques such as vicious knee strikes to the groin, stomach, head, etc. Hair pulling, throws, takedowns, and tiger hand attacks to the throat were used with great skill. Kicking techniques were practical, effective, and delivered with devastating power.

Strategy

The pankration fighter's strategy was to use his kicking techniques to break through his adversary's guard or to come close enough where he could strike his opponent with rapid, violent blows. Once inside, he would use throws, takedowns, reaps, and sweeps to take the opponent off his feet. He would then employ various techniques to finish off his opponent. They usually consisted of grappling torture holds that could maim or kill his opponent. These lethal grappling techniques were a combination of holds that resemble jujitsu and Western catch-as-catch-can wrestling.

Many of the ancient wrestling techniques of pankration have survived up to the present time. Western catch-as-catch-can wrestling has adopted these ancient wrestling submission techniques, and they are still used in combative wrestling. In fact, vases, paintings, and statues depict the fighting techniques of pankration fighters: One bronze statue is of a pankratiast attacking with a low front kick thrust. Another statue shows a pankration fighter doing a lunge punch.

Other ancient artifacts depict many different pankration fighting techniques, such as a fighter attacking his opponent with a right vertical punch to the chest and also delivering a kick to the groin. Another artifact shows a pankration fighter deflecting a straight right punch from his opponent with his left. He knees his opponent in the groin with his left and palm-strikes him in the face with his right. On another ancient vase is a pankration fighter on top of his adversary, who is on his back. He seizes his opponent by the throat with his left hand and punches him in the face with his right fist. On one particular vase a pankratiast applies a standing submission arm lock on his adversary. This technique is almost identical to a classical Japanese jujitsu joint lock. Many other ancient artifacts demonstrate different throws, blows, kicks, joint locks, chokes, leg locks, and counterattacks.

Modern Rebirth of Pankration

Many so-called bare-knuckle fighting tournaments, such as the Ultimate Fighting Championships, Vale Tudo Matches, Brazilian jujitsu contests, Pancrase, and Shoot Wrestling, are modern-day forms of ancient Greek pankration.

Jim Arvanitis considers himself to be the father of modern-day pankration. He has spent most of his life researching the history and concepts of Greek pankra-

tion. He has trained in Greco-Roman wrestling, freestyle wrestling, combat wrestling, Greek boxing, Western boxing, Muay Thai boxing, boxe francaise savate, combat judo, and submission grappling.

Arvanitis is especially upset with martial artists claiming to practice pankration. He considers these individuals to be plagiarists. Arvanitis said, "There are many now claiming to be practicing pankration. The fact remains that I was the very first to revive this ancient art. I transformed it into a contemporary cross-training art and popularized it around the world."

Arvanitis calls his system Mu Tau pankration. He told me that his system is designed solely for unrestrained street combat. It combines submission grappling and ground-fighting techniques with kickboxing. His modern-day pankration style is based on leverage and technical efficiency rather than brute strength. The student of this hybrid dynamic style is an all-around decathlon fighter. He is skilled either as a kickboxer or a grappler. He is effective in a standing position or in a grappling position, where many fights are terminated.

Arvanitis's future plans are to spearhead a movement to include pankration as a special Olympic event at the 2004 games in Athens, Greece. He is planning seminars and training programs with Greek officials and other Europeans in preparing competitors for the 2004 Olympiad. Arvanitis is developing a set of rules for acceptance by the IOC (International Olympic Committee) for 2004 Olympic pankration.

He is the author of two books: *Mu Tau: The Modern Greek Karate*, Todd & Hoeywell, N.Y., 1979 (this book is out of print), and *Mu Tau Pankration: Concepts and Skills of "All-Powers" Combat*. The latter is his latest book and is now available to readers. It is an excellent book on his style of modern-day pankration.

Jim Arvanitis wants to spread the Greek art of modern-day pankration throughout the world. He teaches and coaches other martial artists, kickboxers, wrestlers, film writers, bodyguards, law enforcement officers, SWAT team members, and elite members of the U.S. Armed Forces.

Regardless of what system of modern-day pankration you follow, whether it is Arvanitis's system or another similar system, all have merit. Pankration can only improve your knowledge and skills as a martial artist, and that is what the martial arts are all about.

JIM ARVANITIS'S TRAINING PROGRAM

Endurance Training

Running: 70 to 80 miles per week

Biking: 120 miles per week

Jumping rope: 15 minutes, four days a week

Strength Training

Weight training routine:

Monday and Wednesday he trains his back, chest, and arms.

Back

1. leverage bar rows
2. pull-ups
3. power cleans from the floor

Chest

1. bench presses
2. push-ups
3. dips
4. flyes

Biceps

1. barbell curls
2. reverse barbell curls
3. wrist roller (for the wrist and forearms)

Triceps

1. tricep dumbbell curls
2. dips
3. reverse tricep dips

Exercises he does on Tuesday, Thursday, and Saturday:

Abdominals

He does a variety of abdominal exercises, such as incline sit-ups, twisting sit-ups, leg raises, bent knees to the chest, jackknives, crunches, side bends, etc.

Shoulders

1. press behind the neck with a barbell
2. dumbbell presses
3. dumbbell lateral raises

Neck Exercises

Head strap and various bridging neck exercises with weights

Skills Training

Speed bag, double-end bag, and heavy bag (3–5 rounds, 3 minutes each)

Sparring (three times per week each)

1. *pug–lak*, Greek kickboxing with gloves and head guard
2. *kato pale*, Greek submission ground grappling

He also practices special grappling drills three times per week. He has followed this program, or a program similar to this, religiously for the past several years. Training and fitness is a way of life for him. He trains seven days a week for 3–5 hours a day.

This material originally appeared in the November 1998 issue of Inside Karate.

The Grapplers of Ancient Rome

Norm Leff

The ancient Roman people were warlike and belligerent. They were aware of the importance of physical exercise and hand-to-hand combats. The unarmed hand-to-hand combats were wrestling, pankration, and boxing.

The Romans were superb wrestlers and fighters. They had a much greater interest in wrestling than in other sports activities. It was the favorite sport of young Roman aristocrats, and the fighting techniques of wrestling and pankration were used by Roman soldiers on the battlefield.

Roman wrestling, pankration, and boxing were greatly influenced by the Greeks and the Etruscans. Many Greeks had migrated to Rome, and their culture had an enormous impact on Roman civilization.

Roman emperors trained in wrestling. Marcus Aurelius, his son Commodus, Caracalla, Alexander

Severus, and Diocletian were outstanding wrestlers. Gaius Julius Caesar, Vespasian, Trajan, Hadrian, and other Roman emperors greatly contributed to the development of wrestling and combat sports.

Many of the Roman generals, army officers, soldiers, statesmen, writers, poets, etc., were excellent wrestlers and pankration fighters. Besides being practiced by Roman aristocrats, wrestling was also practiced by warriors, shepherds, and slaves. A Thracian shepherd whose name was Maximinus became emperor of Rome due to his wrestling ability. Maximinus was a herculean giant who stood almost nine feet tall. He was the strongest man in the land. He could kill a horse with a blow from his fist. He crushed stones in his hands as easily as a man can crush eggs. He could lift, from the ground to an overhead position, 300 pounds with one arm. Maximinus was born a peasant, but because of his huge size, strength, and wrestling ability, he emerged a Roman emperor. This is an amazing true story of how a poor man became emperor of the ancient world through his skill, physical strength, and athletic fighting prowess.

In all the athletic Roman games, wrestling was the most important sport. Wrestling champions were rewarded with expensive prizes. Besides the prizes, they received other privileges: citizenship, appointment to a public office, and other benefits and material goods. Emperor Augustus personally gave out prizes.

A wrestler could make a teacher's yearly salary in one day. Popular wrestlers, pankration grapplers, and boxers were highly rewarded for their accomplishments. Roman culture promoted physical culture. At that time they had huge arenas to stage sporting events. The Colosseum could seat 87,000 spectators. The biggest stadium was the Circus Maximus, which could seat 385,000 spectators.

Pankration fighting was very popular at that time. This type of fighting was extremely brutal and violent. Roman pankration was more savage than the Greek version. It consisted of kicks, punches, strikes, vicious knee thrusts to the body, brutal grappling holds, and locks. These techniques were used to kill, maim, or force the opponent into submission. Strangleholds were probably the grapplers' favorite techniques.

Roman wrestling was also cruel, violent, and painful. Roman wrestling consisted of standing and ground techniques, and all of the throws and holds were extremely dangerous. Roman wrestlers were masters of submission grappling.

Boxing was also very savage. Boxers fought with the deadly *caestus* gloves, the brass knuckles of the Roman time. They were made out of stone and leather—a lethal weapon! All boxers and pankration grapplers had to wear the deadly caestus gloves. The caestuses were frightful weapons, and they caused horrifying injuries to the fighters. These lethal gloves had several different versions. Some covered almost

the full length of the arm, with space left for the fingers at the ends of the bindings. All were vicious looking, and they were extremely harmful. In the book *QuoVadis*, the author describes the cruelty of the sport. The hero, Craton, says, "Master, just visualize the fight. His backbone is cracking in my hands, and after that I smash his dirty face with my fist."

In order to satisfy the blood lust of the Roman spectators, the wrestlers, pankration grapplers, and boxers often fought to the death. Besides having weapons training, the Roman gladiators also trained in wrestling, pankration, and boxing. It is said that the gladiator combat matches were of Etruscan origin. Generally, the gladiatorial fights were preceded by wrestling, pankration, and boxing contests.

The Roman spectators became intoxicated on the bloodshed of the wrestlers, pankration fighters, boxers, and gladiators who fought in these stadiums. These bloody and brutal contests aroused the spectators' inhuman and barbaric emotions.

The Romans destroyed the Olympic spirit with their lust for cruelty, brutality, bloodshed, and violence. The games became characterized by the shedding of blood and savagery. Due to this corruption and evil, Emperor Theodosius prohibited the Olympic Games from taking place. The Olympic Games were abolished in A.D. 392. With the end of the Olympic Games, pankration died out, and wrestling never regained its worldwide popularity.

Techniques of Roman Pankration Grapplers

A good pankration grappler was a wrestler who could fight with his fists and kick like a donkey. Pankration champions were treated with great respect and awe. They were worshiped as heroes. Many ancient Roman writers portrayed them in this manner. Other writers had a low opinion of this kind of fighting. The pankration fighters were fantastic kickers. They used violent blows, devastating throws, powerful takedowns with sweeps, reaps, complex locks, and deadly strangling techniques.

Many pankration fighters came from Asia Minor. Most of them were poor, underprivileged rustics, slaves, captured soldiers, and men who liked to fight. There were those who were seeking glory, riches, and fame, and they were willing to pay the physical price of getting killed, maimed, beaten, or disfigured for their moment of glory.

The pankration fighters were tall, very strong-looking, agile, supple, and brave. They had very muscular and powerful physiques with necks like bulls. They were able to give and take the most violent blows and administer the most tortuous locks. They would prefer to die than be vanquished in a contest. Often a match ended in the death of one of the competitors.

Greek pankration, even though it was a bloody affair, had more prohibitions than Roman pankration. Roman pankration was truly a "no holds barred" fight in which everything was permitted.

Roman pankration began in a standing position and usually ended on the ground. When one of the pankration grapplers threw the other grappler to the ground, he held the other wrestler in that position by striking him or using various submission techniques on him until he gave up, was knocked senseless, or was beaten or strangled to death. It was not a sport for the fainthearted.

Biting, punching, and kicking the groin and sticking fingers into the eyes were permitted in Roman pankration. It was said that after several years of pankration fighting, the fighter could not be recognized by either his family or friends.

The wrestling techniques of pankration were the forerunner of catch-as-catch-can wrestling. Also, many of pankration's locks, chokes, and torsion techniques resembled the holds of judo, jujitsu, and *sambo*. The punches, strikes, and kicks were similar to those of boxing, kickboxing, and karate. Most of the wrestling techniques were the same as modern-day submission grappling methods.

A good pankration fighter was a deadly fighter. He was an expert in the lethal art of submission grappling. His punching, striking, and kicking techniques were delivered with power, speed, and deadly accuracy.

What Motivates the Fighters of Today

Today's fighters have the same ambitions that the ancient Roman fighters had. Technology has changed with time, but human nature has not. The same driving force that motivated the fighters of antiquity motivates modern fighters. Regardless of the times, these fighters have a consuming hunger to dominate, excel, and be the best in their fields of fighting. Based on the simple fact of survival, the ancient Roman fighters probably knew more about wrestling, pankration, and boxing than the fighters of today. If they wanted to survive, they had to be deadly competitors. A loss to a modern fighter entails a loss of prestige and money. A loss to an ancient Roman fighter could entail his death or being crippled for life. Ancient grappling, wrestling, and boxing were thus risky sports. The vast majority of these warriors did not experience old age.

The ancient Roman grapplers were our teachers, and their fighting techniques continue to live on.

A Lesson to Learn

The ancient grapplers fought, suffered, bled, and died in the dusty arenas of the ancient Roman world. They fought in front of people who had an insatiable appetite for bloodshed, cruelty, and brutality. What desensitized the Romans to brutality, death, cruelty, violence, and suffering? Why did they lack humanity and human compassion? Perhaps their environment corrupted and brutalized them. They became cruel sadists and were entranced by human slaughter, suffering, and torture.

The German philosopher Schopenhauer believed that man outdoes the tiger and the hyena in pitiless cruelty. Man's beastlike quality lies dormant but is always eager to spring forth in an instant when angered or provoked.

Ancient Roman civilization's attraction to carnage, bloodshed, savagery, and vice indicated a malevolent, harmful, venal, and degenerate society. These vices finally led to the collapse and demise of the Roman Empire.

The lesson to be learned is that whenever man loses his humanity, he descends to the kingdom of evil.

This material originally appeared in the April 1999 issue of Inside Karate.

Savate

Forerunner of Modern French Martial Arts

Dr. William Durbin

Although modern savate is known as a kicking and boxing art, the original art was primarily grappling and much more akin to jujitsu.

Bill Beach has had a wonderful, varied martial arts career. He has studied Kodenkan jujitsu and expanded his Oriental knowledge in the same way that Henry Seishiro Okazaki studied many forms of martial arts in order to found his system. And just as Okazaki studied non-Oriental arts to expand his knowledge, Bill Beach has followed the same tradition and expanded his knowledge by studying the French art of *savatte*.

And no, the spelling is not wrong, though it is different from what is used by many people today. Some feel that modern savate is a hybrid of original French foot fighting (savatte) merged with Oriental skills during the modernization of the art.

During the mid-1800s, savatte was looked down upon by the aristocracy, yet it was during this same time that jujitsu began to spread beyond Japan. The emperor of Japan, wanting the Japanese people to modernize their nation as quickly as possible, sent emissaries to other nations, seeking to learn the ways of the West in order to strengthen their then-primitive country.

The Savatte-Jujitsu Connection

Representatives went to most countries in Europe. In England in the early 1900s, Sadakazu Uenishi introduced Tenshin Shinyo-ryu jujitsu to many European students. This led to a student of Uenishi, Guy de Montgailhard, opening a dojo in France. Other *Jujutsuka* demonstrated in France, creating a renewed interest in empty-hand fighting. While savate had a revival, it was basically a modified form, which was very beautiful and graceful. Some of the rough-and-tumble aspects of the original street-fighting savatte were removed, leaving a very elegant art.

Practitioners of the original savatte, however, had gone underground and found kindred spirits in the jujitsu teachers. Many of the old savatte practitioners became friends and colleagues of the Jujutsuka. This trend would continue as other martial arts came into France.

Karate in particular, with its kicking techniques, influenced the development of modern savate as the art was introduced into the country. However, those practitioners of the older form, which was a complete fighting art, still felt closer to the rough-and-tumble jujitsu men.

Original savatte used the feet and legs to block, kick, throw, choke, joint lock, and dislocate. Many times the legs were used in combination with hand grabs to accomplish many of the techniques, especially in regard to throws, joint locks, dislocations, and chokes. These techniques were largely deleted from the later savate, in many cases vanishing from the curriculum, as the sport of La Boxe Francaise Savate developed.

Just as karate has split into sport karate and self-defense martial arts, savate also split. Some forms of French savate training became more gymnastics than fighting, while others began to resemble kickboxing, with the use of boxing gloves and an emphasis on kicking.

But there were those who preserved the more original savatte and maintained the connection with jujitsu practitioners, like those in France in the early 1900s. This is what opened the door to Bill Beach's introduction into the world of savatte.

Bill Beach's Introduction to Savatte

In the winter of 1955, Bill was teaching judo and jujitsu classes at the local YMCA in Jacksonville, Florida. A student by the name of Lefebure joined the class. Being a man of infinite mirth, he enjoyed showing the class throws and takedowns using only his feet. Not jujitsu techniques, they sparked an interest in Bill Beach, so he paid close attention to the young man's skill.

Lefebure started spending time after class with Beach, explaining his throwing methods and explaining the origin of his techniques. During this private time, Bill learned the many techniques of this young man's savatte, seeing an effectiveness that could contribute to his overall knowledge of combat. Bill remembered how his instructor Ray Law had told him that Master Okazaki absorbed knowledge from any source, not just Japanese jujitsu, but also from Okinawan karate, Chinese martial arts, and Hawaiian Lau. Thus he decided that he should learn all he could about this French fighting art, since it was based on legitimate self-defense skills.

During these private sessions, Lefebure explained how he and his uncle, Louvois, had moved to the United States from Canada. His uncle had been the one who had taught him savatte. His uncle had settled in New York, while Lefebure had moved to Florida, but he kept up his training in what he felt was a family tradition. He was drawn to Bill's jujitsu dojo, since original savatte had maintained such close ties to jujitsu in France.

While Lefebure was a nice person in general, he tended to be disruptive in class. It was partly due to his intrinsic energetic nature and partly because he was extremely competitive. He used his savatte skills to give him an advantage over the jujitsu students. Once when Bill Beach had to be away from class due to family considerations, Lefebure told the class that it was very important to watch an opponent's feet more than any other part of his body, whether in competition or practice. This was of course in direct opposition to good judo and jujitsu combat philosophy.

In those days, each class ended with *randori*, freestyle practice, giving the students a chance to work on and develop the spontaneous use of their skills.

When Bill returned for the next class, he found the students using Lefebure's method of watching the feet. He knew he needed to correct this serious mistake, so he asked Lefebure to join him in a randori, and the young man eagerly accepted. The entire class came to a standstill to watch the match. The two men bowed and began to move about the mat. As was his tendency, the young man tilted his head downward to watch Bill's feet. Being jujitsu Flandori, as opposed to sport judo play, all techniques were allowed, so Beach lightly head butted Lefebure, who, being so intent on watching the jujitsu instructor's feet, was caught completely by surprise and dropped to his knees. The class erupted with laughter. Lefebure, with good humor, and after shaking off the effects of the head butt, admitted that watching the feet was not the best strategy. In a situation where two people agree to only use their feet, it is possible to only watch the opponent's feet; but when the whole body is a weapon, as in jujitsu, it is necessary to watch the opponent, not only one part of his body. The class understood the lesson, and as randori practice resumed, the students watched each other properly. As did Lefebure.

Bill Beach's Modern Savatte Teachings

Shortly thereafter, Lefebure moved without leaving a forwarding address, but Bill Beach continued to practice the savatte skills he had learned and merged them with his jujitsu. Then in 1956, Beach was sent to the Naval Air Station in Lakehurst, New Jersey, for special training. While there, he took time to arrange some meetings with Louvois, Lefebure's uncle. During these meetings, Bill was taught more about the history and background of the art to which he had been introduced.

Louvois explained to the jujitsu master why savatte was so different from savate. Most important, Louvois explained that modern savate tends toward sport and pretty gymnastics, while the original was geared more for the street self-defense situation.

Bill Beach feels fortunate to have learned the art of savatte in its original purity, with its fascinating, effective, and unique techniques. So much so, that he put the skills he learned into a specific curriculum that he teaches to his jujitsu students.

These skills are not, however, typical kick-a-person-in-the-head-or-body skills normally associated with the sport of savate today. These skills are applicable to actual self-defense. The techniques actually use the legs to effect takedowns and throws. From hooks and presses to traps and chokes, as well as joint locks and throws that are designed to hurl a person to the ground in an injurious manner, savatte was designed for effective fighting. Original savatte techniques were compatible with the jujitsu of old, which is why in the old days, savatte teachers and jujitsu instructors became friends.

Today students who train in the Hawaiian Jujutsu System of Bill Beach learn not only the complete *Kodenkan* jujitsu of Henry Seishiro Okazaki, but also the savatte techniques that Bill learned back in the 1950s, an original French fighting system geared toward real combat and self-defense.

This material originally appeared in the February 1989 issue of Inside Karate.

10

Boxe Francaise Savate in the Feminine

Salemn Assli

By the 1850s, full-contact savate fights flourished all over France, especially in Paris. Unfortunately for the practitioners, in 1856 (the year of her son's birth), Napoleon III's wife, the Empress Eugenie, asked for a ban on all fights. Even the name of *Boxe Francaise* and especially savate had to be concealed under the name *Adresse Francaise* (French Skill). This sounded more gracious and less bloody. So, except for the underground fights, the practice of fighting arts became more like gymnastics.

In the early 1900s the popularity of Boxe Francaise savate, codified by Joseph Charlemont, started to grow dramatically. Suddenly, the schools were full. The Charlemont Academy in Paris that opened in 1877 was so popular that all the members of the nobility took classes at this location. Amazing for the era, Joseph Charlemont and his son Charles not only enrolled men, but by transforming a street self-defense method into a truly graceful and elegant art, soon attracted the ladies as well.

It was indeed the first time that the European women really found an attraction for the fighting arts. Soon it became a craze, and women started to put their gloves on and learn La Boxe Francaise. They learned how to punch, kick, and wield the cane in regular classes. We still sometimes find, in the flea markets around Paris, some nostalgic postcards in black and white of those female pioneers, practicing the *coup de pied bas* wearing their hair up, a divided skirt, slippers, and boxing gloves. In the 1960s black tights replaced the divided skirts, and toward the end of the 1970s, everything was replaced by the one-piece unitard, which covers all the body except the arms. The Boxe Francaise shoes replaced the slippers, and today as in the beginning of the century, women wear boxing gloves.

The Boxe Francaise Savate competition for women is a fairly new event. Until recently it was out of the question for women to spar, let alone to have full contact. However, in 1979, in Vincennes outside of Paris, the first women's Boxe Francaise competition was held under the name of National Challenge, thanks to a handful of men and women who were convinced that competition for women would truly help to popularize Boxe Francaise Savate. Many women were attracted to the sport, but the nonexistent competition had caused most of them to turn their studies more toward arts like Muay Thai or kickboxing.

Competition started progressively. First of all, exclusively under the form of assault, the matches were judged on technique and precision of the blows. Power was to be controlled and violence excluded. In the first few years the technical level was not very great and the combinations were slow and often the same, with a lot of difficulty in control due to lack of experience. Five years later, however, the level had drastically improved such that the women's competition event occurred the same day as the men's and in the same ring. Following this success, the Boxe Francaise Savate committee decided, after a lot of thought, to allow women to participate and finally, to enter combat. Boxe Francaise Savate in the feminine was born.

Now the combat is open to women who have achieved great proficiency in the assaults level. Up until 1982, the France Championship was open to the yellow gloves and the technical silver gloves. Later on, only the bronze gloves and the competition silver gloves could participate. Today, besides the tremendous technical evolution, the women, like the men, are competing against women from other countries. Since recently, being now truly equal to men, the women can't wear headgear or shin guards in all the national and international competitions.

Savate's Appeal to Women

What exactly attracts women to practice Boxe Francaise Savate, raising the number of active practitioners from a mere couple hundred a few years ago to over five thousand today? It's actually not surprising. First of all, from a self-defense point of view, the effectiveness of savate doesn't need to be demonstrated. Women learn how to use their natural weapons (and their shoes) using various types of blows effectively and accurately, which is the best way to reply in a real situation.

Also, in the case of Boxe Francaise Savate, a certain element appeals particularly to women and has motivated them from the beginning. This seems to be the aesthetic aspect of this sport, where everything is based on distance. They learn the proper footwork, how to pivot, spins, jumps—all of this combined with skillful kicks and punches thrown at various angles and levels with a complete and flexible extension of the body.

Many women practice Boxe Francaise Savate for the sake of physical fitness. The women who practice this sport soon develop terrific muscle tone and endurance.

Because of the evasive nature of the defenses, savate naturally lends itself to a female physique. From a physiological standpoint women are smaller and lighter; so in a manner of speaking, they lack the "shock absorber" (ability to take a blow) that men have. However, they tend to be a little quicker in terms of reflex response time and better coordinated, especially in the legs; so the evasive aspects of the defenses, such as bobbing, weaving, and angulation, as well as the concept of distancing, makes this art perfect for women.

Boxe Francaise Savate in the feminine may have had its origins on the violent streets of France in the last century. It is proving to be, however, the ideal combative art for the violent streets of today.

This material originally appeared in the April 1997 issue of Inside Karate.

Capoeira
The Forbidden Sport

Debora Martins

As feet fly gracefully through the air and hands spin swiftly across the floor, the sound of percussive and stringed instruments fills the atmosphere.

What is going on? Is this some kind of martial art? Is it some type of exotic dance? Maybe it's just a game. Like a chameleon that changes its color according to its surroundings, *capoeira* had to change and adapt to survive for almost five hundred years.

So, what is capoeira (pronounced Ka-po-air-a)? Capoeira is a blend of various elements such as martial arts, dance, music, philosophy, ritual, acrobatics, theater, and game. Although capoeira began as a style of fighting, Brazilians today call it "a game that is played and not fought."

It is believed that the word capoeira came from the Bantu word *kapwera* (to fight). African warriors practiced a ritual folk dance called *n'golo* (dance of the zebra). This name came about because the dancers imitated the zebra's fighting movements. As the zebra balanced on its front legs, its hind legs kicked forward. These quick leg movements are common in the capoeira style of fighting.

A circle called *roda* (pronounced Ho-duh), is made, and while music is played, everyone sings and claps their hands as two players play in the middle. The leading musical instrument used is the *berimbau*, a one-stringed, bow-shaped instrument with a gourd attached to the bottom end to give resonance. A drum called *atabaque*, a tambourine called *pandeiro*, and double cow bells called *agogo* are also used.

Within this music-filled circle, the *capoeiristas*, those who practice capoeira, skillfully perform their art by demonstrating a complex process of kicks, leg sweeps, flips, and handstands.

"Portugues" (far left), "Carapato" (center), "Peixe Boi" and "Chile" (far right) train the *ginga* (fundamental capoeira movement) as Mestre Delei looks on.

A roda (circle) is formed while Nichole "Anaconda" Rodriguez (left) and Barbara Ramos (right) get ready to enter the game by the foot of the berimbau.

Both Nichole "Anaconda" Rodriguez (left) and Barbara Ramos (right) begin the game with an au (cartwheel).

While "Caboclinho" and "Mao" play the berimbau, Bradley plays the agogo. Nichole "Anaconda" Rodriguez (right) performs a negativa (defensive movement) and Barbara Ramos (left) finishes a role (attack movement).

Turbulent History

To better understand the roots of this exciting art form, we must travel back to Brazil during the sixteenth and seventeenth centuries.

Like the United States, Brazil also had slavery. The slaves came from various cultural regions of Africa. Once in Brazil, the slaves were dropped off in the states of Recife, Bahia, and Rio de Janeiro. The slaves, tired of their captivity, rebelled against their tobacco and sugar plantation owners.

In Recife, a group of slaves decided to escape by killing all the whites and burning down the plantation house. Free from the white man and with the help of the Indians, they were able to find a safe spot in the mountains. The free slaves later named this place Palmares because of the large numbers of palm trees they found.

In this place the former slaves built a new African community. Tribes that were once strangers and enemies in their native Africa were united to fight for their freedom. In this newly formed community, capoeira was born.

Barbara Ramos (in white pants) counterattacks Nichole "Anaconda" Rodriguez's *parada de mano* (handstand) with a *meia–lua* (spinning kick).

Nichole "Anaconda" Rodriguez (right) performs an au (cartwheel) and Barbara Ramos (left) a role.

Barbara Ramos (right) avoids "Anaconda's" *meia–lua de frente* (front spinning kick) with a role.

In the roda both "Calango" and "Bizorro" perform a parada de mano (handstand).

Capoeira became their weapon and their symbol of freedom. With it they were able to cause considerable damage to the white man. They were able to beat both Portuguese and Dutch armies on various occasions. These armies were ambushed by unexpected attacks. Using swift and tricky movements of capoeira, the slaves were able to defeat the experienced and well-trained Portuguese and Dutch soldiers.

Back in their safe haven, the slaves practiced their secret weapon. But they soon had to alter their practice, because those who were caught were sentenced to death. By disguising their deadly art with added music, dance, and ritual, they were able to fool and amuse the plantation owners by leaping, tripping, and kicking their opponents. They would then avoid a strike by slithering across the ground like snakes.

Outlaws Outlawed

In 1888 slavery was abolished, and some slaves returned to Africa. Those who remained were not able to find jobs in either the plantations or cities. Because of their skills in capoeira, a few were lucky and got jobs as bodyguards for politicians, but those less fortunate became dangerous gang members.

Two young players perform an *au* (cartwheel).

"Cabeza" and Bruno are in combat while "Caboclinho" and Mestre Delei control the game speed as they play the *berimbau*.

Then in the 1890s, capoeiristas were viewed as a danger to the Brazilian government. Capoeiristas were being hired to trash government assemblies, causing the art to become illegal until 1920. Anyone caught practicing capoeira was forced to leave Brazil. But capoeiristas kept capoeira alive by disguising it as a folk art, and this made its practice more acceptable to society. During this time of havoc, capoeiristas, like the group called Mautas who wore silk scarves around their necks, used blades on their feet. The razor was the only weapon the capoeirista would use during a fight.

In 1937 the most important master of capoeira, Mestre Bimba, was invited by the Brazilian president to perform his art in the capital. After an outstanding performance, Mestre Bimba was allowed to open the first Brazilian capoeira school. Years later the senate passed a bill that established capoeira as a national sport. In Brazil capoeira is now practiced everywhere. You can find it in elementary schools, universities, clubs, and military academies. It is also practiced all over the world in countries such as the United States, Germany, Australia, Denmark, New Zealand, Canada, Italy, Portugal, England, Spain, the Netherlands, and many others.

Capoeira offers to its students training in flexibility, strength, endurance, and self-defense, along with a knowledge of the music, culture, and traditions of Brazil. The practitioners of capoeira wear white pants held by a *cordano* (cord). Just like in martial arts, the color of the cordano represents the student's level of expertise. In each level technical aspects, dedication, character, discipline, and knowledge are taken into consideration. When a student is committed to capoeira, he or she must go through the *batizado* (baptism) ceremony. During this event the student will receive an *apelido* or *nome de guerra* (nickname given as part of the batizado initiation).

Musical Martial Art

As two participants at a time enter the roda and play with each other, the game is controlled by the music and the abilities of each capoeirista. Capoeira's most important musical instrument is the berimbau. It is a very simple instrument made up of a piece of wood, a wire, and a gourd. The person playing the berimbau controls the speed of the game. The music sets the rhythm for the players' actions by encouraging the capoeiristas to move faster, slower, or smoother. Capoeira songs are sung in Portuguese, and they reflect the cultural origins of capoeira and the actions that are occurring within the roda.

Many circular kicks are used in capoeira, along with many dance movements. Because music has been an important part of African culture, it has influenced capoeira by making it appear like a dance. That is why it is always practiced to music. You might even say that capoeira looks like break dancing.

The underlying development of the techniques used in capoeira has practical and philosophical reasons. Because slaves were often chained by their hands, they had to resort to other types of strikes to fight. And from a philosophical standpoint, in African culture, the hands were not used for destructive purposes. Hands were only used for creative purposes like hunting, harvesting, or building.

In capoeira many moves are used, such as handstands, kicks, and cartwheels. The capoeiristas may balance on one or both hands while giving kicks to their challenger's head or body. They also use ground-fighting techniques, such as sweeps and trips. Some of these movements are called au (cartwheel), *bencano* (front kick), *boca de siri* (crab's mouth movement), *cabecada* (head butt), *cocorinha* (squatting movement), *floreios* (acrobatic movements), *martelo* (hammer kick), *meia-lua de compasso* (compass half moon, a spinning kick), *piano* (spinning top), and *rabo de arraia* (stingray's tail kick).

The first open capoeira tournament in the United States was scheduled for May 1999 in Miami, Florida. This event was organized by the capoeirista Mestre Delei and his capoeira group Abolicano (abolition).

Some of Mestre Delei's students have chosen to practice capoeira because of its uniqueness in style, as opposed to other forms of martial arts. He also has students as young as two years of age.

Famous Stock

Mestre Delei started playing capoeira at a very young age, but he officially began practicing at an academy when he was nine.

"In Brazil capoeira begins from father to son. The father teaches his son," says Delei. "The first person I ever saw do an au (cartwheel) was my father."

Delei's father was not a mestre, but he was of African descent. He played the berimbau, sang, and loved capoeira. His own father lived during the period in which capoeira was prohibited and thus did not want any of his children involved in its practice. Even when Delei entered into an academy, capoeiristas were discriminated against. Once in the academy, Delei started helping his mestre.

"I never did anything else in my life, (so) I made it my profession."

Delei trained a lot, but he had no discipline and self-control when he was around the age of 15. Because he was young and a troublemaker, he would use his talent in capoeira to get into fights. It was

"Coral" Bianca (left) and "Mano" (right) are locked in a *banda de frente* (front trip movement).

"Mano" (left) attacks "Coral" (right) with a bencano (front kick), which is avoided with an *esquiva* (escape movement).

A banda de frente (front trip movement) is used by "Mano" (right) as "Coral" (left) counterattacks with a role.

A *chibata de presa* (leg sweep) is performed by "Coral" (right) as a *rasteira de frente* (front sweep) is used by her opponent.

through his master's guidance that Delei became more disciplined.

"I was always by my master's side, but he never gave me the *mestre cordano* until he saw that I was responsible." At the age of 17, Delei finally became a master instructor.

Mestre Delei's academy has just recently opened in North Miami Beach, Florida, but his capoeira group Abolition (Grupo de Capoeira Abolicano) has been around for more than three years. When asked why he decided to call his group Abolition, Delei said, "It was capoeira that caused the abolition [of slavery in Brazil], because they [the whites] were already feeling the pressure from the blacks. That is why I picked this name for my academy."

What's in a Name?

When giving a nickname (apelido) to his students, Mestre Delei begins by observing them from the time they first enter his academy. According to what they do and how they act, he will see which apelido will fit. He also takes into consideration their personalities and styles.

Mestre Delei's real name is Narciso Wanderlei de Oliveira, but his family called him Delei. So when he started practicing capoeira, they already knew him as Delei. As he trained, his master always compared him to a strong piece of Brazilian wood, coincidentally called Delei. And that is why he was baptized with the apelido Delei.

"The practice of giving a capoeirista an apelido stems from tradition," Delei notes, adding that it was "Mestre Bimba (Manuel do Reis Machado) who invented the apelido to prevent the police from discovering the real identity of the capoeirista."

The colors of the belts (cordano) used in Delei's academy are the same as in the Brazilian flag. These colors and their respective ranks have been recently accepted by various groups of capoeira in Florida. The belt colors are different in Brazil, and they also change within groups because each capoeira group has a different way of thinking. The colors used by Mestre Delei are green, yellow, and blue. Then comes red, which represents the blood spilled during slavery by the blacks, and then black, which represents the slaves in capoeira. The last color is white, and that is given to the capoeirista who has achieved the highest level within capoeira. Usually, that occurs when the capoeirista is around 60 years old.

"The difference between capoeira and the other martial arts is that capoeira is Latin American and not Oriental. Capoeira has this spirit and energy that the other martial arts don't have," says Delei.

The capoeiristas feel the pulsating music and work the whole body. They use their legs, arms, head, and knees, and they also use the floor. "Capoeira is a complete martial art (form). It isn't like boxing where you use (only) hands, or tae kwon do where you use mostly legs, or karate where you use legs and arms but are fixed. Kung fu has beautiful moves, but not force. . . . So, capoeira, in my opinion, is a complete martial art. It's more than that. It's even hard to explain. It's something you need to try in order to feel it."

Mestre Delei's students, to earn their cordano, need to learn how to play all four instruments and sing the capoeira songs. They need to learn its history so that they can understand and appreciate its cultural origins and the many struggles it had to overcome throughout history.

Capoeira is famous for the balance and flexibility of its gymnastics, the strength and grace of its dance, the speed and trickery of its fight, and the intoxicating rhythms of its music. These elements are all blended to create a unique game, which is now practiced throughout the United States and the world.

As the capoeira song goes, "*Capoeira e defesa e ataque e ginga de corpo e malandragem*" (Capoeira is defense and attack, it's movement of body, it's trickery).

This material originally appeared in the September 1998 issue of Inside Kung-Fu.

The Fighting Animals of Korean Martial Arts

Jane Hallander

Everyone knows about China's Shaolin Temple five animal fighting forms and techniques. Why, however, limit animal martial art studies to China? Other Asian countries have wild animals. What about them?

Korea borders China at its northern end, giving it many of the same animals that inhabit China and many similar mythical animals, such as the dragon. The Korean martial art of *Kuk Sool*, while itself a contemporary fighting art, is based strictly on Korean martial arts, with roots as far back as three thousand years. Its founder, Houston, Texas–based Grand Master In Hyuk Suh, spent many years of his youth researching and resurrecting those ancient arts to present them as authentically as possible in today's Kuk Sool.

Among the many different facets of Kuk Sool are its animal fighting techniques and forms. These are not reproductions of the Shaolin five animals or any other Chinese animal fighting style. They are approached differently than are the Chinese animal techniques.

Disappearing Arts

When the Japanese occupied Korea (1910–1945), the knowledge of ancient Korean martial arts took a drastic nosedive. While under Japanese domination, martial arts study was not allowed in Korea and many valuable records and books were lost forever. After the Japanese occupation was over, martial arts in Korea made a comeback through forms such as Kuk Sool Won. Kuk Sool Won is based on three ancient traditional Korean martial arts: *koong joong mu sool* (royal court martial arts), *sado mu sool* (family or tribal martial arts), and *buldo mu sool* (Buddhist martial arts). From these ancient arts came a full range of instruction involving Korean animal forms.

Grand Master In Hyuk Suh's first dragon hand technique blocks Kuk Sool Won master Barry Harmon's kick.

Suh's other dragon hand technique blocks Harmon's punch.

Then Suh goes into action by grabbing Harmon's head with both hands . . .

. . . and twisting it . . .

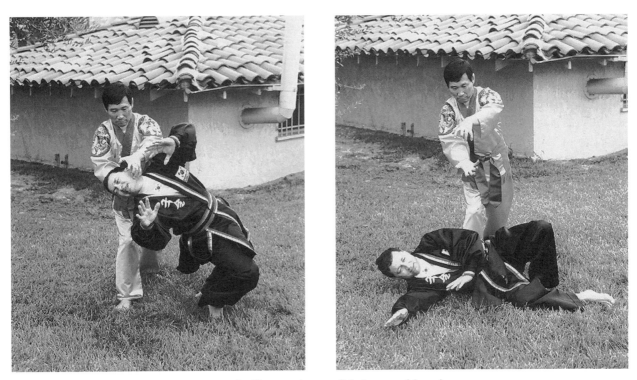

... to take Harmon down, off balance and in pain.

While Chinese martial arts appeared to place a greater emphasis on individual animals by establishing whole systems around a single creature (praying mantis kung fu, for instance), Korean martial artists studied animals, on the whole, as an important source of fighting knowledge.

"Early man had to eat, and from this basic need, hunted for his food. Humans are both plant and meat eaters, so he foraged for plants and hunted for meat, much the same as the animals he eventually studied for martial arts," explains In Hyuk Suh.

"As he hunted and foraged, he watched and copied the hunting and survival tactics of other animals. Sometimes he applied his new knowledge to the animals he hunted, and occasionally he also used these skills against the larger animals that found man as suitable prey. Pretty soon, man had developed a crude form of martial arts, begun mostly through trial and error (costly if he lost) and through imitation of other animals' fighting behaviors."

As the human race grew and established territories and nations, martial arts in those territories expanded, particularly when these countries went to war with one another. War between nations gave man the opportunity to further develop his martial arts into ever more advanced forms; some of these would become a way of life and a code of ethics for martial artists. As he watched an eagle catch a rabbit, two tigers fighting, or a snake capture a frog, the budding martial artist added not only more techniques but also the spirit and fighting principle of each animal.

Becoming the Animal

Keeping with the Korean philosophy of basic practicality, Kuk Sool Won animal forms vastly differ from those of other countries' martial systems. Kuk Sool practitioners believe that merely to imitate the animal is not sufficient. People are not like other animals, because humans use cause-and-effect reasoning, rather than just reacting. Humans also have a different body structure—two legs instead of four. Therefore, just imitating an animal's motions doesn't make a powerful, effective technique. Only by careful conversion of an individual creature's fighting principles into human requirements do animal forms become effective. Then, not only are they effective methods of fighting, but they greatly enhance and expand the human warrior's strength and capabilities.

In Hyuk Suh refers to the ancient theory of five elements to explain the importance of studying more than just one animal.

"The five elements of martial strength," he explains, "are speed, internal power, correct breathing, body balance, and practice. These are important, not only to martial arts, but to the animals we study. Even the animals adhere to the five element basics when they practice their fighting tactics in the guise of play."

Just as kung fu's five elements (water, fire, earth, metal, and wood) have different qualities and relationships, the Kuk Sool's five-element theory dictates that each animal has different strengths and weaknesses over other creatures. To elaborate, no single animal is completely free of enemies and natural predators. The snake runs from a crane, while the crane, in turn, flees from an eagle. As in the Chinese description of the five elements, there is a continuous circle where each animal counters another creature and is countered by still another.

That's why, in Suh's opinion, no martial artist should be satisfied with the knowledge of only one type of defense, animal or not. For instance, if a small person has to defend himself against someone larger, he shouldn't have to rely on the tiger form, which requires great strength. Instead, he might call upon his knowledge of the snake's fighting habits, placing his body power into his defensive counterattacking blow.

Although there are other animal forms to be found in Korean martial arts, not all suit the individual practitioner, and the student should choose only those that do. Suh, himself, has five favorite animals.

Dragon

Most Westerners think of serpents or dragons as creatures of evil bent upon destroying anything that stands for the betterment of mankind. Only in Asia does a certain reptile take on the form and meaning of a benefactor to mankind. That serpent is the dragon, known also as a mythical animal who plays an important role in the animal forms and imitations of certain Asian martial arts.

Although strictly a mythical creature, the dragon represents the highest level in the animal kingdom. He consorts only with royalty, affects the balance of nature in both the heavens and below the seas, and symbolizes an explosive combination of both internal and external strengths.

Situated midway between China and Japan, Korea has always been in a position to incorporate ideologies from the other two countries and, at the same time, influence them with its own culture.

Perhaps China contributed the lore of the dragon to Korea when the religion of Buddhism moved down into Korea from the north. The dragon holds a special significance in Buddhist doctrine, since it is considered to be a key spiritual animal. As Buddhism enveloped Korea and became its primary religion, belief in the qualities of the dragon moved into Korea's martial arts in the form of special training designed to imitate the superiority of the creature.

In Korean martial arts there are two types of animal imitation. One depicts the physical aspects and personalities of wild beasts such as the tiger, panther, and bear. These are animal forms more suited to external martial art training, since they take the best qualities of each animal's fighting style and adapt them into techniques and attitudes that fit their human counterparts.

The other type of animal form is called *sa leon* (imaginary animals). The animals that fall into this category include both mythical animals, such as the

Against a punch from Kuk Sool master Marlin Sims,
Grand Master In Hyuk Suh first blocks it with a snake
hand technique . . .

. . . then immediately counters with an open hand snake grab to Sims's throat.

Here is a tiger fist action aimed at pressure points. Suh blocks Sims's initial punch.

Then, while Sims is still off balance, Suh pulls both hands back to form tiger technique fists.

Suh strikes forward, hitting pressure points located in the floating rib area.

dragon, and animals that actually exist but have characteristics traditionally attributed to them that go beyond reality. In this class are the dragon, the Korean crane, the *kerin* (an animal known for its ability to catch snakes), and the giant tortoise. These animals either rely upon their internal (ki in Korean, chi in Chinese) strengths to make up for their lack of external power or, like the dragon, use their calmness, concentration, and ki to express themselves in many different fighting forms. Of all of Kuk Sool Won's martial art animals only the dragon has the ability to change his form and nature into any of the other animals.

Ancient Korean warriors placed so much value on their belief in the powers attributed to dragons that if they visualized a dragon in any dreams before combat, they felt sure to win the battle.

From a Buddhist concept, dragons were prevalent both in the sky and under water. They controlled the actions of the heavens and the tides of the seas. Dragons brought rainfall to relieve drought-ridden lands. At the same time, an angry dragon could raise a massive tidal wave to scold negligent people.

Korean martial artists took the Buddhist beliefs and expanded them into techniques attributed to the mythical animal's nature and habitat. They decreed that he has three directions from which to strike—from under the ground or ocean (*bokyotig*), down from the sky (*gatigyong*), and up toward the sky (*dung chun*).

Each animal contributes special attributes to the martial artist. Tigers, for instance, lend an aggressive nature, speed, and power to each technique. As an instrument for internal development, the dragon presents his own particular attitude, techniques that can be either hard or soft, and the ability to change easily from one animal to another.

The dragon's attitude is called *sim wha* (fire of heart). This attitude is of total aggressiveness—it is never defensive. The dragon stylist's aggression, however, is not one of violence. Instead, it's a calm, cool reaction to any situation.

Kuk Sool dragon form techniques are sometimes likened to thunder coming from clouds. They include the palm strike, which can also become a grab and joint lock. The dragon resting underground or under the ocean is seen in low spin kicks and upward attacks initiated from close to the ground.

Every dragon technique is coupled with a strong low stance that gives the stylist the foundation from which to make his powerful strike. A typical sequence of dragon techniques in a self-defense situation might look like this: First, the Kuk Sool dragon stylist blocks or covers his attacker's punch with an open-palm cross-block, which turns into a downward open-palm (dragon descending from the sky). The palm becomes a wrist grab that pulls the attacker forward and into a low grab to the thigh (dragon rests below the ocean). From there the dragon defender strikes straight up into his opponent's face with either a fist or palm (dragon ascending toward the sky).

Dragon techniques also involve grabbing and snatching movements. Unlike the praying mantis, who lends circular and angular grabbing techniques to martial arts, dragon grabs are always straight up, down, or horizontal movements. One might advance for a grab, which in turn pulls an opponent into range for the next advancing attack.

The difference between fist and palm strikes is a trademark of the dragon. One of the most important principles of dragon techniques is the balance of *urn* (yin) and yang. Palm strikes represent yang energy, since when the palm is open, power is made, which flows out easily. Fists, however, are closed and retain their power, just like urn energy. The urn energy of a fist doesn't come out until the fist strikes its target.

The balance of energy during practice of the dragon form is so important that incorrect training can cause energy to be depleted, with recovery difficult. Incorrect practice of dragon techniques can cause the internal energy to stop flowing normally.

The dragon is so special to Kuk Sool Won that it is said those who practice the dragon form often see the dragon in their dreams, which means everything will turn out the way they wish.

Snake

One of the greatest challenges in empty-hand combat is flawless execution of animal fighting techniques, and the snake is no exception.

Ancient Korean martial arts valued techniques taken from the study of many different animals, including the tiger, leopard, bear, crane, eagle, and the snake. Of these animals, the snake lends perhaps the most unique and advanced fighting techniques to the martial arts.

Sa hyung hak, the study of snake motion, occupies an ancient place in Korean martial arts history. The first recorded snake form in Korea's history dates back to about 57 B.C.

Snake meat and organs have always been popular in Korean culture. Many times the people who supplied the public with these snakes were martial artists and had ample time to observe their prey to see how it moved and attacked other animals. It is possible these snake handlers originated the snake-oriented maneuvers and fighting techniques.

In keeping with a basic Korean philosophy of practicality, Kuk Sool snake forms are not similar to those of other martial arts. Since people are not animals, to merely imitate the animal is not good enough. Powerful techniques cannot therefore be created by imitating the animal's actions alone. Only by carefully converting each animal's fighting principles into human requirements can animal techniques become effective.

The snake seems an unlikely creature to include in martial arts since it has no legs for quick movement, no arms to strike with, and by nature is generally a calm animal. For exactly those reasons, however, the snake has played an important role in the development of higher forms of martial arts.

Since the snake has no limbs, it must move with a zigzagging, twisting action of its body. To fight effectively, it must compensate for its lack of appendages.

A snake accomplishes that goal in two ways. First, it can coil its body in a springlike fashion and rise straight up into a striking position, as does a cobra. From that coiled position and with devastating accuracy and speed, it straightens its body and strikes its prey. The snake gains a tremendous amount of power from the momentum and rotating action of its strike and in this manner can defeat even the strongest opponent.

For defensive purposes, a snake has a quick, active motion that gives it the ability to move easily between several objects. Since it can bend, straighten, and coil, it remains flexible and strong at the same time—an attribute highly prized by martial artists. When imitating the snake motion, a martial artist should be able to move quickly to the left or right to counterattack as he winds his body around his opponent's fist.

Another attribute of the snake, perhaps even more important than its unique movement and striking techniques, is its ability to develop and release ki with every strike. Within the martial arts, this same cultivation and use of ki power is what gives the fighter a penetrating strength far superior to that of ordinary external blows.

Since the snake is a calm, relaxed creature, it possesses much more ki than do other animals. When it combines its internal energy and strength with its external striking techniques, the snake becomes a formidable and powerful adversary.

In Kuk Sool Won, the study of snake motion means two things to the martial artist. First, he must clear his mind in a natural manner, allowing his ki to reach its fullest development. Second, he will train his body to become fast and active, preventing any opponent from finding an opening in his snake defenses. He will be flexible as well as straight, and rotational from a single position as well as quick with his footwork.

At the onset of a snake technique, the martial artist's body will contain positive (yang) ki in some areas, negative (urn or yin) ki in others. As he moves into his snake techniques, both opposite ki powers will concentrate into the portion of his body that actually performs the strike. The initial body movement that

Grand Master In Hyuk Suh blocks a punch from Kuk Sool Won master Barry Harmon with an eagle blocking technique.

Suh simultaneously reaches for a pressure point on Harmon's neck.

While controlling Harmon's hand with one eagle technique . . .

. . . Suh takes Harmon down with the pressure-point manipulation at his neck

Suh stops Harmon's kick with one crane technique.

Suh then blocks Harmon's punch with another crane hand technique.

Suh finishes the confrontation with a crane strike to a vital pressure point at Harmon's armpit.

resembles a snake's motion (coming from the lower abdomen) activates the two ki powers and causes them to merge into the final, powerful product.

According to In Hyuk Suh, "As your body gets used to the snake form and you feel the smoothness in your body, the urn-yang ki energy should flow from inside the body. Just as the sky becomes clear and transparent, your mind or spirit should become as clear as the moonlight on a winter night. If you don't feel the smoothness in your body, you will find difficulty moving properly, and your spiritual power (ki) won't work. If you understand perfectly, your mind will be as precise and perfect as a snake's reaction or motion."

Because of its relaxed, floating-like movements, the snake differs from other animal styles because it can deliver a force that is both hard and soft. Most animal styles elicit a tense, aggressive power to strike down enemies. For instance, the tiger form has strictly hard, external strength. Whereas the snake's energy is quiet and internally motivated, tiger stylists are active, forceful, and loud. Snake practitioners make no sound and deliver soft, penetrating blows.

When a snake is relaxed, its body is merely a long, ropelike tube. Upon sensing danger, however, it immediately prepares itself for battle. When it coils into a defensive position, the snake's entire power is transferred to its head, the actual striking area. The fighting principle borrowed from the snake is that of defensive attack from a prepared position, which allows the entire body force to transmit through the practitioner's striking hand or foot. While snake techniques are both offensive and defensive, the offensive techniques are always based on defensive needs. In other words, snake techniques start with defense, rather than attack.

In order to obtain success while using loose, flexible power, it is necessary for the snake practitioner to focus his intent and energy into one point and to place his body weight into the striking surface (the fingers, for instance). Snake techniques then become quick, circular, short-range, almost wrapping actions, similar to the coiling and uncoiling action of an actual snake.

A snake practitioner's footwork is also soft and fluid, employing movements that penetrate deep within an opponent's defenses, allowing him no escape.

If a snake is faced with a larger adversary, it will often wrap its body around its foe to crush and immobilize it. Kuk Sool Won snake techniques follow the same principle. A Kuk Sool stylist might capture his opponent in a choke hold by faking a high kick and suddenly wrapping his leg around his opposition's neck.

Offensive snake techniques are characterized by penetrating palm and fingertip attacks. Pressure-point strikes, made with two fingers bracing one another, are popular defenses within the Kuk Sool snake form. The pressure points are vital areas of the body that, when stimulated, can cause excessive pain, paralysis, or even death. Some of the more sensitive pressure points are located at the temple, eyes, throat, solar plexus, armpit, and groin regions. Other hand and foot techniques are also occasionally employed, such as low, sweeping kicks and head butts.

Snake techniques are of the advanced martial level where blocks and strikes are employed simultaneously. Defense becomes offense and vice versa. For instance, coiled or circular snake techniques begin defensively, then quickly change into straight, penetrating strikes. Speed and fluidity play important roles in the snake form.

Tiger and Eagle

Horangi (the tiger) is strictly an attack-oriented animal. Suh makes it clear that Kuk Sool Won's tiger is not completely represented by the popular claw hand seen in other martial arts. The animal uses its speed and heavy body weight to pounce upon and break the backs or necks of its victims. Then it bites victims in a vital area to finish them off. Although a tiger will use its paws and claws in fighting situations against opponents of similar size and weight, it employs the greatest power when hunting and killing prey.

Therefore, Kuk Sool uses a solid, palm-breaking technique rather than a scratching action to represent the tiger. This same palm is used to break boards and concrete that simulate a human foe's body.

Another characteristic of the tiger is that it always attacks the front portion of the prey's body. The front exposes more vital areas of the victim's body to the tiger's bold, aggressive attack. In Korean history, the tiger was the most important nonspiritual animal.

The tiger and eagle represent two of the most aggressive, ferocious animals in nature. They are also noble, up-front creatures who use some of the most effective fighting techniques in the animal world. What better creatures to have add their techniques to a martial art.

Eagle (*doksuri* in Korean) targets are small pressure points, just like those attacked by the animal itself with its beak or claws. Tigers are smart and more patient than the other big cats, attacking at just the right moment. Kuk Sool tiger techniques are large, using raw speed and power—very different from the delicate precision of eagle techniques.

The history of tiger and eagle fighting techniques in Korean martial arts goes back to the foundation of sado mu sool (tribal martial arts). Eagle techniques were seen as grabbing and thrusting actions against pressure points. Sado mu sool rock- and dirt-throwing techniques represented tiger movements.

The tiger and eagle are good representatives of two fighting styles. For instance, tigers attack from the ground, leaping upward. Eagles, on the other hand, descend from the air above to catch their prey. Kuk Sool tiger and eagle techniques reflect the ascending and descending characteristics of their animals. Tiger techniques are open-palm actions that demonstrate the way tigers attack other animals. For instance, a tiger attacks a zebra, knocking it down with its claws, then killing the zebra with its sharp teeth. In Kuk Sool, tiger open-palm techniques attack blunt areas with devastating force. Striking the chest with open palm is a common tiger fighting technique.

The eagle uses its open claws to capture its prey, then kills the prey with the same talons. Eagle techniques pinpoint small pressure points and typically grab sensitive areas like the wrist and neck. From an eagle wrist grab, it's easy to attack pressure points in the wrist and forearm.

Each animal type requires different kinds of push-ups to develop expertise. Push-ups on the palms, with no pressure on the fingers, strengthen hands for tiger strikes. Push-ups make wrists flexible and palm heels strong. Also, practice palm training on rocks and bricks develops the heel of each hand for tiger strikes. Striking soft bean bags helps make a power connection for impact from forearm to wrist to palm heel. Tiger techniques require strong forearms, which also come from Kuk Sool staff (*bong*) and sword practice.

Eagle techniques require different push-ups. Fingertip push-ups, done two different ways, are best for eagle strikes. One way is with the fingers splayed outward and the other clawlike, with the fingers bent to strengthen the joints. Kuk Sool practitioners also work with beanbags, throwing from one person to another and catching them in the air with a claw-finger grab. The bag is caught very lightly with the fingertips. An eagle fighting technique that comes from beanbag training is a shoulder grab with the fingertips that not only holds the opponent, but also drains his power.

Tiger techniques are different, pursuing the opponent on the ground and continuing the attack after first stunning him with a palm strike. Typical Kuk Sool tiger techniques include palm strikes to the face, neck, or back of the head. Even the back of the hand is a weapon for tiger techniques, striking the kidney area of the opponent's back. Not all tiger techniques are strikes. Some are strong-pressing downward blocks against kicks. Whatever the technique, tiger actions denote sheer power techniques.

Eagle techniques include grabbing movements, using the fingertips to manipulate pressure points or vital areas, such as the face. Pinpoint pressure-point strikes to shoulders or knees characterize eagle techniques. Devastating joint locks to the elbow or wrist also mark Kuk Sool eagle techniques. While tiger techniques knock the opponent away with one or two powerful palm strikes, eagle techniques often use both hands—one to grab and hold the opponent as the other finishes him with a pressure-point strike or lock.

Neither tiger or eagle is better than the other. Each has its merits and advantages. What determines the success of each technique is the one using it. That's why Kuk Sool practitioners try to place their own interest in the animal techniques that suit them best.

Crane

While the eagle techniques are geared totally to offense, the crane (*hak*) set of techniques, although based on a creature that is 100 percent the aggressor, comprises loose, relaxed, and quick moves, manifesting a much softer power than the eagle's power.

In Asia the crane represents longevity and good luck. It's known as an animal with a good heart—a noble and spiritual animal.

Since the crane isn't a physically strong animal, it combines relaxed, soft power with extreme speed to capture prey. To obtain success with loose, supple power, the crane must focus intent and energy into one point. The snake also focuses power toward one point, and for that reason, both creatures place the whole body weight into the head, which is used as a striking surface. However, the crane uses long-range, relaxed movements, while snake action is short and hard.

High-level among martial arts techniques, crane movements use lower stances than other animal forms. If attempted too early in a martial artist's training, crane stances can damage joints. The Kuk Sool crane form has over 130 individual movements, with the crane practitioner staying in a low stance for each movement. Suh likes to say, "When you learn the crane form, it's like weight training for your lower body."

There is also a lot of body and joint twisting and turning within crane techniques. A difficult form to learn, the difference between the Kuk Sool crane form and lifting weights is that you can stop lifting weights whenever you get tired. With the crane form you cannot stop until the end of the form. Kuk Sool's crane form is a combination of power and lightness—the legs are powerful, yet the footwork is light for mobility.

Within the Kuk Sool crane form are many fighting applications, with each technique being a crane strike representing different parts of the crane's body—beak, legs, and wings. Crane fighting techniques are often joint twisting movements that lead to crane strikes with explosive power, each motion generating more power for the following crane strike.

Suh notes that, within Kuk Sool Won animal forms, crane movements never allow the martial artist to expose his body, as do some other martial arts that imitate cranes with their wings outstretched. He reemphasizes that people are not animals and, since only the animal's basic fighting principles are important, there is no reason to try to resemble an animal.

Concluding Remarks

When several animal fighting principles have been mastered, Kuk Sool stylists put them together into rapid, successive combinations of fighting techniques. From each animal, martial artists take its unique fighting habits and combine them with their human thought processes to further enlarge their martial expertise.

This material first appeared in the May 1998 issue of Inside Kung-Fu.

Imperial Palace Paqua

China's Royal Martial Art Comes to America

Jane Hallander

There are three recognized internal martial arts in China—tai chi (*taiji*), *Hsing I* (xingyiquan), and *paqua* (*bagua*). All originated in Northern China and are deemed internal since they use a combination of external wise force (*chou jing*) and internal energy (*qi* or chi) to overcome opponents.

All three are considered among the highest levels in Chinese martial arts training and were once taught only to wealthy families who could afford to hire a martial arts master to teach their immediate family members. Only in this century were these three martial arts made available to the Chinese public. Since then they have become popular throughout the world.

Paqua, in particular, was known as the scholar's martial art. It bases many of its principles on the *Yi Jing* (*I-Ching*) *Book of Changes*. Today when most people think of paqua, they think of walking the circle

and the eight palm techniques that characterize paqua, much the same as eight trigrams characterize the Yi Jing.

Paqua's Many Faces

Like its cousin tai chi, paqua has different styles. Some appear more oriented toward health, while a select few emphasize practical, no-nonsense fighting techniques. Imperial palace paqua (*gong ting* paqua in Chinese) is perhaps the most practical of all paqua styles, while still keeping the mysticism that makes paqua so universally appealing.

Gong ting paqua's foremost teacher is Gong Zhong Xian. Gong came to the United States from Shanghai, China, in 1988 and now teaches his art in

Gong Zhong Xian demonstrates imperial palace paqua principle number 4—*ban* (moving).

In the application, Gong faces off with his student, Quan Zhuan Canh.

Gong avoids the punch by stepping to the side and behind Quan while placing his hand behind Quan's shoulder.

With only one finger, Gong generates enough force to bring his opponent forward off balance . . .

. . . and into a position where Gong delivers a back-of-the-palm strike to the opponent's head.

Here Gong shows how the principle *twei* (pushing) looks in the paqua form. Notice the back-and-forth twisting motion of his body as he puts internal power into the technique.

The application of *twei* starts from a ready position.

Then Gong deflects Quan's punch . . .

. . . and traps his punching arm as he distracts and takes Quan off balance with a strike to the face.

Then Gong finishes his opponent with a two-handed straight push to the opponent's centerline.

An example of imperial palace paqua walking the circle. Gong starts with short, tight steps and knees turned inward.

The steps are short throughout, with the feet lifted straight up, rather than the heel or toe.

Los Angeles. Gong's paqua lineage is impressive. He is a fourth-generation instructor of imperial palace paqua.

Born in 1924, Gong started his martial arts studies at an early age, learning both tai chi and Hsing I. His imperial palace paqua teacher was Wang Zhang Fei. Wang was a student for over fifteen years of Gong Bao Tien—a personal bodyguard of the emperor of China. Gong Bao Tien, in turn, was a student of the famous paqua master Yin Fu. Yin Fu learned his art from the creator of paqua, Dong Hai Chuan.

Gong Bao Tien guarded the emperor in the last years of the Qing dynasty before the Nationalist government ruled China. When the Japanese invaded China everything became chaotic, and Gong Bao Tien was invited by Wang Zhang Fei to live quietly at his house. Gong was a famous martial artist, recognized by the Qing dynasty and given a high position within the Imperial Guards. Therefore, it was essential that he not fall into Japanese hands. While living with Wang, he taught Wang the many secret techniques that were previously available only within palace confines. Wang passed these secrets on to Gong Zhong Xian.

The differences between imperial palace and other paqua styles are basic. In the old days, gong ting paqua was used exclusively to protect China's emperor and high-ranking officials. Therefore, many techniques were not exposed to the public; instead, they were kept secret to ensure that the emperor's enemies would not know any countering techniques.

Secret Art

Only Qing dynasty supporters and officials who were directly involved with the Chinese government were allowed to learn imperial palace paqua. On the few occasions it was taught outside, it was conservative and many techniques were kept from the public.

On the actual fighting technique level, other paqua styles walk a larger circle, which makes the movements sometimes less effective than the smaller, tighter circle that characterizes gong ting paqua. Gong asserts that for fighting purposes small, tightly stepped circles are effective because they strengthen a martial artist's internal energy. When you strengthen your

Sideways *twei* (pushing) technique.

From a ready position . . .

. . . Gong stops Quan's oncoming punch.

Then he steps to the side, behind Quan . . .

. . . and pushes the already off-balance Quan.

Gong demonstrates *por* (lifting).

From the ready position . . .

. . . Gong moves his hand under the opponent's elbow and lifts upward . . .

. . . forcing the opponent off balance . . .

. . . and allowing Gong to strike the opponent's face.

Lan, which means stopping an opponent from further advancement.

From a ready position . . .

. . . Gong intercepts Quan's punch by touching the punching hand.

Gong then grabs the punching hand.

Gong pulls Quan forward into a position where Gong can strike his face . . .

. . . moves around behind Quan . . .

. . . to strike his head, then pushes Quan off balance.

Here Gong demonstrates *ban* (moving).

From a ready position . . .

. . . Gong deflects Quan's punch.

He then steps around Quan . . .

. . . and places his arm behind Quan's shoulder with one finger on his opponent's spine to take him off balance.

internal energy with tighter footsteps, you also increase your striking force.

"Practice a small circle and your whole body feels very light. Then you will walk very light and strike very fast," Gong explains.

Gong ting paqua also has a health aspect. According to Gong Zhong Xian, gong ting paqua strengthens the digestive tract and calms the central nervous system. The tightness of the steps and body twisting of the eight palm techniques are good ways to lose weight, because you perspire a lot. Smaller and tighter than most paqua styles, imperial palace paqua's circle has a radius of approximately two shoulder widths.

There are eight basic palm techniques in gong ting paqua. The original eight palms expand into 64 separate animal forms, including the phoenix and tiger. The original eight palms are modified gradually until they reach the final total of 64.

Gong demonstrates *lan*, pulling down.

From a ready position . . .

. . . Gong grabs the opponent's punching wrist and pulls straight downward.

Then Gong pushes the opponent off balance.

Gong Ting Paqua's Eight Palms

- Twei translates into "pushing." Although it looks like a tai chi technique, the internal principle of twei differs in gong ting paqua. It is a body-twisting motion—similar to squeezing water out of a wet towel—that starts at the paqua practitioner's toes and extends to the head. Twei crosses the paqua stylist's body, starting at the shoulder and twisting outward to the palm itself. According to Gong, twei may be done in two directions—straight from the body centerline or from either side. You can push with one hand and protect with the other or use both hands to push.

- *Lan* describes stopping an opponent from further advancement. For instance, an opponent comes at the paqua practitioner with a straight punch. The paqua stylist intercepts, which is not the same as a simple block, by touching the opponent's hand and turning his own palm to a position where he can grab the opponent's wrist. From this grab, the paqua stylist pulls the opponent forward and down. Either the left or right hand may be used to twist the opponent down on either side. Again, lan uses the same full-body motion, as does twei.

- *Dai* means "carry or bring over." It is a larger degree of movement than the previous techniques. Against a right punch the paqua stylist moves his palm to redirect an opponent's body as far as possible to either the left or right. Once redirected, dai takes the opponent completely off balance. The paqua stylist's palm lightly touches the opponent's punching hand, uprooting him and opening a target for the paqua practitioner's counterstrike to the opponent's side.

- Ban translates into "moving." When a punch comes, the gong ting paqua stylist moves his arm behind the opponent's shoulder, with one finger touching the opponent's spine. This generates a force that sets the opposition's arm out of control enough to miss its target. The paqua stylist moves behind the opponent's line of attack and moves the opponent's power and striking direction to one side.

- *Por* is a term that describes a lifting motion. As a punch comes toward the paqua defender, his hand moves under the opponent's punching elbow and lifts upward. This forces the opponent's body upward and backward. It puts his center of gravity so far back that he loses his balance. It takes only a small amount of por force to set an attacker off balance.

- *Co* is a hooking action. Against a straight punch, co is like touching your palm to the opponent's face. Simply raising the palm and coming forward to the opponent's face with a dropped elbow and slight twist of the wrist sends an opponent off balance to one side. As the punch comes forward, the paqua stylist's hand raises until it touches the opponent's punching hand and the punching fist touches the defender's elbow. Then the paqua stylist advances his elbow forward, allowing his palm plenty of room to strike the opponent's face.

- *Ling* means "leading." A smaller circular technique than dai, ling doesn't require the paqua stylist to move his body, only his hand. However, the body root or balance is the same and locked in that place, rather than pulled off balance. The opponent is actually being trapped in one position. The opponent's punch is touched, much the same as touching a circle and leading the opponent's force in that circle, although the opponent remains in his original position.

- *Te* is a term for "intercept." As the punch comes, both of the paqua stylist's hands wrap around the opponent's arm, twisting and breaking his elbow. Te works with other techniques, such as ling, dai, and twei, as a secondary motion that breaks the opponent's elbow. Force is placed on one side of the opponent's hand while the other hand presses against his elbow. One hand twists outward to break the opponent's elbow.

Imperial Palace Footwork

Besides walking the circle when practicing gong ting paqua, there are three principles of imperial palace paqua footwork. The first is divided into eight points with each step landing on one point. The point radius is two-and-a-half times the size of your foot.

Next is a small nine palace footwork—nine circles that join together, with the paqua stylist required to move back and forth in different directions within that circle. Later, the paqua practitioner doesn't need the circle anymore. The large nine palace footwork is the third type of movement. It is more difficult and harder to visualize staying in line with the paqua walking points.

There are two reasons to walk the paqua circle: first, for paqua's fighting techniques, and second, for the health benefits. According to Gong Zhong Xian, walking the circle makes your internal energy stronger by centering the chi energy into the body's *dan tian* pressure-point area, which is located three fingers below the navel. The imperial palace paqua walk is lower and more focused than in other internal martial arts. Lowering the body as you walk is important. The more you walk, the more the internal organs are strengthened.

Gong ting stylists believe that leg strength is based on the footwork. The way you walk the paqua circle strengthens your legs and thereby strengthens your body. On the martial arts side, you also learn to be a moving target.

When walking a small paqua circle, your feet should be close together. Imagine a small circle with one foot landing on one point of the circle and the circle so small that one foot wraps around the other. Both toes twist toward one another, with the knees pointing toward each other. Lower your body and walk this way for thirty minutes to an hour. You will feel your back muscles expanding, while at the same time your body remains straight. Since the toes and knees point together, it is similar to a triangle.

When you walk, you must lift your knees high. Your toes must grab the ground—although you are walking flat, lifting the toes first and placing the foot flat on the ground.

Sometimes we forget that the internal martial arts were once known solely for their superior fighting skills. The health benefits were a definite plus and enabled many tai chi, paqua, and Hsing I masters to live long, healthy lives. However, the internal martial arts really excelled as fighting arts. It's refreshing to see that tradition has continued with gong ting paqua.

This material originally appeared in the April 1999 issue of Inside Kung-Fu.

Original Hung Gar

The Tangled Roots of a Powerful Kung Fu

Gene Ching

Remember when you first began your journey into the martial arts? First, you learned to distinguish between the different martial arts, such as karate, tae kwon do, kung fu, and so forth. Then, after narrowing your focus to kung fu, you found hundreds of different styles of kung fu, such as Shaolin, praying mantis, *Choy Li Fut*, *cha kuen*, and many more too numerous to mention. Beyond that, there were even dozens of variations on each style.

Some of these variations are so drastic (as in the case of *Wing Chun*) that feuds are fought over which variation was more traditional, correct, or effective. What's more, sometimes the variations are so different that it seems a mere coincidence that these two different traditions share the same name. With so many different opinions, which is the real school of kung fu?

Hung Up on Hung Gar

Hung Gar kung fu is a excellent example of how one term can have many different meanings and how confusing this can be. The Cantonese character *hung* (*hong* in Mandarin) means "red." Hung is a common surname, hence the term *gar*, which means "clan." It is also known as *hong kuen* (red fist). Often families had their own style named after them, sort of like Gracie jujitsu. Generally speaking, hung gar refers to the particular kung fu school that descended from the southern Shaolin monk Gee Sim and his student, the layman disciple Hung Hay Kwun.

This lineage includes the legendary folk hero Wong Fei Hung. Wong's exploits have been fictionalized in over one hundred feature-length Hong Kong movies, such as Jackie Chan's *Drunken Master* series,

Canton school salute.

Ha Say Fu school salute.

Canton school tiger.

Ha Say Fu school tiger.

The salute: Canton Hung Gar salutes in a cat stance.

Tiger: Both schools use specific spirit shouts to control their breathing.

Canton school butterfly swords.

Ha Say Fu school butterfly swords.

Canton school dragon.

Ha Say Fu school dragon.

Butterfly swords: Ha Say Fu Hung Gar butterfly swords flip the blades back along the forearm.

Dragon: Canton Hung Gar dragon begins internal power training.

Canton school snake.   Ha Say Fu school snake.   Canton school panther.   Ha Say Fu school panther.

Snake: Ha Say Fu Hung Gar snake uses a pressure-point striking hand known as the "snake's tongue."

Panther: Both schools emphasize speed and the panther fist strike.

Canton school crane.   Ha Say Fu school crane.

Crane: Ha Say Fu Hung Gar crane is performed almost entirely on one leg.

The unique weapons of Ha Say Fu Hung Gar:

The double tiger-head shields.

The *gen* (a precursor to the Okinawan *sai*).

The nine-pointed rake.

The dragon-head wooden bench.

The double-headed dragon chain whip.

Jet Li's *Once Upon a Time in China* series, and the world-record longest movie serial, Kwan Tak Hing's *Wong Fei Hung* series. Most of the great Hung Gar masters in the United States, such as Buck Sam Kong, Kwong Wing Lam, John Leong, Y. C. Wong, and Frank Yee, are part of this lineage. Many of them emigrated from Canton or Hong Kong, where this school is very popular, earning it the colloquial name of "Canton" Hung Gar. But this is just one school of Hung Gar. There is much more.

First, it is important to point out some of the ambiguities of the term hung gar. A parallel society known as Hung Tong (Red Fraternity) was an underground society of rebels against the Ching dynasty. They took their name from the founder of the previous dynasty (Ming), Emperor Hung Wu (A.D. 1368–1399). Their motto was "overthrow the Ching, restore the Ming." Many of these rebels practiced Hung Gar, and many Hung Gar masters, such as Hung Hay Kwun, were active in the rebellion, but these two groups were somewhat distinct. Not all Hung Gar practitioners were rebels, nor did all the rebels practice Hung Gar. There was so much overlap, however, that this rebellion cannot be separated from the martial art. Legends and popular movies have further muddled this relationship between politics and kung fu, so this distinction is quite bewildering.

Poor translation has brought about a new problem. Hong in Mandarin is phonetically similar to Hong in Cantonese, which can mean "hero." The words have different inflection pronunciations and different Chinese characters. Entirely different words, but they sound the same in English, so they have been mistaken for each other. Another completely different style of kung fu is called hong kuen, meaning "hero's fist."

In Mandarin, the same character "hong" (red) is also frequently used in reference to Shaolin Temple kung fu, because two of the primary forms of Shaolin are both called "hong," *xiaohongquan* (small red fist) and *dahongquan* (big red fist). Unlike "hero" kung fu, both schools use the same Chinese character.

Although Hung Gar descends from Shaolin, xiaohongquan and dahongquan have no apparent relationship to Hung Gar.

Once the puzzling references to Hung Tong rebels, "hero" kung fu, and xiaohongquan are eliminated, still more different schools of Hung Gar remain. Most of these are divided by region. Apart from Canton Hung Gar, there are Wubei Hung Gar, Szechuan Hung Gar, as well as some others that are very obscure. There is also the esoteric Ha Say Fu Hung Gar, or four lower tigers red clan. These schools are completely different from Canton Hung Gar.

Original Style

It would be foolish to dismiss these other schools of Hung Gar as inauthentic or nontraditional. Even though the lineage of Canton Hung Gar can be clearly traced back to Gee Sim, a Shaolin monk from the Southern temple, these other schools have also stood the test of time and have a valid claim to the name Hung Gar. Unfortunately, none of the other styles are as popular or well-documented, so they will always be in the shadow of the Canton school. Who knows when or where they separated or whether they even came from the same root?

Perhaps their shared name is entirely coincidental. Wubei and Szechuan Hung Gar bear such a minimal resemblance to Canton Hung Gar that it is hard to imagine they were once the same style. Ultimately, it does not matter much. The fact that these other schools have survived for generations testifies to their effectiveness. After so much time, it would be foolish and futile to be possessive of the name.

Fortunately, the past two centuries of Canton Hung Gar history are well-documented. Deep within its past is an interesting chapter of its origins that may explain at least one of these other schools. Early texts describe the original Hung Gar as having short-hand techniques and focusing upon close-distance fighting.

Its horse stance was described as small, only the width of the hips plus a half. Furthermore, it contained no jumping movements and could be practiced in a four-tile square (which is about a square yard).

The monk Gee Sim made three journeys from the Fukien Shaolin Temple to Canton. There he observed different styles of fighting and determined that his Hung Gar short-hand techniques were good for defense but lacked offensive capabilities necessary for Canton's brutal city streets. So he did what any master would do. He modified the system. He added longer hand techniques and widened the horse stance. He increased the focus on offense. Eventually, this modification grew to become Canton Hung Gar.

The earlier version of Hung Gar may still exist. Ha Say Fu Hung Gar fits the description of the original Hung Gar. It focuses on short-hand techniques and defense, its basic stance is narrow, it does not have any jumping, and it doesn't take up a lot of floor space to practice. Perhaps this is a vital clue to the roots of Hung Gar.

The Four Lower Tigers Meet Canton

Sifu Kwong Wing Lam of Sunnyvale, California, trained in both Canton Hung Gar and *Ha Say Fu* Hung Gar. He teaches both schools as complementary parts of his Hung Gar curriculum. His students begin with the Canton Hung Gar, then progress to the Ha Say Fu Hung Gar later. This is because the Ha Say Fu is a little more sophisticated, with a much deeper emphasis upon internal power and many esoteric weapons.

Hung Gar is famous for its animal sets. The Canton school is famous for a set known as *sup ying* (ten forms). These forms are the five animals (dragon, snake, tiger, panther, and crane) and the five elements (gold, wood, water, fire, and earth). Frequently, students neglect the elements, giving rise to the set known as five animals. The dragon form uses intense internal power exercises while the other four animals train fighting techniques that mimic the spirit of each respective beast.

In Ha Say Fu Hung Gar, these five animals each get their own respective set. Each set has a different focus upon internal power. Each animal set relies heavily upon *yee chi kim yeung ma* (withdrawing the gonads horse stance) instead of the *sei pihng ma* (four corners horse stance). This stance is shorter, the width of your hips plus a half, with the toes pointing inward like the Wing Chun stance.

The Hung Gar salute has an elevated mystique. Because of its associations with Hung Tong, secret gestures were used so underground rebels could recognize each other, as with the Masonic handshake. This carried over into Hung Gar. The salute is a fist and a tiger claw, made with two steps forward then two steps backward. Both the salutes of Canton and Ha Say Fu Hung Gar fit this description, but their salutes are distinct. The Canton school steps forward to a cat stance, while Ha Say Fu uses a stance with the heels together and the toes pointed outward.

One of the most fascinating aspects of Ha Say Fu is its emphasis upon unusual ancient weapons. Ha Say Fu contains many weapon sets seldom seen anymore, such as the thunder hoe, the double tiger-head shields, the gen (a precursor to the Okinawan sai), the nine-pointed rake, the dragon-head wooden bench, and the double-headed dragon chain whip. Both schools share the same distinctive weapon, the butterfly swords. However, each school has its own individual version of this set.

Another fascinating aspect of Ha Say Fu is that it has a unique iron palm training method. Ha Say Fu Hung Gar favors the tiger claw for attack, just like the Canton school. So, its iron palm trains the tiger claw strike in addition to palm strikes. This iron palm method uses a special training table where the iron-filled striking target can move. The moving target is struck, grabbed, and moved with the tiger claw within the designated sequence of palm strikes.

Sifu Wing Lam believes Ha Say Fu may well be monk Gee Sim's original unmodified system, but acknowledges the impossibility to prove it. It does fit the descriptions in the history books and preserves many of the characteristics of Canton Hung Gar. Furthermore, according to Wing Lam, the feel of Ha Say Fu is deeply rooted in traditional Shaolin. If it is the true original, the modification was far too long ago to have been properly documented. Unlike the Canton school, the lineage of Ha Say Fu is murky.

A Mysterious Master

Sifu Wing Lam was introduced to his Ha Say Fu Hung Gar teacher, Leung Wah Chew, through a mutual friend. Sigung Leung would make house calls to Wing Lam's tiny apartment, always arriving by a different route. Since open floor space was scarce, they would practice on the rooftops above Hong Kong's crowded urban sprawl. They had the minimal resources for a school—just a teacher, a few students, and a meeting time. Often, they fashioned the unique weapons of Ha Say Fu Hung Gar out of whatever they could acquire, usually substituting wood pieces for metal, just so they could transmit the teachings. Wing Lam never learned his teacher's complete martial lineage. Leung's reputation and skill were enough for him to feel privileged to train under him.

Leung had connections with the "dark society" of Hong Kong, what we might call organized crime. He had a kung fu school in Macao that he closed when he immigrated to Hong Kong. In Hong Kong, he was the boss of a major underground casino (gambling casinos are legal in Macao, but not in Hong Kong). His fighting skills were sharpened constantly by this business. Wing Lam remembers when Leung brought over a friend to assist coaching fighting skills. Although this fighter was impressive, the very next day he was ambushed in the streets of Hong Kong by a rival gang, who cut him to death with long Chinese watermelon knives. Wing Lam never again heard anything else about his teacher's notorious guest.

Leung Wah Chew was a good friend of another great master, Um Yue Ming. Together these martial brothers answered the challenge of the first Asian public kung fu tournament of the twentieth century, the famous Chinese Taiwan Kuoshu ("national art") Association Invitational of 1957. Competitors from Macao, Taiwan, and Hong Kong sparred against each other, comparing a wide range of styles such as Shaolin, Choy Li Fut, *yau kung moon*, snake, white crane, mantis, *law hron moon*, and more. Leung represented Ha Say Fu Hung Gar and Um represented *hop gar*. They joined thirty other competitors from Hong Kong. Unfortunately, neither placed very well. Since neither had trained with sparring gloves or tournament rules, both were eliminated before the finals. This loss did little to affect their pride. Um Yue Ming's school used a black lion for two consecutive Chinese New Years to collect lucky money. The black lion symbolizes an open martial challenge to duel with any and all comers. In those days, this was no idle boast. Such challenges seldom went unanswered. Eventually, Um immigrated to San Francisco, where he opened a school and clinic on Powell Street. Some say he overstepped his boundaries. In the 1970s, he was gunned down at the door of his school.

Wing Lam had heard that Leung recruited his students into dark society; however, he never got the chance to find out the truth. After studying with Leung for five years, Wing Lam immigrated to the United States, possibly escaping a life of crime.

By Any Other Name

It is impossible to prove which is the original school of Hung Gar, so it also is impossible to know whether Ha Say Fu Hung Gar is really the original. The ancient mists of time have shrouded the truth from us forever. Ultimately, it does not really matter. While we must

Canton Hung Gar snake. When the adversary attacks to the middle gate . . .

. . . Sifu Wing Lam smothers the first punch with both forearms. When the adversary follows with an attack to the high gate . . .

. . . Wing Lam counters with a high block and snake hand strike to the throat.

Ha Say Fu Hung Gar snake. The defense to the same attack is identical.

The only difference is that Wing Lam counters . . .

. . . with a "snake tongue" strike instead of a snake hand strike.

Canton Hung Gar favors closing the gap.

When the adversary attacks to the upper gate, Sifu Wing Lam blocks the punch upward.

When the adversary follows with an attack to the middle gate, Wing Lam blocks it to the side.

When the adversary follows with a second attack to the high gate, Wing Lam again blocks upward, while simultaneously closing the gap for an elbow strike.

Ha Say Fu Hung Gar favors sticking to the adversary.

When the adversary attacks to the upper gate, Sifu Wing Lam deflects the punch to the side.

When the adversary follows with an attack to the middle gate, Wing Lam seizes the arm and pulls him forward.

As the adversary attempts to recover, Wing Lam slides up his arm to jab into the armpit.

Canton Hung Gar favors offense.

When the adversary attacks to the middle gate, Sifu
Wing Lam blocks it to the side with one arm.

When the adversary follows with an attack to the high
gate, Wing Lam simultaneously blocks and chops to the
throat.

Ha Say Fu Hung Gar favors defense.

When the adversary attacks to the middle gate, Sifu Wing Lam blocks it to the side with both arms.

When the adversary follows with an attack to the high gate, Wing Lam again blocks it to the side with both arms.

This two-arm block is stronger and it provides a better opportunity to seize the arm. However, it commits the defender to defend. He cannot simultaneously block and attack.

Canton Hung Gar favors simultaneous blocks and strikes.

When the adversary attacks to the middle gate, Sifu
Wing Lam smothers the first punch with both forearms.

When the adversary follows with an attack to the high
gate, Wing Lam counters with a simultaneous "crane
wing" block and kick.

Ha Say Fu Hung Gar favors joint locks and pressure-point attacks.

When the adversary attacks to the middle gate, Sifu Wing Lam grabs his wrist.

Wing Lam twists the adversary's arm, while seizing an elbow pressure point.

With the adversary's arm in a lock, Wing Lam finishes with a kick to the hip joint.

always honor our martial ancestors for their sacrifice, we cannot dwell so deeply in the past that we lose track of the moment. Like computer programs, it is not the first version that we need to know—it is the most up-to-date version.

The most important issue here actually concerns knowledge. We live in a time where information is abundant, but only if you are willing to seek it out. So many people today are willing to accept the first easy answer and worship it as the truth. In kung fu, this attitude is a terrible disservice. The greatest treasure of kung fu is its long and diverse history. From a modest seedling, it has grown to a mighty tree that has born many fruits. It would be such a shame to see any of those fruits go to waste when so many people are hungry.

It is the responsibility of each earnest student to delve deeply into this wealth of knowledge. Only a fool will lean upon his own misunderstanding. While we might dedicate our lives to a particular discipline, we should not limit ourselves so much that we fail to see the forest for the trees.

FOUR SCHOOLS AND WHAT THEY FEATURE

Canton Hung Gar
Comments: most popular school of Hung Gar outside China.
Characteristics:
   kiuh sau (bridge hand)
   sei pihng ma (four corners horse stance)
Major hand sets:
   kung gee fook fu (taming the tiger)
   fu hoc sheung ying kuen (tiger and crane fist)

sup ying kuen (ten forms fist)
tiet sing kuen (iron thread fist)

Ha Say Fu (Four Lower Tigers) Hung Gar
Comments: fits descriptions of the earliest Hung Gar.
Characteristics:
   yee chi kim yeung ma (withdrawing the gonads horse stance)
Major hand sets:
   bao ying kuen (panther)
   fu ying kuen (tiger)
   she ying kuen (snake)
   hoc ying kuen (crane)
   lung ying kuen (dragon)

Wubei Hung Gar
Comments: creation is attributed to the first Song emperor.
Characteristics: focus on open-hand strikes over closed fist.
Major hand sets:
   jung sao (big combination hand)
   fong sao (jamming hand)
   gum gong sao (gold general's hand)

Szechuan Hung Gar
Comments: contains sets and principles that are consistent with modern Shaolin Temple kung fu.
Characteristics: attacks along the centerline, seldom sidesteps.
Major hand sets:
   siu hong kuen (small red fist)
   da hong kuen (big red fist)
   hong moon choy (red door strike)
   hong moon sao (red door hand)

This material originally appeared in the January 1999 issue of Inside Kung-Fu.

15

Da Mo's Secret Shaolin Temple Chi Kung

Dr. Yang Jwing-Ming

The Shaolin Temple

In the first half of the sixth century, a Buddhist monk named Da Mo arrived at the Shaolin Temple in Henan province, China. The arrival of this traveling Indian monk would have a great effect on both the temple and Chinese martial arts.

Da Mo, also known as Bodhidharma, was a prince of a small tribe in southern India. From the fragments of historical records that exist, it is believed he was born about 483. At that time the Chinese considered India to be a spiritual center, since it was the source of Buddhism, which was becoming very influential in China. Many Chinese emperors either sent priests to India to study Buddhism and bring back scriptures or else invited Indian priests to come to China to preach. Da Mo was an invited priest.

Da Mo is considered by many to have been a bodhisattva, or an enlightened being who renounced nirvana to save others. Buddhism is a major religion based on the belief that Gautama, the Buddha, achieved nirvana, or perfect bliss and freedom from the cycle of birth and death, and taught how to achieve this state.

Da Mo was of the Mahayana school of Buddhism, which includes Tibetan Buddhism and Chan, or Zen, Buddhism. He came to China in 526 or 527 during the reign of Emperor Liang Wu of the Liang dynasty. Da Mo went first to the Guang Xiao Temple in Canton. The governor of Canton recommended Da Mo to the emperor, who invited Da Mo to visit. The emperor, however, did not like Da Mo's Buddhist theory, and so Da Mo left the emperor and traveled to the Shaolin Temple in Henan province, where he spent the rest of his life.

When Da Mo arrived at the temple, he found that the monks were in poor physical condition because of their lack of exercise. Many were weak and sickly and would fall asleep during meditation and lecture. Da Mo was so distressed by the monks' physical conditions that he retired to meditate on the problem and stayed in retirement for nine years. When he emerged, he had a solution—Da Mo's *Yi Ji Jing wai dan* exercises.

For more than 1,400 years, the monks of the Shaolin Temple have trained using these Da Mo chi kung exercises. These exercises used to be secret, and only in the twentieth century have they become popularly known and used.

These exercises are easy, and their benefits—good health, improved strength and muscular endurance, and the development of internal power—can be experienced in a short time. The Shaolin monks practiced these exercises to circulate chi and improve their health. Later, the Shaolin monks coordinated their wai dan exercises with martial techniques. This built their internal power by concentrating chi to affect the appropriate muscles and also helped to establish the Shaolin Temple as an important center of martial arts training and development.

Da Mo's Yi Ji Jing is a chi kung exercise based on the theory of wai dan, or "external elixir." Wai dan, pronounced "Why Dan," is the practice of increasing chi circulation by stimulating one area of the body until a large energy potential builds up and flows through the chi channel system.

The principles of wai dan chi kung practice will be explained first, followed by Da Mo's famous Shaolin training method.

Wai Dan Theory

Wai dan exercises increase chi circulation in the body. Chi flows through the body via a network known as the chi channels, which act like rivers. According to acupuncture theory, the chi channels are connected to the internal organs. If chi is circulating smoothly, then the organs will function normally. If an organ is not functioning normally, then increasing the chi flow in the corresponding channel will help restore its normal function. Good health is the result of strong, balanced chi circulation.

To train wai dan chi kung, you repeatedly tense and relax a specific muscle or part of the body as you concentrate on that muscle or body part. When you exercise a part of the body in this way for several minutes, both chi and blood are collected in this high-potential area. Then when the muscles relax, the highly charged chi and blood will spread to nearby areas with a lower energy state and so increase the chi circulation.

When doing this type of exercise, be sure to use as little tension as possible, because great tension will constrict the chi channels and prevent the flow of energy. Some practitioners do not tense their muscles at all, but merely imagine tensing them. Others tense them just enough to aid concentration.

In wai dan exercises, you concentrate on your breath, and at the same time imagine guiding energy to a specific area. The chi channel system and the brain are closely connected; so when you concentrate, you can control the circulation of chi more efficiently. This results in the muscles being able to exert maximum power, known as wai dan internal power.

For example, to guide the chi you have generated to the center of your palm, imagine an obstacle in front of your palm and try to push it away without tensing any muscles. The better you imagine, the stronger the chi flow will be. Frequently, when an object seems too heavy to move and you have tried in vain to push it, if you relax, calm down, and imagine pushing the object, you will then find the object will move. Therefore, when practicing the wai dan exercises, you should be calm, relaxed, and natural. The muscles should never be strongly tensed, because this tension will narrow the chi channels. Concentrate on breathing from the dan tian (approximately one and a half inches below the navel) and on guiding the chi.

In chi kung training, concentration is the key to success; the mind controls the flow of chi, just as it controls other body functions. You may have experienced ways in which the mind causes reactions in your body. Thinking about frightening things can make you sweat. Thinking of a tense situation can cause you to tighten your muscles so much that your whole body becomes sore. In this case your mind causes a chemical reaction (i.e., the generation of acid) in your tight muscles. Your mind can also relax your body just by thinking about it. Many people are using this approach to control their pulse or blood pressure without drugs.

There is a disadvantage to wai dan exercises. Because of the repeated tensing and relaxing of the muscles during training, the muscle itself will be built up, as in weight lifting, and can become overdeveloped. This overdevelopment will slow you down and at the same time will constrict the channels. When these overdeveloped muscles are not regularly exercised, they accumulate fat, which further narrows the channels and causes the chi and blood to become stagnant. Common symptoms of this phenomenon are high blood pressure, local nerve pain, and poor muscle control. In the Chinese martial arts this is called *san gong*, or energy dispersion. As long as you avoid overdeveloping your muscles, san gong will not happen.

Da Mo's Yi Ji Jing Exercises

When practicing the Da Mo exercises, find a quiet place with clean air. Stand facing the east with your back relaxed and naturally straight, and your feet a shoulder-width apart and parallel. Facing the east takes advantage of the Earth's rotation and the energy flow from the sun. Keeping the legs apart will relax the legs and thighs during practice.

Keep your mouth closed and touch your palate with the tip of the tongue without strain. In Chinese meditation this touch is called *da qiao*, or building the bridge, because it connects the yin and yang circulation. You will find that saliva accumulates in your mouth. Swallow it to keep your throat from getting dry.

The key to successful practice of this exercise is concentrating on the area being exercised and on your breath. Without this concentration, the original goal of chi circulation will be lost and the exercise will be in vain.

In several circumstances practice should be avoided. Do not practice when you are very hungry or too full. If you are very hungry, it interferes with proper concentration. If you have eaten, wait at least 30 minutes, and preferably one hour, before practicing so that the chi is not concentrated in the digestive system. Avoid practicing one day before or after having sex. Do not practice when you are so tired that your attention wanders uncontrollably. Do not practice after drinking alcohol. And finally, do not practice when you are very worried, for it will be too difficult to concentrate.

The forms should be done continuously, one after the other, to conserve the energy you build up. For example, the first form will build up the energy at the wrist. The second form will transfer the energy already built up at the wrist to the fingers and palms

Form 1: Keep your hands beside your body with the palms open and facing down, fingertips pointing forward. Keep the elbows bent. Imagine pushing the palms down and lifting your fingers backward when exhaling, and then relax them when inhaling. This form will build the chi, or energy, at the wrist area, and your palms and wrists should feel warm after 50 repetitions.

Form 2: Without moving your arms, make fists with the palms facing down and thumbs extended toward the body. Imagine tightening your fists and pushing the thumbs backward when exhaling, and then relax when inhaling. Keep your wrists bent to retain the energy built up in the first form.

Form 3: Again without moving your arms, turn the fists so that the palms face each other, and place the thumbs over the fingers, like normal fists. Imagine tightening your fists when exhaling, and then relax when inhaling. The muscles and nerves of the arms will be stimulated and energy will accumulate there.

Form 4: Extend your arms straight forward at shoulder height, palms still facing each other. Making normal fists, imagine tightening when exhaling, and then relax when inhaling. This will build up energy in the shoulders and chest.

Form 5: Lift your arms straight up, palms facing each other, keeping your hands as fists. Imagine tightening your fists when exhaling, and then relax when inhaling. This builds energy in the shoulders, neck, and sides.

Form 6: Lower your arms so that your upper arms are parallel with the ground, your elbows are bent, and your fists are by your ears. The palms face forward. Imagine tightening your fists when exhaling, and then relax when inhaling. This builds energy in the sides, chest, and upper arms.

Form 7: Extend your arms straight out to the sides with the palms facing forward. Imagine tightening your fists when exhaling, and then relax them when inhaling. This form will build energy in the shoulders, chest, and back.

Form 8: Raise your arms out to the sides of your body with the palms facing forward and your elbows bent to create a rounded effect. Imagine tightening the fists and guiding the accumulated energy through the arms to the fists when exhaling. Relax when inhaling.

Form 9: Pull your fists toward your body, bending the elbows. Keep your fists just in front of your face, with the palms facing out. Imagine tightening your fists when exhaling, and then relax when inhaling. This form is similar to form 6, but the fists are closer together and forward, so a different set of muscles is stressed. This form intensifies the flow of energy through the arms.

Form 10: Lift your forearms vertically. Your palms face forward and your upper arms are out to the sides and parallel with the floor. Imagine tightening your fists when exhaling, and then relax when inhaling. This form will circulate the energy built up in the shoulders.

Form 11: Keeping your elbows bent, lower your fists until they are in front of your navel, palms down. Imagine tightening your fists, and guide the energy to circulate in the arms when exhaling. Relax when inhaling. This is the first recovery form.

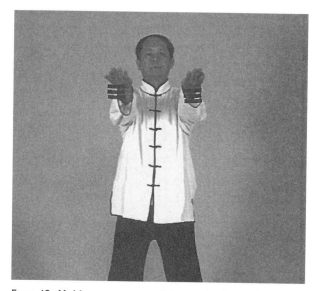

Form 12: Hold your arms straight out in front of your body. Open your hands so that your palms face up. Imagine lifting up when exhaling, and then relax when inhaling. This is the second recovery form.

Bodhidharma, or Da Mo, once a prince of a small tribe in India, was considered by many to have been an enlightened being who had renounced nirvana to save others. He created an exercise program for the monks of Shaolin.

while continuing to build up energy. The third form will transfer the energy from the palms and wrists to the arms, and so forth.

Repeat each form 50 times. A repetition consists of inhaling while relaxing the muscle or limb, and then exhaling while imagining that you are tightening the muscle and simultaneously imagining energy flowing to that area. The muscles may be slightly tensed. The arms should not be fully extended in these forms. After 50 repetitions, begin the next form in the sequence without stopping.

Beginners may find it hard to complete more than five forms if they do 50 repetitions of each form. Do not be concerned. Five forms is a good number to practice, because this means a practice session will take approximately 15 to 20 minutes. Alternatively, you can practice all 12 forms and do fewer repetitions of each. For example, 20 repetitions of each form of the complete Da Mo set would take approximately 20 minutes. If you practice once or twice a day, you should be able to complete the entire form in six months. If you continue this training regularly, you can build a tremendous amount of power and energy. These exercises will increase your nerve and muscle efficiency so they can be used to their maximum in martial arts. If you are practicing for health purposes only, five forms daily is sufficient.

After practicing, stand for a few minutes with your arms hanging loosely at your sides. You can also lie down and relax completely. Breathe regularly, relax, and feel the energy redistribute itself.

Conclusion

The Da Mo set is a simple yet effective method for developing strength, power, and improved health. It builds extra energy (chi) in your body and helps you to use this energy more efficiently; for example, it allows you to strike with tremendous power or to resist the penetration of an opponent's power into your body. It is also a good chi kung set because the simple motions make it easier to concentrate on your breath and the flow of chi.

For more information on chi kung training, including further wai dan practices for the martial arts, please refer to the book *Qigong for Health and Martial Arts* by Dr. Yang Jwing-Ming (YMAA Publication Center).

This material originally appeared in the August 1998 issue of Inside Kung-Fu.

16

Baguazhang
Art of the Chinese Bodyguard

Jerry Payne

I rooted out the enemy above and below;
I made an end of war;
I promoted the welfare of the land;
I have sheltered them that need me in my strength. . . .
—KING HAMMURABI, BABYLONIA (1792–1750 B.C.)

Dr. John Painter in traditional costume assumes the Jiu Long Baguazhang "wandering dragon" posture.

The caravan of trucks and horses heading north out of Chengdu made its way across the narrow pass entering the southern section of the Daba mountain range. Lin, the lead driver, was nervous. Continuous battles over territory beginning with the birth of the Chinese republic in 1911 to well past 1929 had fueled the greed of many Chinese warlords who preyed on travelers and merchants as they made their way along the unguarded roads from province to province.

Rounding a bend in the narrow road, the lead truck skidded to a halt. Boulders blocked the path. All eyes darted from one crag of rock to another. Suddenly their worst nightmare was realized as Chang Peifu (a notorious Fetui), holding a rifle and accompanied by three other men, one with a pistol, the others with shining sabers, stepped from behind the boulder.

Dr. John Painter instructs senior student Hoan Ngo in the proper position for the twin heaven palm posture.

Dr. Terry Berryman, a Jiu Long Baguazhang study group instructor from Vail, Colorado, practicing Jiu Long *qigong* standing meditation posture—"hands float on water."

"Give us your horses and trucks," Chang demanded.

Lin pointed to the triangular banner floating in the breeze attached to the hood of the truck by a slender pole. "Leave us alone, we are protected by fierce bodyguards," he said.

With those words Chang spat on the ground as he ripped the banner from the truck and broke it over his knee. Tossing the flag into the ravine hundreds of feet below he leveled his rifle at the driver.

"Hold up there. Let us go in peace and no one will be harmed." The voice came from behind the bandit's group. Wheeling, Chang and his men saw an older man with long graying black hair tied in the back and wearing a padded jacket. He was on horseback. A younger man beside the horse was on foot. The two

had suddenly appeared from around the bend without warning. The elder man spoke as he dismounted his horse, moving toward the bandit with a curious, sliding walk.

"My name is Li Zhang-lai and this is my son Long-dao. We want no trouble. Please leave our employers alone and we will not harm you." With a sneer Chang leveled his rifle at the small man's chest. At almost the same instant, the older man darted to one side and seemed to glide forward, both palms outstretched, forming the Jiu Long Baguazhang heaven palms wedge posture.

A sharp report split the mountain air as the rifle discharged. But it was no longer in Chang's hands. Chang was falling back as the rifle flew over the cliff's side. Reeling from the blow, the bandit made a grab for the pistol at his hip. As if by magic, suddenly an M96 Mauser pistol appeared in the elder Li's hand. There were two sharp cracks as he put a bullet through Chang's heart and another through his head. The odd-looking gun seemed to snake beneath his left armpit as he whirled to face the other gun-wielding bandit. A third and fourth bullet found their way through the head and heart of the second Fetui, who was just leveling his own pistol at Master Li.

The two sword-wielding bandits turned to flee and found themselves cut off from escape by Long-dao. They both attacked him simultaneously. Dodging deftly past a downward stroke, the first man suddenly found his hands empty, wrist broken, and his own body flying over the cliff after his sword. The second man sliced horizontally. Longdao seemed to spin inside the cut and then disappeared. The last thing the man felt was a pair of powerful hands grabbing his head from the rear. Then all went black as he collapsed to the ground with a broken neck.

"Not bad, first son," said the elder Li as he returned the smoking Mauser to its shoulder holster.

Jiu Long Baguazhang develops tremendous whole-body power combined with mental energy to release the *nei gong,* or internal energy. Here Dr. Painter snaps a 12-foot solid pine post set three feet in the ground with the Jiu Long Baguazhang "mountain" palm during a 1997 T'ai Chi Farm workshop.

Instructor David Briggs from Richboro, Pennsylvania, develops *wai gong* (outer power) strength with the Jiu Long iron sphere circle-walking exercise. The spheres, originally made of iron or hollow clay, are now made of rubber filled with water. Weights range from 5 pounds to 50 pounds. The exercise develops whole-body connection to the earth and power in the lifting muscles of the entire torso.

Dr. Painter works speed, timing, and "dragon coiling" energy on the double-ended speed bag as part of the combat Jiu Long Baguazhang training.

Hoan Ngo walking the circle in the Jiu Long "dragon upholding heaven" posture.

"Although, your weight floated just a bit on the dragon circles the heavenly moon when you took the last bandit."

"I will try to do better, father," the young man replied. In a few hours the rocks were cleared and the caravan resumed its journey. It was just another day in the perilous life of the Chinese *Baobiao*.

Chinese Bodyguards

I never tire of hearing Dr. John Painter recount the many stories about his teacher's adventures. They are always tales of survival and hope from the legends of the Li family of Sichuan province, China, who had been taken from poverty to wealth as Chinese bodyguards responsible for the safety and lives of their many merchant clients.

For almost thirty years John Painter, a captain with the American Rangers Law Enforcement Training Institute and a naturopathic physician, has trained in and used Jiu Long Baguazhang in his work as a professional bodyguard and law enforcement defensive tactics trainer. Painter is now the North American representative of the Li family Jiulong Baguazhang Association. He conducts classes and workshops in both the healing and martial art methods of this fascinating system for law enforcement officers and the general public.

The men who had attacked the caravan were the Fetui (bandits). Fetui were ruthless thugs who, in a country with little or no local law enforcement, became quite a problem for the local citizens and merchant caravans. Merchants who transported goods were easy prey. The best way to move safely about was to hire the Baobiao (armed escorts) who

Dr. Berryman squares off in the boxer's stance, ready to punch Hoan Ngo. Ngo assumes the "heaven twin yin" posture in preparation for the attack.

Berryman lunges with a right hook and Ngo counters, stepping into the "dragon upholding heaven" posture. His right palm creates uplifting force while the left spears to heart meridian point number 1 at the axillary plexus under Berryman's armpit. This blow is very dangerous, often resulting in temporary or permanent paralysis of the arm.

specialized in protecting caravan travel routes along which merchandise was shipped. A few of these bodyguard families became well known for their work as Baobiao.

Caravans under the protection of the Baobiao would be accompanied by these armed guards, all skilled in hand-to-hand combat, traditional weapons, and modern firearms. The head wagon would carry a large triangular flag upon which appeared the Chinese characters for the name of the head Baobiao. If the *wushu* (martial) man was famous enough, just the presence of his banner on a caravan was at times enough to guarantee safe passage.

The Art of Choice

The Baobiao were not like ordinary house guards or bouncers. They were often educated and highly skilled in military tactics, healing, and martial arts. One of the most popular methods for hand-to-hand and weapons fighting employed was that of baguazhang (*Pa Kua Chang*), an internal martial art noted for its use of deft footwork and the palms instead of fists for striking.

The other advantage of this method was that, unlike other styles of combat, baguazhang seemed to have been designed to deal with multiple and armed

Sliding his left hand under Berryman's arm, Ngo steps into a spinning step as his body presses into Berryman's torso. The left forearm and shoulder produce a *Qin Na* lock to the elbow. The spinning action of this move can easily fracture the delicate elbow joint.

Ngo's momentum, combined with the lock, throws Berryman forward. Here Ngo uses the "twin yin heaven" posture to step into Berryman's center of balance and project him away.

opponents. The art contains strikes, throws, locks, and avoidance techniques, making it one of the most effective and complete systems ever devised. Even today, this four-hundred-year-old combat system is still the art of choice for the Chinese special police and government bodyguards.

What Is Baguazhang

Baguazhang translates as "eight shapes palms." No one knows exactly who created the first baguazhang, although most experts agree that the most widely circulated forms can be traced to one Dong Hai Chuan

(1796–1880). Dong's martial art, which he claimed was taught to him by an ancient Daoist sage, was so effective that it became the official technique of the palace guards protecting the Qing emperor.

Today, truly effective combat-oriented baguazhang is quite rare. The combat arts of baguazhang, like those used by the Baobiao during the early 1900s, are unlike the more-modern cousins designed after the Communist revolution. These new methods retain few combat-effective (*zhandouli*) principles and are mostly for aesthetics, aerobic exercise, and tournament display.

The original old forms of combat baguazhang training are both internal and external, developing the

Dr. Painter applies a Qin Na shoulderlock to student Robert Castaldo during a baguazhang push-hands practice. Note the position of Painter's front foot as he prepares to throw Castaldo. At fast speed the enemy's ankle and possibly knee will be dislocated.

Senior instructor Andrew Garza disarms saber-wielding senior instructor Alan Marshall using the Jiu Long "heaven" tai chi posture. Methods used for disarming edged weapons at close range are also used with firearms control by Jiu Long experts.

muscles, tendons, ligaments, and bones, as well as the internal energy. Combat baguazhang is a difficult taskmaster requiring strict discipline and rigorous physical and mental training. Instructors with true combat training experience in baguazhang are rare today even in China. Among the rash of schools springing up around the world, there are very few individuals in this category.

One system of baguazhang that became associated with the Li family of Sichuan province was called Jiu Long Baguazhang (nine-dragon eight-shapes palm). This style was said to have been first conceived by Daoist sage Li Ching-yuen. He taught this system to his cousin Li Zhang-lai (1850–1946), who developed it into a devastating martial art making use of the mind/body connection to fuel the great power that is the hallmark of the Jiu Long system. Li Zhang-lai taught the method to his son Li Longdao (1880–1980), who then passed it on to John Painter after moving to the United States.

The Same, but Different

Although there are many external similarities, Li's family style of Jiu Long Baguazhang differs from Dong's version in a number of ways. Training consists of internal and external exercises comprising standing meditations, martial arts and qigong practices, balance work, strength and speed developmental routines, linear and circle-walking forms holding and applying each of the postures, and the study of defensive tactics.

In Jiu Long Baguazhang the word *palm* actually means the shapes assumed by the whole body, incorporating upper- and lower-body positioning. This shape embodies all the body's energies. The shapes become entire attitudes permeating the entire psychological and physiological makeup of the student.

Jiu Long forms are not fixed techniques but outer expressions of the energy revealed by the *Yi Jing* symbols expressed in mental attitudes and movements of the body. Training in the Jiu Long system is much more than just memorizing set patterns or forms. Each of the eight postures is studied individually, almost as eight separate martial arts, with each containing a special type of energy.

When a student comes to understand the numerous variations of a single shape mentally and physically, these forms become natural and intuitive. The ultimate goal of Jiu Long Baguazhang is to learn to move naturally with such power, grace, and balance that no matter what happens, you are able to go along with the "now" moment, merging and emerging with external forces while preserving your own energy.

Captain John Painter in battlefield dress assumes the "wandering dragon" posture. Jiu Long principles for military CQB (close-quarter battle) were recently introduced at an Israeli military combat training school by senior Jiu Long instructor Ben Hazan, a military combat instructor in Israel. Hazan reports that many of the soldiers expressed surprise and interest at the efficiency and ease with which the methods function.

Jiu Long's Heaven Palm

The first palm in Jiu Long is the heaven palm, symbolized in the Yi Jing by three strong lines of the *qian gua* representing yang energy. Its actions are swift and as unforgiving as the cutting edge of a sword; they are nonjudgmental. The heaven palm is the master energy source of expansive power from which arise the other seven energies of

1. earth (energy of spiraling power)
2. fire (explosive power like a cannon shot)
3. water (flowing energy as in the ocean waves)
4. wind (penetrating energy like an ax splitting)

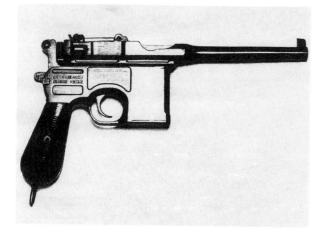

Shown here is the ten-shot Mauser M96 semiautomatic pistol used by the Li family bodyguards. Mausers were created in Germany in the 1890s. Large quantities of this semiautomatic pistol were imported by China during the birth of the Chinese republic in 1911. Later, the Chinese manufactured copies of the powerful firearm at small factories. This is reputed to be the same pistol used by Li Zhang-lai when he killed the Fetui bandit Chang Peifu. His son, Li Longdao, smuggled the weapon out of China when they escaped in 1945. This treasured memento of the Li family can be found in the collection of Captain John Painter.

5. thunder (the shocking force of an earthquake or sonic boom)

6. lake (deep rolling energy that draws things into the depths)

7. mountain (uprooting power of the inner mind)

The Jiu Long Baguazhang heaven boxer moves into the opponent like a flying dragon, surrounds him, winds him, and wraps him with his heaven energy. The rushing force and power of the Jiu Long wedge principle overwhelms his center of balance. As the oppo-nent loses control he experiences the fear of sudden loss of control.

From the first touch there is a feeling of control exerted from the heaven boxer into the spine of his enemy that produces confusion and disorientation. As soon as the enemy feels himself being pushed in one direction and attempts to adjust, the force keeps shift-ing like a swirling maelstrom. Because whole-body energy is used in striking, the heaven palm power is devastating, sending uplifting or pressing downward shockwaves through the torso and head that have such intensity they can disrupt internal organs and break bones. Throwing and locking arts designed to instantly disable a weapon-wielding attacker are also part of the heaven boxer's arsenal of weapons.

Today, as in the past, those who practice Jiu Long Baguazhang are sworn to uphold a strict moral virtue. This code is part of the system of the Li family admo-nition to not teach any undesirable people who would use the art for personal gain at the expense of others' safety.

To the Li family, Baobiao justice and right action prevail whenever the art must be used in defense of one's self or others. The Jiu Long boxer of today, as his brothers from the past, can truly say, "I have sheltered them that need me in my strength!"

This is the legacy of the Chinese baguazhang bodyguards.

Jerry Payne, a longtime student of Dr. John Painter and the Li family's daoqiquan *internal martial arts, is a freelance writer living in Arlington, Texas. This material appeared in the June 1998 issue of* Inside Kung-Fu.

PART TWO
Techniques

How to Develop a Fighting Strategy

A Lesson Plan for Becoming a World Champion

Roger Haines

With a sense of urgency, Roger L. Haines worked into the late hours of the night putting together fighting strategies for his well-known student, Aisha Thornton, a World *Tang Soo Do* Champion. Master Haines, a police self-defense instructor and Eighth Dan Black Belt, teaches Tang Soo Do and tae kwon do to teens within the inner city. His lesson plans resemble a Webster's dictionary. Master Haines teaches his champion student essential sparring strategies for how to attack, counter, and checkmate her opponents in the competition ring. One of the most important things in teaching strategies is to have good communication between instructor and student. It's vital that both people be on the same page.

One very useful tool for students and teachers alike is a checklist with comments on techniques and performance. Use a checklist when you go over your fighter's and student's good and bad points. As a tournament competitor, a student needs to know where he or she stands in order to have a point to build from. Communication between the student and instructor is a must. The student has to believe that the coach can make him or her a champion.

Defense Strategies

For World Tang Soo Do Champion Aisha Thornton, the name of the game is to beat your opponent off the line. Aisha is one of martial arts' fastest female kickers in competition. She explodes off the line with six to eleven kick combinations without placing her foot down. This type of strategy and offense system was put together by coaches Master Haines and Master Steve Allen. Its intention is to make Aisha's opponents move backward. If the opponents try to counter her, then she blocks the counter and attacks them. She must always remember to keep pressure on her opponents and try not to give them a chance to come after her.

Defense Fighting Strategies

Aisha Thornton and her coaches never go into competition fighting on the defensive. When the situation occurs, however, Aisha has to react by blocking and then counter-turning a defensive situation into an offensive one. She does this by using offensive kicking techniques. As an opponent attacks her with front and back kicking techniques, Aisha will use a front-leg swoop hook kick. The swoop hook kick wraps around the opponent's guards in a circular motion. She kicks at the same time her opponent is launching an attack on her. The best defense is a good offense! However, a coach must have a good menu of techniques to teach students. Other techniques include a defense backhand, ridge hand, and defense counter-punching. Some defense kicking techniques are a defense jump back kick and spinning hook kick. The counter reverse wheel kick covers the distance over a long range.

Aisha Thornton uses the reverse wheel kick when an opponent is taller than she. Timing is crucial! As soon as the opponent brings his or her leg up, you bring your leg up to close the gap and hit him or her in the head.

Angle Kicking Techniques

Aisha never throws the same kicking techniques twice from the same angle. She has been blessed with the ability to kick from any angle she chooses. It's hard for her opponents to block something when they don't know where it will come from.

How to Train to Win

The top of any coach's agenda is sparring practice. Aisha tries to get twenty rounds of sparring per workout with different partners. It's also important to condition and stretch for two hours a day. Make sure students spend just as much time working on their weak points as they do on their strong ones.

The Video Room

One of the most intriguing things about training for competition is studying opponents on videotape. To use videos as a tool for training students, a coach must know what to look for and have a plan on how to take that information and implement it in the classroom or gym. After watching videotapes of the best female fighters on the open circuit, tae kwon do and Tang Soo Do circuits, and the National Karate circuits, Master Haines has Aisha make a list of her opponents' strongest points and what she will have to defend against. Master Haines and Aisha work as a team, looking for the opponents' weakest points and what they have to attack. An opponent might have a good side kick, back kick, or reverse punch.

Master Haines and Aisha look to see how many times an opponent might throw a side kick or round kick. Then they write that down as the number one technique to practice against. If the opponent's next strongest technique is the spinning wheel kick, they write that down as the number two technique to practice, and so on.

Good Sparring Partners

Good sparring partners are sometimes hard to find. Aisha works out with a group of black belts who are champions from the NASKA (North American Sport Karate Association) circuit. One of her top sparring partners is Master Brian Nixon. Master Nixon adopts the fighting styles of different opponents after he watches them on videotapes. He might be a tae kwon do fighter on Monday, and then he is an NBL (National Blackbelt League) or NASKA fighter on Tuesday. This type of training makes Aisha Thornton work harder and be at her best for any type of competition.

This material originally appeared in the March 1998 issue of Inside Karate.

18

Transmutation
A Lock Is a Block Is a Blow Is a Throw

Tony Annesi

Every art has predetermined techniques, and every technique has a series of transitions
that may be more of an art than the techniques themselves.

Changing from one shape to another, one changes through a series of other transitional forms. This is the essence of the analytical principle called transmutation. But you do not have to be a chameleon or a shape-shifter to make these changes. You make them all the time, though you may not recognize the transitional postures as valid shapes, forms, or postures because you do not retain them for an appreciable amount of time and you do not see them photographed in books about technique or kata. But you have a wealth of hidden application within (or between) almost every movement sequence, short or long, that you practice.

The idea is simpler than it sounds. Consider doing a basic kata movement from karate or a basic technique from jujitsu. Your style has an orthodox method that helps its students consistently learn the same thing and prevents them from getting confused by

adding too many variations too soon. That orthodox way has a form. Sometimes you represent the form to yourself by a mental snapshot, sometimes by a mental video sequence. Either way, static or dynamic, the form has a recognizable shape as a specific art or even a specific style of a specific art. What if your art really was secreting elements of other arts in the very movements you do every training session?

Form Without a Name

In Japanese, that recognizable shape or form is called either a *kata* (prearranged form) or a *waza* (prearranged technique). Each art not only has an orthodox way to perform the form but also has an orthodox way to interpret the form. Thus, a karate technique called *jodan age uke* (upper-level rising reception) is seen as a block to protect one's head. An aikido technique called *sokumen irimi nage* (lateral-entering throw) is seen as a throw moving sideways. The name limits the technique and thus limits what we can see in the form. However, it doesn't have to. What if we could see the form without a stylistic bias and without a predetermined application?

What if we studied martial shapes, static and dynamic, from an objective viewpoint and drew possible applications not from their names or from the art they are associated with, but from our own knowledge of what the body can do? Admittedly, it is difficult for many martial artists to see beyond the surface of a movement. We are used to seeing definite postures, poses, and still lifes. Even in our video-oriented world of one-second takes and quick scene changes, our minds slow down or stop the action for the sake of recognition. We identify A as a music video, B as a newscast, and C as an adventure flick.

We make judgments based on our emotional evaluations of A, B, or C. Therefore, a martial arts movement gets quickly categorized as "my style" or "not my style," as functional or nonfunctional, as this or that, depending on our previous experiences, preconceived notions, and emotional evaluations. It is hard to see that upper block as anything but an upper block or that throw as anything but a throw. That is where the study of transmutation comes in. It is easier for people to see divergent results and then connect them than it is for them to see how a karate movement, for example, can be anything else than what it first appears to be.

Transmuting a Basic Technique

Let's start with the basic karate upper block. Let's further assume that we will finish with something totally different—let's say, the basic aikido side-entering throw mentioned earlier. Each transitional change may be very minor, but the accumulated changes will transmute one technique into the other. We are famil-

iar with this effect from the movies. When, in *Terminator II*, the villain robot dissolves and re-forms before our eyes, he is "morphing" thanks to new computer technology. Transmutation is a sort of "morphing" from a martial arts point of view.

The attacker comes at you with a right lunge punch. You step back with your right foot, executing a left front stance upper block. Simple enough.

Now, to develop a quicker, more efficient response, you augment your left upper block slightly. This time you use a little more body angling (*hanmi*) and parry with your right arm before performing the upper block. The attack is blocked with the parry and the block becomes a strike.

Ah, but you are not finished with your cleverness. Next, you use even more hanmi and meet the same attack with a receiving thrust (*uke tsuki*). This deflects the incoming punch and almost simultaneously strikes the attacker's face.

Now, instead of blocking, parrying, or physically deflecting the strike, you shift your weight momentarily to the right leg, which steps back only half as far as before. This minor change allows you to lunge forward a half-step inside the opponent's thrust. His lunge pulls him into your left arm, which is used as an intercepting elbow strike.

But if you can intercept with a blow, you can just as easily enter and slide your forward arm past the attacker's face. This time, you do not full enter inside the opponent's attack but allow your lead leg to stay outside. He is wedged between your forward leg and your rising arm. The resulting brushing action arches him backward, and your forward motion combined with just the slightest amount of hip rotation throws him to the side. From here, very little augmentation is needed to get a lateral *sokumen irimi nage* from aikido.

Now, what we have done forward can be done "in the looking glass." It should be obvious to any aikido person who wishes to make his application more atemi-oriented (atemi is body-striking) that his sokumen irimi nage can easily be turned into an intercepting strike with just a rotation of the forearm. From here we can work backward until we arrive at what looks like a karate upper block.

Thinking out of the Box

In June of 1993, I organized a two-day seminar with Hanshi Bruce Juchnik of the Sei Kosho Shorei Kai called "Transmutation: A Lock Is a Block Is a Blow Is a Throw." The event was quite successful, and we were able to record it on videotape. During the seminar, Hanshi Juchnik illustrated techniques similar to each other but applied with the attitude of arts from various countries; I demonstrated how a shape used by a soft art could be slightly modified to result in a shape used by a hard art and vice versa.

For years I had been doing seminars and clinics with the idea of "What You See Is Not What You Get," reversing Flip Wilson's famous seventies' aphorism.

This time, another martial artist not only agreed with my perceptions but could contribute his own insights to them. A year later we worked on a yet unpublished video, tentatively titled *Boundless Budo*, in which we did at least a dozen more transmutations to the very upper block in the previous examples.

Tony Annesi, a martial artist since 1964, has earned clan ranks in judo, aiki ju-jutsu, and karate; he also has studied aikido and researched numerous other arts. Annesi is the director of Bushido-Kai Buidoya, which markets martial arts videos, manuals, and other educational materials. He also serves as chief officer of Bushido-Kai Kenkyukuai, an organization dedicated to the development of traditional martial arts in the modern world. This material originally appeared in the April 1998 issue of Inside Karate.

Winning Wing Chun Fighting Stances

Alan Lamb

Wing Chun's basic training stance, the yee chi kim yeung ma, is sometimes referred to as the "internally rotated adduction stance," or the "goat's head" stance. It relates to the *yoy dachi*, or ready position, of Japanese martial arts.

The classroom command for the ready position in Cantonese is *oy*, almost the same as *yoy* in Japanese. The main difference in position, however, is that Wing Chun stylists adopt a "knees in, heels out, and pelvis forward" posture, which is awkward and difficult to move from but, in reality, quite practical.

As with many Wing Chun techniques, the stance varies from school to school. Some practitioners stand with their knees in, but with the toes pointed straight. Others turn their heels past 45 degrees, with their knees almost touching. Who is right?

Everyone—stance differences are merely variations on a central theme. The trick is hard training and adapting to all situations. You must be able to fight effectively from any position. If you have trouble turning, sliding, stepping, or angling from the basic stance, you are either doing it wrong, or you have not put enough time into the basics to get it right.

Take surfing as an example. How many people can stand on a surfboard without training? It takes long hours to develop balance and feel comfortable on the board. Once they have it down, however, good surfers can ride virtually any wave and adjust to all conditions because their legs and bodies have been conditioned and trained to do just that. They are "rooted" to their board.

Like Riding a Bike

The analogy of riding a bike is similar to the kung-fu concept of "rooting," which is crucial to the stance. Once you've got the stance down, you don't have to

Yee Chi Kim Yeung Ma Stance

1. Feet together, back straight.

2. Breathe in, raise palms.

3. Elbows back, sink breath, bend knees.

4. Toes out.

5. Heels out, sink and root.

6. Left turning stance.

7. Right turning stance.

8. Left fighting stance.

9. Right fighting stance.

Flanking Step or Sit Ma Stance

1. Side guard stance.

2. Side step.

3. Advance 45-degree step (*sit ma*).

worry about it. It's like riding a bicycle. Once you've learned how to do it, you don't have to worry about it; it just happens, and your basic training and forms will maintain your stance by keeping your legs strong and in good shape.

The martial arts have a variety of fighting stances, all of which have strengths and weaknesses. Much depends upon the style, mobility, and techniques being emphasized at any given time. A good fighting stance will keep you balanced and safe against attacks from the front or rear, as well as from the side. It will also allow you to adjust to flanking attacks, which cut in at 45-degree angles to your centerline.

The basics begin with the nucleus of all Wing Chun stances, the yee chi kim yeung ma. This is the basic Wing Chun parallel leg training stance. To open the stance, stand erect with feet together, back straight, hands resting on the thighs, body relaxed, and eyes gazing toward the horizon. Next, draw the hands up into the double palm-up *tan sau* position as you breathe in through the nose. Bend the knees and sink your breath into the lower abdomen, or dan tian, area. Next, turn your toes out to approximately 45 degrees, then the heels out to approximately 45 degrees. The word *approximately* indicates that you can assume a position, within that range, that will be com-

fortable for your body size. The feet are usually about a shoulder-width apart. Push the pelvis forward by tucking in the tailbone and contracting the buttocks. This turned-in position of the knees creates an imaginary third leg, forming what is called the lower Wing Chun triangular base. It is important to keep your center of gravity low for stability. If you imagine that you are holding a "bucking goat"—with its head between your knees—that is trying to free itself by pulling backward, you will be able to get a better understanding of the basic stance.

Have someone pull forward on your arms to test your stance. Then visualize the goat and put strength in your knees. Repeat the test and you will feel a difference in your stance. By focusing the strength in your knees, you should feel firmly rooted to the ground.

Another way to develop a good rooting position is by practicing the one-legged stance called *fung gerk*. This posture is formed by picking up the forward leg and holding the foot in the toes-out, fung gerk blocking position, while keeping the hands ready to be used in follow-up techniques on the centerline. It is important to know that *chi gerk* is based on the fung gerk stance. Therefore, it is valuable for beginning Wing Chun students to practice it and understand how it is related to more advanced routines.

From Basic Stance to Fighting Stance

Once you have developed a strong basic stance, you can begin practicing the rotation from the basic stance into the fighting stance—one leg forward, heel in line—called the *how ma*. This action of turning from the basic stance into the fighting stance is called *tren ma*, which means "turning stance." This turning action gives you the correct foot positions for the fighting stance. Methods of rotating the stance also vary from school to school. In Wing Chun, an experienced practitioner may choose to turn on the heels, middles, or balls of the feet. The toes-out, heels-out, opening of the basic yee chi kim yeung ma stance suggests this.

The two basic methods that a beginner should use, however, are the vertical or nonvertical axis rotations. The vertical, or central, axis method of turning the stance requires that you rotate on your centerline, keeping the weight forward on the middles or balls of the feet. This allows you to preserve your power curve as you turn your hips, making for a very strong simultaneous block-and-punch combination—as in palm-up block, *tan-da*, or palm-down block, *gun da*—by striking with your fist at an angle of 45 to 90 degrees from your centerline.

Wei Gerk, or Knee Rotation

1. Forward knee push.

2. Counter knee push.

3. Knee press to unbalance.

4. Knee press, counter, step back, low side kick.

5. Setup for leg sweep.

6. Application of leg sweep (sit ma).

Pivot and Slide Step Counter

1. Pivot, palm-up and punch counter.

2. Slide in, slap block and palm attack.

3. Slide in, elbow fiinsh.

Vertical and Nonvertical Rotation

1. Vertical rotation defense.

2. Staying in tight for counter.

3. Nonvertical rotation defense.

4. Leaning to compensate for attacker's left hand.

Fung Gerk Position

1. Leg sweep attack—slide into block.

2. *Fung gerk* to rear leg.

3. Throw down.

The nonvertical, or oblique, method of rotating requires turning on the heels, then sitting back on the rear leg. The rear leg supports your body weight, as well as forms a strong root. This adds a third dimension to the equation, because when you rotate, the negative or defensive side of the body moves away from the line of attack. In this nonvertical method of turning, 70 percent of the body weight is on the rear leg, which frees the forward leg for blocking or kicking. You can use this stance to completely avoid incoming blows. First use a slide step to get to the side of your opponent, rotate the stance into the tren ma position, and then block and strike. This combination of sliding and turning the stance is *noy sin wy ma*. This maneuver puts you outside the line of attack, while keeping you close enough to counterpunch.

All other forms of stepping in Wing Chun are derived from the basic yee chi kim yeung ma stance or the tren ma turning stance. The most common steps are the flanking step, *sit ma*, or the forward sliding step, *serng ma*. Knee trapping or rotation, *wei gerk*, is achieved by pinning the opponent's forward leg with your knee as you advance. The position of the front knee can be adjusted by shifting your knee position from over-the-ankle to over-the-toes, as you trap or push your attacker's leg to control and weaken his base.

Conclusion

My purpose with this chapter has been to provide you with a basic understanding of Wing Chun stance work. To use a Chinese analogy, "If your body is a house, the stance is your foundation." Therefore, a weak stance makes for a weak body. Think of the stances not only as your base of support, but also as a means of generating backup power into your hands.

Because the feet, hands, and body move as a whole, the stances are the glue that holds them together. Always keep in mind that Wing Chun is a fighting art. When using Wing Chun for self-defense, think of being proactive rather than reactive. In other words, use your stances and footwork to take the fight to your opponent. When you are training, think of your legs as instruments to carry the body into the fight.

When attacking, you can use your stance to its maximum potential by employing the slide step for attacking and maintaining pressure. When retreating, maximize stance potential by using the angle step to evade, zigzagging as you move backward. Focus on applying all techniques with speed, accuracy, and power. Being able to use correct stances and footwork will take time to master, but will definitely make you a winner.

This material appeared in the August 1998 issue of Inside Kung-Fu.

Combat Wing Chun Techniques

A Direct Approach to Close-Range Fighting

Gavin Blackburn

Close-range combat Wing Chun kung fu is a traditional martial art that is also an explosive, modern self-defense system. The principles and applications taught throughout the Wing Chun forms can be applied in thousands of variations and are limited only by the practitioner's imagination. These applications are called the "nonclassical" stage of development because they give Wing Chun fighters the freedom to express techniques and principles their own way, drawing upon knowledge gained at each level through personal experience. A Wing Chun proverb says, "Upon achieving the highest level of proficiency, the application of techniques will vary according to the opponent." This flexibility to respond to an attack with a unique technique is one of the factors that makes Wing Chun such a practical and useful martial art.

Although Wing Chun is a very structured fighting system, at its higher levels it allows tremendous freedom for creating a spontaneous defense for any situation a practitioner might face. Wing Chun's concept of freedom within a structure is similar to the game of chess. Although strict rules of movement and utilization apply to the individual game pieces, there is complete freedom to use those pieces as seen fit. Depending on strategy, experience, and skill, one player can capture a game piece in a trap set many moves in advance. In the same way, a Wing Chun fighter can use any hand or foot technique, combined with any strategic principle, to control a situation.

Sequence One: Gavin blocks Randy's jab with *woo sau* (guarding hand).

Randy quickly counters with *pock da* (slap block/strike), which Gavin blocks with *pock sau*.

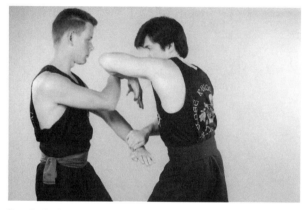

Randy leaks around and over Gavin's block with *gwai jaaan* (downward arcing elbow) . . .

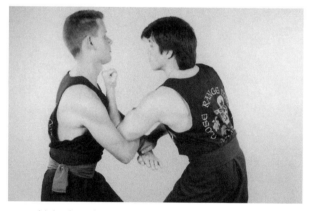

. . . which claws into and pulls Gavin's arms down . . .

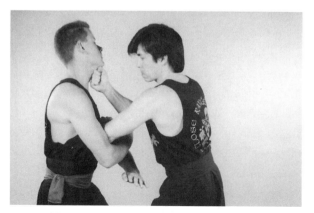

. . . enabling Randy to uppercut using *chau kuen* (drilling punch) . . .

. . . followed by a layover trap using *lon sau* (L armbar) and a finishing punch.

Sequence Two: Randy blocks Gavin's jab with *boang sau* (wing arm deflection) . . .

. . . then counters with *lop da* (grab / punch) . . .

. . . and traps Gavin's shoulder with *loy pock sau* while using a *cheong kiu ngahn woon* (long bridge alternating wrist swap) forearm strike to his throat . . .

. . . followed by a lon sau choke. Long bridge motions develop power from the shoulder rather than from the elbow and allow the hand to be shot down the open line to the target using *cheong kiu lick* (long bridge strength) instead of either retracting the striking arm or circling it slightly, allowing the opening to disappear.

Sequence Three: Randy stops Gavin's lead hook using a *woo/pock sau* complex block. This is in accordance with a Wing Chun principle that states "if a punch is already off the centerline, keep it off; if it's on the centerline, take it off."

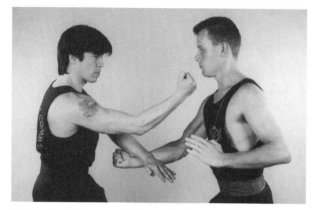

Gavin then follows up his attack with an uppercut, which Randy quickly blocks with a *gahng da* (low sweep block/strike).

Gavin attempts a second hook, which Randy blocks with *poh pai sau* (chest breaking palm). He does not block with woo/pock again because he is too close, so he uses the twin palms technique, which stops the hook on the shoulder and chest.

Randy then pulls Gavin into *loy doy gock gyeuk* (inward diagonal knee strike) using *pon geng sau* (neck pulling hand), which adds power to Randy's strike and also traps Gavin's body. Using woo/pock to block hooks causes great pain to the attacker's arm because it blocks two soft areas with powerful techniques that, in effect, attack the arm.

Sequence Four: Randy blocks Gavin's jab with boang sau . . .

. . . and counters with *lop/fun sau* (grab/outward horizontal chop).

Randy then quickly follows up with *huen da hay jahng* (circle strike/raising elbow).

He then armlocks Gavin and pulls him into *tai sut* (raising knee strike) . . .

. . . and *dyeung jing gyeuk* (nailing front kick). Two kicks done in sequence, without putting the foot down, is known as *moh ying gyeuk* (shadowless kick), which refers to an opponent's difficulty seeing or feeling a Wing Chun kick coming until it is too late. A double kicking attack should not target the same area twice, because it can upset structural balance and is less effective than a double kick. This kick works so well because it whips from the high line to the low line to deliver "whirlpool energy," caused by the hip and knee shifting from one kick to another with a body twist.

Sequence Five: Randy blocks Gavin's jab with a *woo da* (guarding hand/strike).

He then traps with *pock da jing jyeung* (slap block/vertical palm strike) . . .

. . . and quickly retraps Gavin's arm with a reverse woo sau trap and strikes with *chahng dai jyeung* (low spade palm). The reverse woo sau trap limits Gavin's ability to move or counterattack, giving Randy time to attack.

Sequence Six: Gavin blocks Randy's jab with *jom sau* (downward/inward chop block) . . .

. . . which chops inward toward the centerline plane (*joong seen*). Randy capitalizes on its inward motion and counterattacks with *ngoy doy gock kuen* (outward diagonal punch) . . .

. . . excluding Gavin's arm to the outside. He then follows up with *lop/chai wahng gyeuk* (grab/stomping side kick).

This breaks down Gavin's defensive structure. As he lands, Randy grabs Gavin's hair and pulls his head backward.

He finishes him with *chum jahng* (sinking elbow) to the exposed throat.

Sequence Seven: Randy blocks Gavin's jab with a *kau da chop kuen* (hooking/strike/low punch).

He then quickly locks Gavin's extended arm with *chum nu* (double inward twisting joint lock). *Kau sau* is normally used as a catch-up block when the opponent's attack has achieved defensive penetration. Because kau sau is a hooking motion that snags an opponent's punch, similar to pock sau, it enables the opponent's arm to be hyperextended, making the *chum kiu* motion an ideal follow-up.

21

Shotokan's Fancy Footwork

Keith Boggess

Traditional Japanese karate thrives on good basics, solid forms, and sparring tactics. Who would have believed that Okinawan village boxing would become one of Japan's most popular martial arts? Most martial arts historians agree that Gichin Funakoshi, the founder of Shotokan and the reputed father of modern karate, led that climb to popularity in Japan and, eventually, in other countries. In a way, karate would be different today, no matter what the style, if it were not for the Okinawan middle-school teacher who devoted his life to teaching the world karate.

Funakoshi had the ambitious dream of spreading karate worldwide as a means of improving life, but he also faced many fraudulent karate teachers who gave karate a bad name. In order to address both issues, Funakoshi's students formed the Japanese Karate Association (JKA). Through the organization's intense study of kinesiology and physiology to teach the ever-questioning American servicemen assigned to Japan after World War II, its members perfected basic techniques and forms.

But Shotokan also led the development of tournament karate. With tournaments, *karateka* for the first time had the chance to create strategies that were not widely taught. They also had to respond to situations not found in Okinawan karate circles.

One of the important situations these early Japanese competitors struggled with was how to seize the opening in an opponent's position. To answer that, they developed footwork based on their own deep martial heritage—sword fighting.

For generations Okinawan masters centered karate practice around kata. They practiced self-defense based on moves from the kata, but with little mobility. In the spirit of kata-based teaching,

Funakoshi isolated kata techniques, modified them for safe practice, and taught them first in *gohon kumite*, or five-step sparring. In gohon kumite, the aggressor attacks with an assigned technique, and the defender blocks with a particular defense for five repetitions and then counterattacks on the fifth move. That brought mobility to karate techniques and provided a way to practice footwork.

From there Funakoshi and his students developed the other traditional sparring methods: *sanbon kumite*, or three-step sparring, which is composed of three moves instead of five; *ippon kumite*, or one-step sparring, which is composed of one move; *jiyu ippon kumite*, or semi-free sparring, where the attack is called but the attacker can move freely for the opening; and *jiyu kumite*, or free sparring.

Although free-sparring practice began in 1935, tournament sparring remained absent from karate practice. After Funakoshi's death in 1957, Masatoshi Nakayama, one of Funakoshi's senior students and chief instructor of the JKA, promoted tournament karate by formulating rules based on one-point matches emphasizing no contact to the opponent. In the two-minute preliminary matches, the competitor who scored a full point, which signified a killing blow, was declared the winner. The competitor who scored three full points in the final five-minute match was declared the winner. A winning blow required a powerful blow with correct timing, distancing, and proper focus. Instead of conducting sparring from in-fighting range, which is more effective in self-defense, two men fought each other from a considerable distance in contest. Footwork naturally emerged to bridge that gap between competitors.

The Ingredients for Footwork

Effective footwork, especially in the stress of competition, requires learning several vital elements. One of the most important elements is something the Japanese are masters of—relentless practice. Training requires high repetition of the moves in order to hone them into reflex action. Since feudal times, the Japanese warriors have separated the brain knowing from the body knowing, and that practice continues in modern karate practice.

Correct body alignment is also important for good power development. The explosive movements and constant body shifting in sparring demands excellent balance. When the body assumes a low posture, as often seen in traditional tournaments, the spine forms the shape of an S, which misaligns the body's vertical axis. The inner ear is the human's "balance control center." When the body is tilted, the balance is off. To maintain balance in a low posture, the hips need to be tucked inward so that the navel points slightly upward. This allows freedom of movement and preserves balance.

Also important is the posture taken during competition. The basic sparring stance resembles a coiled position, and without the stance the footwork cannot be initiated quickly and deceptively. The head is straight, and the hips are tucked to align the spine. The shoulders are relaxed to promote total body connection. The lead leg is bent over the toes for explosive spring forward and backward. The rear leg is bent with the foot pointing about 45 degrees. The stance described is a popular one, but stances vary according to individual and situation. Fighters are always in a position to explode and shift.

Another element in footwork is critical distancing. Distancing refers to the amount of space between two competitors. Critical distancing means that one is at such a distance from his opponent that either a step forward brings the hand and foot into attack or a step backward safely avoids the attack. It also represents the ability to not get too close to the opponent nor too far away from him, but to be in a position so that the technique has maximum effect. This requires a defense that keeps the opponent's attack one or two inches from the defender's body so a successful counterattack can be made at full focus. Such an attack would be hard to defend.

Footwork also depends on the technique, stance, and strategy being used. That is not to say that technique dictates footwork, but it positions the fighter so that weapons can be used in their best way. To sum it up, footwork is dictated by the opportunity seized.

Shotokan's Three Kinds of Footwork

Structurally, the legs and body generate only a few motions. In any kind of movement, each leg plays one of two roles, either as the pivot leg or the moving leg. The pivot leg drives into the ground to create motion and energy, and for effectiveness, it must be connected to the ground. The moving leg slides over the ground to its destination. One foot at all times is either the pivot leg or the moving leg, and good footwork comes from being intuitively aware of which leg is doing what.

In body motion, hips control the movement. The hips rotate either right or left and forward or backward. Turning motions of the body use either the right or the left hip as a fulcrum. Also, the center of the hips can be used as an axis for a combined linear and circular movement.

The legs also have only a few possible ways of movement in a contest. Footwork forward, backward, left, or right by cross-stepping, by changing the pivot leg, or by maintaining the stance constitute the main categories of traditional karate footwork.

All of these movements, however, can be categorized into three broad areas: circular footwork, linear footwork, and combined circular and linear footwork. Each type of footwork has its place in tournament competition. The combined method is the hardest to learn, but it must be mastered if you want to control your opponent.

Circular Footwork

Circular footwork uses hip rotation to propel the body in circular motion. When used, it is primarily a counter technique: the fighter defends by avoiding the punch or kick while his hands or feet attack the open-

ing created by the opponent's commitment. For example, as the opponent steps in with a same-side punch (*oi zuki*) with the left hand, the front leg acts as the pivot leg while the waist leads the body in a turn left to avoid the attack. The rear-moving leg follows the waist anywhere from 45 degrees to 90 degrees, where it plants for the right backfist. Further rotation of the hips generates the power for the backfist.

Linear Footwork

The linear footwork category is more frequently used than the circular. It encompasses moving forward or backward, side-stepping, and angling in or out. Most novices learn sparring linearly with basic kicks, punches, and blocks by working five-step, three-step, and one-step sparring.

A good example of linear footwork in five-step sparring is moving backward while maintaining critical distance. Upon an opponent's front kick, a move straight backward into a forward stance while keeping the critical distance, a skill that requires much practice, gives the fighter the chance to execute a block sweeping from the outside to the inside with the two outer bones of the forearm. That allows an opportunity to score a reverse punch against the opponent by shuffling into range without hesitation. Both competitors should recover back into a balanced posture after the snappy strikes.

Another example of linear footwork is angling forward and to the opponent's outside at a 45 degree angle as he executes a straight technique. The side step evades the attack while the counter punch scores to the ribs. The move is done in one motion, exhibiting the spirit of a samurai swordsman.

Linear/Circular Footwork

Against a skilled karateka, it is almost mandatory to use the combined linear and circular footwork. With that category, the body becomes mobile and deceptive, scoring hits in the most unlikely places. An excellent example of the combined motion is when the opponent throws a same-side punch. The move backward from a right forward stance, with the left, rear leg as the pivot leg, is the linear motion. The circular motion occurs when the hips rotate as the right leg continues backward, circling out of the line of attack. Then a counterattack is executed, usually a reverse punch or a strike.

Another favorite footwork maneuver also uses the combined motion. As the opponent attacks with a right front snap kick, the fighter charges in with a right face punch. But as the front leg is about to plant, the fighter rotates the hips and the rear leg so that when the punch lands, the body is angled 45 degrees to the opponent.

A third example of the combined motion is switching the pivot leg. The opponent attacks with a right same-side punch. The fighter steps left with the rear leg and pulls the right, lead leg back and around to the left leg to deceive the opponent into misjudg-

ing the distance. The fighter drives the right foot into the ground for the lunge and scores. By the time the opponent realizes he has misjudged the distance, it will be too late for him to recover.

Observing tournament champions shows the importance of footwork. Their steps are light, their hips flexible, and their legs strong. Practicing these examples through the traditional methods of sparring can give the traditional tournament fighter the edge to win. But these fighters have also mastered *kihon* (basics) and kata (forms). Without first excelling in those areas, successful sparring will always be out of range.

This material originally appeared in the May 1998 issue of Inside Karate.

22

Finally! Pressure-Point Techniques for Women

Chris Thomas

Interest in pressure-point combat (*kyusho jutsu / dim mak*) has increased. In the past, only a handful of people could actually perform genuine pressure-point techniques (though they rarely shared this knowledge), but now several legitimate martial arts teachers with a high level of proficiency and understanding actively and publicly teach these methods.

Certainly, some of the interest in pressure-point techniques is just an example of the notorious habit many martial artists have of following the latest fad. Anything new, anything that seems to offer instant invincibility (for only $39.95) is immediately snatched up by those who are convinced there must be a secret of the martial arts that does not involve hard work.

It is certainly disappointing for these fadists to discover that, while *kyusho waza* (pressure-point techniques) require minimal physical exertion to perform, they do necessitate study and practice. Kyusho jutsu is a refined, elegant art, and its proficiency takes diligence.

Serious martial artists, however, once they are exposed to pressure-point knowledge, tend to incorporate it into their particular style. The reason is simple: kyusho jutsu makes sense. It's sensible strategically, it's sensible physiologically, and it makes sense of all those traditional techniques that seemed for so long to be nonsense.

In short, kyusho jutsu explains kata (forms), and that alone makes it worth studying. Kata has long been misunderstood, and its movements have long been explained in useless and ineffective ways. Kyusho jutsu fills the missing gap and shows how effective kata techniques are when properly understood. This understanding makes living, fighting kata possible, and is hastening an end to the day of kata as merely a series of pretty movements.

Unlocking the Secrets

As a result, however, the primary emphasis in kyusho jutsu teaching has been on kata, applying pressure-point concepts as the key to unlock the fighting techniques of the ancient masters. Because of this emphasis, an important feature can easily be overlooked: namely that pressure points are useful for practical, simple, and effective self-defense. And, since pressure-point techniques do not require overpowering one's opponent, they are especially well-suited to many women's self-protection needs.

Day in and day out women are subjected to brutal attacks and rapes. Some of these assaults occur at the hands of family members, others at the hands of strangers; but one thing is common to virtually all these outrages: they are perpetrated by men.

No one knows why so many men brutalize women. Is it because in many ways our culture devalues women? Or is it because men are trying to hide feelings of inadequacy and powerlessness behind acts of violence against those who are in their power? Whatever the reason, this much is clear: men are physically stronger than women, and women have been socialized not to fight back. These two factors make women "safe" targets for aggression.

In this climate of violence, more and more women are turning to self-defense classes to give them confidence and some measure of protection. To enter these classes, women must reverse years of conditioning just to be open to learning anything of value. (I have seen women who were emotionally unable to practice striking a man even when he is in heavy protective armor! That is how completely the instinct for self-preservation has been crippled by societal shaping.) All too often, however, what these women learn are techniques that simply will not work unless executed by a strong man.

Because the instructors of women's self-defense classes are usually martial artists, they tend to teach the techniques that work for them. But since these martial artists are usually men, they unconsciously rely on techniques better suited to men. And since they often do not know about pressure-point fighting, they have not been able to offer this genuinely useful and effective training for women.

Kyusho jutsu offers a real alternative. These techniques and methods were designed to be used by the frailest martial artists (the old masters) and were generally not taught to younger practitioners who could rely on their strength and speed. These are precisely the techniques most suitable to women. The following two examples should serve to illustrate the advantage of knowledgeable pressure-point instruction over the conventional material commonly taught.

First, in the average self-defense program, women are told to strike with a palm-heel against a point of the chin. This technique, however, does not work unless it is delivered with sufficient force to snap back the attacker's head, something that requires strength to accomplish. An untrained woman is likely only to anger an assailant with such a response.

In a kyusho jutsu–based program, a woman would be taught to attack with an upward angling strike to the side of the jaw. There is a vital nerve target located at a groove near the place where the cheek muscle bulges when the teeth are clenched (designated as Stomach No. 5 in acupuncture nomenclature). When this pressure point is struck with the proper angle, very little strength is needed to stagger an attacker.

Second, in many classes women are taught to respond to a double-hand lapel or shoulder seizure by bringing their arms up inside the attacker's arms and attempting to knock or pry his hands away. This cannot work. The movement of the hands from the center of the body outward (the motion the defender is performing) is physiologically very weak, relying on the small muscles of the back. In contrast, the motion of the hands toward the centerline (the movement the attacker would use to counter the attempt to knock his hands away) efficiently uses the powerful pectoral muscles of the chest.

A Blow to Attackers

The kyusho jutsu response uses vital-point attacks in such a way that the woman uses her body to her advantage. On the outer forearm is a motor-nerve point (Large Intestine No. 10), which causes the arm to painfully cramp. When a woman is grabbed with the two-hand movement, kyusho jutsu stresses striking this point on both her attacker's arms, hitting inward toward her own centerline to maximize her musculature.

Striking these points not only causes pain in the arms, but also sets up the points on the attacker's jaw (Stomach No. 5) for a follow-up attack. Once established, even a light blow simultaneously to both sides of the jaw produces a dramatic effect. An understanding of the relationship between the large intestine point on the arm and the stomach point on the jaw is not necessary for effective self-defense. The advanced kyusho jutsu practitioner studies these relationships to expand the combative options and develop new techniques. But, for the person interested only in methods of self-protection, it is enough to know that the technique works.

One special feature of pressure-point techniques is that they are extremely humane. This is an important consideration for women, because the training they have received in our culture causes them to hesitate to defend themselves for fear of harming their assailant, especially when they know their assailant (such as a family member or coworker). Pressure-point techniques do not draw blood, they do not break bones, and they generally do not even cause bruising. As a result, many women who would find it difficult to practice conventional self-defense responses (groin kick, eye gouge, etc.) do not have as great an emotional barrier to the pressure-point methods.

The bottom line is that a technique is only as effective as a person's willingness to use it on another human being. Many principles and techniques of kyusho jutsu are especially well-suited to the needs of women in self-defense. These techniques have been passed on from the founders of martial arts and represent a great heritage. Historically, few people were privy to these time-honored techniques. Today, however, the most practical and effective martial arts self-defense techniques are available to women of all shapes and sizes.

Trankadas

The Key to the Hand-Trapping and Hand-Locking Techniques of Lapunti Arnis de Abanico

Dr. Jopet R. Laraya

As with most styles of martial arts, immobilization techniques are incorporated in the fighting arsenal to increase and improve the efficiency of the style. A generic application technique is introduced to the practitioner with the hope that he can explore all the possibilities and variations thereof. Consequently, this "personal expression" of the technique becomes the basis for the existence of the different styles or sub-styles.

In Philippine stick-fighting, hand-trapping and hand-locking techniques are integrated in the training of the stylist. Emphasis is given to the principles of leverage, angulation, and force manipulation.

The Safety Factor

Before any trapping or locking technique is attempted, the key question to be asked is, "Is it safe for me to do the technique?" For obvious reasons, traps or locks are close-range techniques, and unless the answer to that question is "Yes," it would be foolhardy, if not downright suicidal, to pursue the application of the technique.

Trapping and Locking Pointers

Traps or locks can be efficiently performed by the practitioner if attention is given to the following pointers:

1. **Assessment of the Situation**: A comfortably accurate analysis of the opponent's body language is an asset. Body positioning, wielding of the weapon, and leg and arm/hand positions will generally indicate the opponent's plan of attack and perhaps the target

point, which can guide you in making the right decision regarding what technique to use.

2. **Choice of Technique**: Your accurate interpretation of your opponent's intentions will guide you in your choice of technique. Keep in mind that despite having chosen the technique, a further modification or "conversion" may have to be resorted to at any point in time during the conflict to suit the changing circumstances.

3. **Speed of Delivery**: The chosen technique need not be changed if performed at a rate faster than your opponent's response to your own techniques.

4. **Feints or Distractions**: Quite often, the use of feints or distracting and diversionary techniques will complement the efficiency and success of your chosen technique.

Application of the Hand Trap and / or Lock

Regardless of who initiates the attack, hand traps and/or locks are always a follow-up technique after the initial exchange of blows. Attacks to your left side are normally delivered by your opponent from the *abierta*, or open position, while attacks to your right side are delivered from the *cerrada*, or closed position. Attacks to your centerline can be delivered by your opponent from either position.

Conclusion

Employing hand traps and locks when engaged in close-range encounters increases your chances of successfully dominating your opponent. While the techniques described in this article appear to be straightforward, the practitioner will find it very gratifying to follow these pointers during training.

Dr. Jopet Laraya is the chief instructor of Lapunti Arnis de Abanico in Oakville, Ontario. This material originally appeared in the November 1997 issue of Inside Karate.

24

Creating the Complete Full-Contact Fighter

Ralph Mitchell

Regardless of the style of martial art you practice, a complete fighter requires both defensive and offensive performance through the development of self-preservation and self-perfection.

I've been practicing both Eastern and Western martial arts and have been in the field of rehabilitative medicine for over thirty years. This experience has helped me train, practice, and develop the Universal Defense System for full-contact fighting.

The foremost and essential ingredient of this system is having a trainer who will ensure your development in three distinct, yet interrelated components:

1. basic training
2. specificity training
3. injury prevention and treatment

It's a special relationship that's being developed between a trainer and a dedicated student. Ultimately, that same winning combination is often seen with professional athletes and teams. The training relationship starts with a thorough assessment that should occur on both sides. Obviously a trainer needs to know the mental and physical attributes and limitations of the student:

- Does this student really want to be a full-contact fighter?
- Is he willing to undertake the intensive training?
- What is his baseline fitness level and athletic and martial arts experience, and are there any underlying health limitations?
- What about his moral character and intent?

Conversely, a dedicated student should also be equally diligent in evaluating his trainer:

- What is his training and teaching background?
- How much "flight time"—"fight time" in any given art?
- Does the teacher possess the same positive mental attitude and objectives that you so desire?

Once this relationship is established, student and trainer are then ready to begin the three phases of training.

Basic Training Component

Positive Mental Attitude

A fighter must already have the drive to endure the training and follow the trainer's advice. Working with a good trainer will help develop a positive mental attitude. A student must have confidence in himself first, then in his trainer to make him into a champion.

The trainer will help work through negative thoughts and insecurities as they relate to skill level.

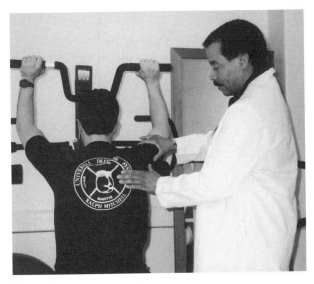

Figure 1.

Strength

Weight training should be a part of the trainer's program for the fighter. Using light poundage with lots of repetitions will give added strength and muscle tone without bulking the student up, especially if she needs to stay within a certain weight class. Weight training should be done systematically along with proper stretching of those muscle groups being trained (Figure 1).

Weight training gives extra strength for the explosive movements. It also helps with confidence during grappling and mat-work training activities, where strength is needed. The statement that weight training will make you slower is an old, outdated myth. Just ask the Super Bowl Champion Denver Broncos if weight training had a negative effect on their game.

Stretching and Flexibility

Along with weight training, stretching and flexibility exercises should be incorporated into the daily training program. Some fighters are genetically looser than others, so depending on the style of fighting, a trainee should spend time developing flexibility in the neck, shoulders, low back, gluteus maximus, quadriceps, hamstrings, calves, and Achilles tendon region. These areas affect kicking performance as well as grappling and throwing ability. Stretching will release the tightness from weight training and reduce the potential for injury to joints and muscles.

Endurance

It doesn't matter if one practices Muay Thai, karate, kung fu, or *kuo shu* full-contact matches. A fighter needs to be able to go three, six, or even ten rounds. Endurance will play a large role in this area. Plyometrics, sparring, jumping rope, and running (especially wind sprints) enhance a fighter's ability to finish each round strongly. Shadowboxing/kicking in front of a mirror also helps the fighter develop his rhythm and endurance while observing the position of his hands, chin, and stance structure. In submission or freestyle fighting, a match can go anywhere from five to thirty minutes, so the trainer must incorporate activities that will develop overall endurance. The quote, "Fatigue makes cowards of us all," says it all. Endurance will give that extra boost of confidence needed to win the match.

Control and Timing

Very often a fighter sees a brief moment of opportunity for either an attack or an escape but fails to capture that flag and run with it to the finish line. Knowing when to punch and kick with the right combinations or pass the guard to seize a dominant position for a submission requires split-second decisions. This knowing is the essence of controlling the moment. Speed certainly plays a major factor in these situations. However, one cannot succeed with uncoordinated, high-speed movement without a definite sense of purpose and effect. You must first attain the ease of self-controlled movement before you can see and sense your opponent's next move.

Timing comes from this relationship between a fighter and his opponent. Basic training must include activities to enhance the fighter's reaction time, decision making, and reflexive response, as appropriate with any given situation, to take advantage of the opponent's weakness.

The idea of control must also include mastering the environment and equipment. A fighter's performance and outcome can often be determined by the type of flooring and the kind of protective gear used. The fighter must gain fighting experience on various kinds of surfaces (e.g., platform, carpeted floor) and in the ring. Proper fitting and personalized protective gear is a must. Can anyone imagine a competition skater or cyclist borrowing a pair of skates or a bicycle from someone minutes prior to entering the competition? The fighter needs to think of the mouthpiece,

head gear, or gloves as an extension of his body that is there to both protect and serve him.

Speed

When we talk about speed, we are talking more precisely about velocity. Elementary physics teaches us, velocity = speed + direction. As previously mentioned, speed without proper direction will result in uncoordinated, spastic movement that seldom elicits any positive outcome. With some fighters, speed is a natural gift; with others it can be developed through drills. Hitting without being hit, switching from one grappling hold to another, and ending with a submission hold or lock requires control of speed. The trainer must develop drills that are specific toward enhancing the fighter's unique attributes.

Tools

Depending on the type of tournament, all tools should be well-oiled. The tools are offensive weapons in stand-up fighting and grappling and submission concepts when working from the mats. Both trainer and fighter should know the fighter's knockout weapons, or, for a ground fighter, what his strong mat-work combinations are based on their effectiveness in the dojo or gym.

Specificity Training Component
Understanding Range

One of the best methods of developing an understanding of range, either kicking or punching range, is using focus mitts and Thai pads (Figure 2). The trainer should set up punching, kicking, kneeing, or elbow drills so the fighter can learn how to adjust his distance for maximum effect. The trainer can be creative and develop many variation drills with the focus mitts and Thai pads. I see many fighters with low hand

Figure 2.

mechanics. The trainer will set up how many rounds should be done on the heavy bag and focus mitts before or after you spar (Figure 3).

Sparring

The trainer must set up quality sparring partners who have different styles of fighting—boxers, kickers, grapplers, and *judoka* (Figures 4 and 5). Many boxing gyms and schools that teach full-contact fighting have very good practitioners who choose not to enter tournaments. A fighter must be challenged in the dojo or gym so that the trainer can assess his weak areas,

guards and their chins stuck way out thinking more of offense while trying to throw bombs or dropping their guards when they throw kicks.

Focus mitts develop hand and foot accuracy and defensive reactions, especially when your trainer pops you in the head if you drop your hands while working your offensive skills. I hear a lot of people say that even the pros drop their guards. Yes, that's true, but their defensive skills are sharper than the average fighter's, even on their "bad" days. Along with focus mitts and Thai pads, the heavy bag also helps develop punching and kicking power. The heavy bag gives instant feedback if one is not using the right body

Figure 4.

Figure 3.

Figure 5.

which can be improved upon before fight night. The trainer must keep the fighter motivated and reinforce his confidence with positive feedback. Just like in boxing, the trainer should monitor the fighter's level of sparring so he doesn't peak too early and burn out by the time he's supposed to fight.

Offensive/Defensive Intensity

A trainer should know if his fighter is stronger offensively or defensively. Some fighters are great offensively with strong intensity, while others are master counter-punchers or kickers (Figure 6). Both types of fighters know exactly when and how to turn up the pressure when needed. Offensive/defensive intensity can be developed through drills and sparring sessions over a period of time. Depending on the fighter's division (novice or pro), he must have this attribute along with the other components to become a champion.

Situation Analysis

The trainer must be able to keep the fighter focused in between rounds and be able to motivate him if his mind starts to drift or if his confidence is being

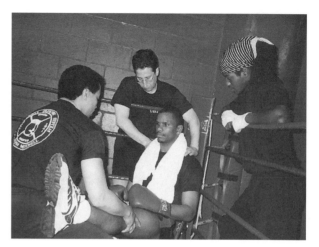

Figure 7.

destroyed by his opponent. The trainer should have people assisting him during all phases of the fighter's training who can help bring out his personal best. I call this concept the pit-stop crew mentality (Figure 7).

Just watch any national race car championship and see how each man has a designated job to perform within seconds to get that car and driver back in the race. During a match the same pit-stop concept can be applied. The two goals that should be achieved in between rounds are providing comfort and reinforcing confidence. The central person is the trainer or another person the fighter trusts to reinforce his confidence. The others should take care of any injuries the fighter may have received.

Strategy and Tactics

Throughout the fighter's course of training, he should discuss tactics and strategy as they relate to the type of fighter he may go up against. He can do this during the various training phases, such as focus mitt and Thai pad training and sparring (in between rounds). By the time a fighter goes into a match, he should have a better understanding of how to switch gears and adjust to whom he's fighting.

In between rounds of a match is not the time to have "discussions" about what a fighter is doing wrong.

Figure 6.

The trainer should follow the "less is more" philosophy, which means getting to the point within the time permitted to get the fighter back on track. The trainer should not "sensory overload" the fighter with, "Do this and do that," etc. A pro should know what he's doing wrong simply by the amount of physical feedback he's receiving from the opponent. As the rounds go by, the trainer's job is to aid the fighter in making the right adjustments to effectively neutralize his opponent.

Cross-Training

Trainers of today's fighters should evaluate training concepts outside their art form to enhance the fighters' potentials. Martial arts are not the only areas with balance or coordination drills. Just look at any of the winning football and basketball teams (to name a few sports that have great drills to develop speed, power, and coordination), and you will find that the trainers and coaches have developed their players to their fullest potential by using various cross-training concepts.

The trainer should be open-minded and aware of the latest information on nutrition, plyometrics, hypnosis, weight training, and other areas that will assist him in developing well-rounded fighters. Trainers should also look at other martial arts that may add to the fighter's skills (Figure 8). Trainers need to break the tradition of not learning other arts if they're trying to develop the complete fighter.

Injury Prevention and Treatment

The trainer will work to ensure the health and safety of his dedicated fighters. Working within the physical, mental, and emotional limits of a fighter is essential in preventing injury and maximizing the potential of that fighter. Basic management of injuries revolves around the RICE principle (rest, ice, compression, elevation) within the first 48 hours. The trainer educates the fighter to prevent injury and treats him when injury occurs. The more effective the prevention, the less need there will be for treatment of injuries. Proper conditioning, strengthening, protective equipment use, stretching, and body movement awareness will serve to protect the fighter.

If injuries occur, however, the treatment and rehabilitation become an essential factor in the training of the complete full-contact fighter (Figure 9). An injury or weakness should be viewed as an opportunity to learn about its mechanism, so that it can be avoided,

Figure 8.

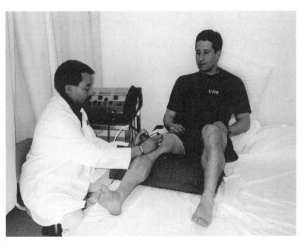

Figure 9.

and to develop the injured or weakened area, so that it becomes a strong and well-controlled one, ensuring a high level of both safety and performance.

Regardless of fighting style the basic goal of every martial arts system is to make movement as efficient and effective as possible for self-preservation and self-perfection. Development of body awareness is a critical aspect in the training of the complete fighter. Efficient and effective movement is essential in improving in any activity.

A fighter should take notice of what parts of the body hold tension, feel weakness, or feel pain. These are clues that are needed to gain increased awareness and control of the affected areas. A simple therapeutic exercise to practice control and gain awareness is to tense one of these areas. You can do an entire limb; hold for 5 to 15 seconds and then relax the area (limbs will feel soft and heavy).

This exercise will serve to increase control and decrease pain in the problem area. If pain increases or is sharp in nature, discontinue activity and seek help from another source (medical).

To enhance the development of efficient and effective movement, it is helpful to have a basic understanding of the muscles, joints, and structures of the body. The trainer should be the source in this process of improving the fighter's abilities. This training should expand the ability to see the opponent's weakness and enable the fighter to capitalize on that knowledge and win the match.

Ralph Mitchell has been a practitioner of the martial arts for over thirty years. He has worked in the field of rehabilitative medicine for more than twenty-five years. His martial arts background includes southern praying mantis, Vee-jitsu, judo, Western boxing, and the Filipino art of kali. *He is a full instructor in the Progressive Fighting Systems. Currently, he is senior vice president of the Eastern United States Kung-Fu Federation. This material originally appeared in the September 1998 issue of* Inside Kung-Fu.

25

The Jeet Kune Do Lead Punch

Ted Wong

As I write this article, it has been years since the passing of a good friend and martial arts instructor, Bruce Lee. During this time, I have stayed out of the limelight and taught only a few, select number of students. I have spent much of the time in further developing my own skills in the ever-changing, ever-developing, ever-evolving manner of *Jeet Kune Do* (JKD). And I have done so more or less in isolation. But, to prevent JKD as Bruce taught it to me from becoming a lost art, I feel it is time to reveal some of the skills he developed in the time I spent with him.

Bruce was always fast to pick up on martial arts techniques, and by the early 1970s, his skill for both observation and execution had reached such a phenomenal level that very few people could keep up with him. Now, I trained with him—I lived, breathed, and trained with him on a daily basis. We were from similar cultural backgrounds, and we both thought in the same mother tongue language, so we could communicate on a more personal level. We were also very close in height, weight, and body size, and we shared similar ranges of body motions and degrees of flexibility. Even though he was the teacher and I was the student, every day we both learned something new, something different. JKD training with him was indeed an ever-changing, ever-evolving, ever-developing process. For example, from week to week, his side kick would look and feel different. Nevertheless, Bruce always emphasized efficiency, immediacy, and above all, simplicity. His art was indeed "the direct expression of one's feelings with the minimum of movements and energy."

To start talking about JKD training, I should stress, right off the bat, the importance of the lead hand/foot weapon. The lead hand/foot weapon, that is, the lead punch/kick, is the backbone of JKD. To understand the art of JKD, one must completely understand this concept. Bruce always stressed placing the lead hand weapon forward. The lead punch, unlike the Western boxing jab, is a devastatingly powerful punch. The lead punch is delivered from an on-guard position, nontelegraphically without wastage of motion during its execution. The punch is propelled forward and explodes right through the target. As some readers might have seen in books, magazines, or other sources, pictures of Bruce throwing a punch and myself holding a focus mitt depict exactly that.

The punch is delivered in such a manner that the hand always moves first, before any other part of the body, in particular, the foot. The punch also lands first, transferring all the energy of the entire body through the punch, before a single ounce of energy is transferred through the landing of the foot. You can practice the lead punch with a partner. First, have your partner hold a focus mitt. Assume a fighting stance with the lead hand aimed toward the focus mitt. With no wasting of motion and no telegraphic movements, strike the pad and recoil back to the same starting position. Begin with a position that is at arm's length from the target, and gradually increase the speed of delivery as you warm up. As you hit the target faster and faster, have your partner move the focus mitt away the instant he detects your movement. This is more like actual combat and will also train your partner to read (or not read) your attack. Gradually, step farther and farther away from the target. Now you must move in with the foot, but remember, the punch must move in before the foot and also land before the foot. This was Bruce's way of exploding through a target from a distance.

In many classical martial arts systems, the foot always precedes the hand in delivering a punch. In Bruce's JKD, it is the reverse. The hand always precedes the foot, and the punch explodes with the whole body weight behind it.

Ted Wong was Bruce Lee's last private student and one of his closest friends. He is presently a director of the Bruce Lee Educational Foundation, a nonprofit organization dedicated to the preservation and perpetuation of the art, science, and philosophy of Bruce Lee. This material originally appeared in the February 1989 issue of Inside Kung-Fu.

26

Backfist Blitz

Mike Soohey

Catching an opponent off guard or before he can react defensively relies on the proper application of a swift and non-telegraphic technique. Not only must this technique possess key attributes such as quickness and accuracy, but it must be simple in nature and travel a relatively short distance to reach its target. It must be lightning fast, follow a straight line to its target, be difficult to defend against, and be easy to learn. It consists of different variations that practitioners can put to use.

This very flexible and versatile forefist punch is the backfist. When delivering the backfist, the wrist is bent back slightly as you make contact with the target area. Depending on which variation of the backfist is used, the striking area can be either the top or back of the first two knuckles of the forefinger and middle finger.

Like the jab and vertical forefist, the backfist can be used as a fast and surprising punch from the on-guard fighting position. With the front hand, the practitioner can rifle this punch out, giving little notice for an opponent to react. The backhand is a very sneaky and often non-telegraphic punch that is used in close-range attacks to the face, solar plexus, groin, abdomen, and rib area. Ideally, with its short overhand delivery, the punch is most effective when attacking different areas of the face, with the temple being a major target. At the same time, the lead backfist hand travels swiftly and directly to its target, relying on very little body movement.

The fighting strategy behind the backfist is to strike quickly, penetrating the defensive perimeter of your opponent from an advanced front position. If you unleash a right-hand backfist, your right leg is forward, putting you much closer to your opponent, enabling you to strike in less time. The concept behind the backfist is to attack or counter with lightning speed and very little body motion.

To summon such swift hand and arm motion, the delivery of the punch is not initiated from the side hip or waist position as many traditional and classical punches are performed. The backfist has a quick hitter's personality. For this to materialize, the practitioner can implement and practice two different deliveries. The first application is purely a speed technique. It centers on no telegraphic arm movement at all. Its attributes are speed, snap, and deceptiveness. The second application is similar to the first, but the punch arm is pulled back slightly across the chest. This technique, while not free of arm movement, still provides a good deal of quickness with added whip and snap. Of the two, it can be termed the power application of the backfist.

The Pure Speed Backfist

In the application of the speed backfist, you unleash your punch without any extra arm movement or added motions, such as drawing your hand back across your chest or to the rear shoulder. You punch directly from the lead hand on-guard position. There is no extra momentum provided by any cocking or drawing backward of the punch hand. It is strictly a short-traveling, non-telegraphic punch that is snapped out with sneaky suddenness.

The practitioner should not be fooled that the speed variation is merely an arm-only punch. While the technique may appear to be a quick hand-snapping-type motion that travels a short distance, the key is to strike with the entire body behind the punch. Your punch arm is a means for transmitting the correct energy flow made by the entire body. You increase the overall snapping force of your arm by having the lower and upper body in sync as you whip out the punch.

The intention of the speed backfist is to attack in a fast assault mode. If your punch arm is held too rigidly or tensely, its delivery will slow down. Even though the punch travels a short distance, a tense punching arm will affect overall power and speed. Remember, speed is instrumental in mounting a power surge. The higher the rate of speed you can mount, the more powerful the technique will be at impact point. Thus it's imperative to relax just before punching into a target area. The moment of impact is when you tighten and contract the muscles of the body. This is the point where one clenches the attacking fist and surges powerfully into and through the impact zone.

While the speed backfist is an easy technique to learn, the martial artist must be aware of certain technical facets. The following fighting tactics will aid in making the speed backfist all the more dangerous and deceptive:

1. Be aware of how your lead foot lands as you punch. If it lands on the ground before you make punch contact, your body weight will move toward the ground instead of pack power behind the blow. Your punch should be slightly ahead of your lead foot's landing.
2. Staying with the lower body, your knees should be slightly bent to take advantage of the large front thigh muscles. With knees bent, you can contract and compress the quadriceps, enabling you to spring powerfully into an opponent. This will help the overall quickness and drive of your backfist attack.
3. To ensure a whipping motion throughout the backfist delivery, recoil your punch hand back quickly and along the same hitting path. Pulling the backfist back at the same speed in which it was thrown replicates snapping a shower towel. When you snap a wet towel like a whip in its forward motion and then recoil it just as fast, it turns into a stinging shot.
4. Keep a tight defense by positioning the punch hand high as you recoil it. This will put you in

a solid ready stance for a possible counter or to strike again with a quick follow-up. Your rear hand should be kept in a good high defensive posture as well. If an opponent can get a countering shot past your front hand, you want your rear hand in good position to catch or deflect the strike. Keeping the rear hand in solid position also gives you the added service of trapping or immobilizing an opponent's arm as you strike with a lead backfist.

5. The last tactic focuses on fighting creatively. Against a smart or crafty fighter, you want to add variety in your backfist application. While your speed backfist may be blazing fast, you don't want to be one-dimensional and fire it the same way all the time. You want to mix up the way you shoot out the punch by sometimes attacking to another area of the body. This will confuse and frustrate an opponent into making the wrong defensive maneuver, which often opens up another vulnerable area. Also, add feinting to your backfist strategy. Faking a low kick or rear hand punch to the body can make the difference when sneaking a wicked backfist into the temple or nose.

The speed backfist is an extremely effective weapon, whether used as a single attack, within a combination, or as a setup for a big finishing shot. As you attack or counter with the technique, keep in mind that your forward advancement must be a coordinated flowing movement. This will put you in sync to take full advantage of the quick hit delivery.

When you use the speed backfist as a single or simple attack, look for the optimum moment to explode at your opponent. You make the simple attack with your mind set on beating your opponent to the punch. The optimum time to attack is when your opponent has dropped his guard, when he's changing his feet pattern, or if he's switching fighting sides. Such movements will assist the swift striking speed of the backfist.

If you are loose and relaxed, you can nail an opponent with the speed backfist just as he's moving forward. Being tense and tight most often telegraphs your intentions, giving an opponent the signal to defend or strike first. If you can stay relaxed, you can attack with smooth explosive speed. You can practice and hone the simple assault with the speed backfist by having a training partner move around holding a focus glove with the lead hand close to the face. Have your partner move around just enough so that he shifts his weight forward at different intervals. The moment he moves or changes his feet pattern, blast into the mitt with a speed backfist.

Like the jab, the speed backfist is an excellent initiation punch. With its sudden stinging impact, it serves as a quick jump start for other techniques. While its effectiveness cannot be denied in a simple punch attack, the speed backfist can be most valuable in setting up a heavy-hitting combination. Since the speed backfist is an explosive punch that can find its mark quickly, the natural flow of attack can develop into a multiple-strike combination. As you punch and force openings with the backfist, you can set your opponent up for a heavy-hitting follow-up. This can be in the form of rear power strikes such as hooks, uppercuts, cross-hands, overhands, reverse punches, and strong back-leg kicks. Speed backfists can also set up wicked turning techniques like spinning crescent kicks and backfists.

The type of follow-up blast will depend largely on the build and agility of the martial artist. For example, a shorter, more-compact practitioner may work his way closer by feinting to a mid- or low-level area. Once on the inside, one can explode with the speed backfist to the face. A powerful follow-up would be to unleash a big hook or uppercut to the body.

An effective speed backfist can stun an opponent long enough for one to gain inside access and administer damaging shots to vulnerable areas. For instance, the speed backfist can be used as a menacing shot to the face, startling an opponent long enough for you to drive a powerful reverse punch or knee thrust to the stomach. If you are diverse at grappling, the speed backfist can cause enough confusion to open an avenue for quickly sweeping in for a leg tackle or single leg takedown.

A taller, rangier fighter can put the speed backfist to good use by taking advantage of longer limbs. A fighter with a longer reach can keep an aggressive attacker at bay by snapping the speed backfist into the face and then quickly following up with a back-leg roundhouse or front thrust kick to an open area. If you have the height and speed advantage over your opponent, you can double up on the backfist by flicking it in rapid succession one right after the other.

The Power Backfist

The power backfist is a technique that can provide more whip and snap by bringing or cocking the punch arm back across the chest. The movement of pulling your punch arm back actually resembles the motion of pulling a rubberband looped around a finger back a little farther to provide extra power. This motion is not an exaggerated pull where you bring the arm far back to the rear shoulder area. Rather, it is intended to be a slight pullback movement to provide extra whipping power behind the backfist. Too much of a pullback or cocking motion will telegraph or give away the sneaky deceptiveness of the punch. While you want to pack more impact force behind the backfist, you don't want to give away its quick suddenness of delivery. One should not forget that first and foremost the backfist is a quick hitter, even the power version.

To get the feel of the power backfist, one can practice its outward application from a side horse stance position. With your arms in a fighting posture, pull your lead punch arm back about eight to ten inches. As you pull it back, check to see that it doesn't go beyond your mid-chest point. This slight pullback is all that's needed to upgrade the hitting power behind the backfist. From here, with your arm parallel to the floor, strike outward with a slight overhand

arc so that the first two knuckles of the back of the hand do the striking. It's important to twist the punch fist at the last moment to accentuate the snapping motion. Once you strike outward, recoil your punch arm and fist like a whip, back to the ready fight position.

From a fighting stance, the outward power backfist is a blistering punch as long as the practitioner maintains a straight-line delivery. The straight-line delivery is the power base behind the technique. One should not attempt to put any extra body swinging or swaying as a means to load up on the punch. This will only diminish the overall hitting surge that comes from the centerline of the body. For the outward power backfist to be devastating, do not miss with the straight-line attack approach. Hit with a quick twist of the waist before your lead leg lands, and keep your body in a relaxed tension state just before you explode into the target.

If you want to put extra body force and strength behind the power backfist, bring the rear foot forward and then raise the lead leg up as you drive forcibly into an opponent. Picking the front leg up and then stomping it down as you fire in the punch compounds the overall striking force. Because this forward surge takes more time to accomplish and can telegraph your intentions, incorporate feints to hide the backfist delivery. Good strategy is to advance, bringing the rear foot forward to close the distance. Just as you raise your lead leg up, fake a punch to your opponent's head with the rear hand. At the same time you are faking a rear-hand punch, pull the lead punch arm back to mid-chest point. As you step down, explode with a power backfist into your opponent's chest or solar plexus. Keeping good body flow and timing the backhand just right can provide a jolting shot to the body. If you score to the solar plexus, this can be a very painful shot, winding the opponent.

The outward power backhand can also be delivered in a rising arc application. In this technique, the punch hand is drawn back to midpoint where it is positioned underneath the guarding rear hand. This type of hand position makes the backhand very deceptive and sneaky as you snap it out toward your target. As you unleash the punch, swing it upward and simultaneously to the right in a whipping motion. This will simulate the overhand striking movement, only started from a lower position. Once again, twist the fist at the last instance before contact to bring the large knuckles of the forefinger and middle finger into play. As you snap out the technique, keep its trajectory in line with the right side of your body if punching with the right hand. This will keep you in a solid centerline posture that generates power and force.

The rising arc application is an excellent punch to whip to the chin or Adam's apple area off a rear-hand punch feint. A good influential feint will make it very difficult for an opponent to defend or stop a well-timed rising arc backhand. The punch can even be directed to the ribs or kidney area if your opponent is bent or turned in a side position.

While the rising arc application travels from a sneaky, low position, the third variation of the power backfist is a technique unleashed in an upper to downward flight. This rendition of the power backfist is referred to as the downward application. The downward power backfist is a strong but little-used punch that makes contact with the back of the fist facing downward. There are actually two ways of delivering this pummeling punch.

1. The first and most common method is done with the lead hand from a side stance or fighting position. This application resembles the outward technique in terms of drawing the punch arm back. But instead of traveling in a horizontal snapping motion, the punch comes in a vertical arc directly over the ear. As you are about to make contact, you turn your punch arm so that the back of the fist is facing downward. You strike into your target with the knuckles of the forefinger and middle finger just as you do with the palm forward outward punch. Snap your hand and wrist hard as you smash into the target. The downward power backfist can be used as a strategic and precisely placed punch to strike over an opponent's defensive

guard. Its downward flight makes it possible to evade your opponent's guard hand and strike rudely to the centerline of the face.

2. The second method of the downward backfist is delivered with the rear hand. It can be applied from either a front stance or side stance fighting position. When performed cohesively with a well-timed rear step forward, it can turn into a real blasting punch. In using a right-hand punch while stepping forward, draw your right fist behind the side of your ear with your palm facing forward. As you step into your opponent, punch forward in a vertical arc directly in a centerline past the ear. Your punch hand is twisted so the back of the fist faces downward as you make contact. Aiming this technique right between the eyes creates a jolting and painful punch. With your full weight behind the hand snap, you can stun an opponent and possibly score a knockout.

The Wicked Spinning Backfist

In terms of summoning overall hitting force, the spinning or turning backfist is potentially the most powerful technique. When the martial artist times this punch just right and makes good solid contact with the target, the results can be devastating. The key in whipping a strong spinning backfist is to turn quickly without losing your balance and your focus on the target as you strike. Much like when performing a spinning hook or crescent kick, you lose sight of your opponent for a split second as you turn. In these techniques as well as the spinning backfist, you want to turn quickly and in a coordinated fashion so that you are instantly right back on track as you zero in on the target zone.

When striking with the right hand, you will be positioned from a left lead fighting stance. To unleash the punch, your first motion is to pick your back, right leg up and simultaneously begin turning your body around. As you spin, quickly turn your head and look immediately over your right shoulder to keep focus on the target. As you are turning, the punch arm, which is positioned at your chest, follows closely behind. Once you make the turn, your punch arm swings in a horizontal overhand motion on a straight course to the target.

The added torque from the spinning motion will provide extra snap and fury as you smash two large knuckles from the middle finger and forefinger into the target. This entire motion happens very quickly and culminates with the punch hand hitting slightly ahead of the right foot landing on the ground. Once again, twist the punch fist at the last moment so the palm faces forward. Your body will end in a direct centerline as you blast into your target.

This wicked technique makes for a powerful head or face shot. The spinning backfist can be made into a very deceptive and sneaky technique by keeping the punch in close to the chest as you make your spin move. If you whip it out too early and at a wide arc, you will give a wary opponent time to react and adjust.

As an attacking technique, the spinning backfist can be thrown off a good low feint. A fake jab or side kick to the body can be implemented to force an opponent's guard down, giving you an avenue to unleash a fierce spinning backhand to the temple. Like the other variations of the backfist, the spinning tactic needs to work off good fighting flow to be effective. This punch can pay big dividends if you catch an opponent relaxing with his guard down. Sometimes you must be patient and set an opponent up, while in other situations you rely on your ability to jump quickly on an opening.

The spinning backfist also carries enough destruction force to be used strategically as a big finishing shot. A fighter with a good stinging jab can break down an opponent's defense, setting himself up for a powerful spinning backfist. Also, when you're up against a very aggressive opponent who charges with wild looping punches, look for an optimum moment to blister the punch. The combined inertia of an opponent coming in and taking the brunt of a spinning backfist can produce a very painful ending.

This material originally appeared in the November 1997 issue of Inside Karate.

27

The Power of the Palm

Jane Hallander

While the fist represents the standard method of delivering a self-defense blow in many martial arts, well-trained martial artists often prefer a palm strike. These people see punches as basic techniques that often lack the power and effectiveness of a well-aimed palm strike.

Why Are Palm Strikes So Highly Regarded?

When a punch lands, it reacts much like a fragmentation grenade that blows apart, depositing little pieces of metal in the target. A punch immediately damages a localized area of the body, leaving bruises and broken bones. A well directed palm strike, however, uses the martial artist's maximum power. It may not leave bruises, but it will shatter nerves and blood vessels, causing far more damage than a punch.

Palm strikes are physically good for martial artists because they can be used to teach beginners without making the hands stiff by having to develop and condition the knuckles. You can think of palm techniques as maximum effect with minimum impact to your hands.

Palm techniques are seen in all martial arts but are more common in styles that separate their fighting techniques into hard and soft or external and internal. For instance, many traditional Korean martial arts place fist strikes in the hard category and palm strikes in the soft or internal martial arts.

Kuk Sool, a very traditional Korean martial art, emphasizes internal, or ki, training as the backbone of successful fighting techniques and certainly the root of so-called soft techniques, such as palm strikes. In Kuk Sool, palm strikes are ranked among high-level self-defense tools.

Grand Forks, North Dakota–based Kuk Sool instructor Ernie Keep has the highest regard for palm techniques. "One reason palm strikes are considered more effective than punches, knife-hands, or spear-hand strikes is that palm techniques, called *pyeong su* in Korean, require the combination of physical conditioning along with internal, or ki, power," explains Keep.

Not only are palm strikes powerful in defense situations, but according to Keep, they are also used to attack the attack. For instance, you might palm strike an opponent's ankle or knee to crush an oncoming kick. You can use a palm technique on an elbow to break a joint lock. Depending on the type of palm technique, it can be either a deep organ strike or a surface strike, using shock to cause pain, disorientation, or unconsciousness.

Kuk Sool has two types of palm techniques: steel palm and open finger palm techniques. Knife-hand and ridge-hand strikes are not considered palm techniques.

Steel palm training involves conditioning and development of the entire hand—palm, fingers, side and back of the hand—enabling Kuk Sool practitioners to break objects with superhuman speed and strength. Steel palm techniques require that the fingers be closed together, making the entire hand the striking surface.

In ancient Korea, when steel palm techniques were used extensively for fighting and self-defense, the angle of the fighter's palm determined whether the resulting blow would be defensive and only injure the opponent or become offensive and cause death. A 90-degree angle was considered deadly, while a 45-degree angle was used for defense only. The blow was made with such speed and force that if steel palm practitioners had no background in internal training, they would break every bone in their hands.

Kuk Sool palm strikes still bear the same destructive qualities of a punch; however, the force is spread out over a greater area. Unlike punches that often bruise tissue, many palm techniques leave no marks behind. Palm techniques that leave no outward signs, but which can cause grave internal damage, use the fingertips and palm heel as the striking surface—never the center of the palm.

Why Not the Center of the Palm Itself?

Making contact with the center of the palm only gives the strike the same amount of power as a punch. It lacks the shock effect of a correctly administered palm technique. The angle of each connecting joint must be correct before the palm strike will exert its maximum force. Also, if the striking point is too low on each finger, it will force the wrist to hyperextend and could damage it.

The correct angle of your wrist during a palm technique depends on the direction of the strike, according to Keep. If the strike is forward, the palms face forward with the fingers spread. For a side strike, the palm is open but rounded, as if cupping a basketball, to allow ki to flow into the hand. Back-of-the-hand or palm strikes have the hand slightly curved to emit relaxed, penetrating power and the wrist is held straight.

Pyeong su palm techniques originated in a branch of ancient Korean martial arts known as sado mu sool (tribal martial arts) over two thousand years ago. They are broken down into three distinct types, each designed for specific uses.

The first type is called *jung pyeong su* (straight palm technique) and is the most elementary of the three. It is a straightforward, penetrating palm strike delivered to any part of an opponent's body. Usually a jung pyeong su strike is made after an opponent's technique has been blocked and an opening becomes available.

The second pyeong su palm technique is named *hae jun pyeong su* (cutting palm technique). These palm strikes come from the side. They can be directed from either the outside toward an opponent or from the inside outward. The primary targets for hae jun pyeong su techniques are joints. A typical hae jun pyeong su strike is made against a punching arm. The palm strike breaks the incoming elbow as the punch is thrown. In this case, the palm technique simultaneously blocks and deflects the punch and counterattacks to break the elbow.

The third technique classified with these palm strikes is called *yop pyeong su* (circular palm technique). It is the most advanced of the three, relying upon a somewhat sticky sensitivity between palm stylists and opponents. Yop pyeong su practitioners make a circle while their striking arms touch their opponents' attacking arms. The circular action redirects the opponent's balance and energy away from the palm stylist. When the redirection of energy and balance has been accomplished and an opening is found, the pyeong su practitioner strikes.

One of the favorite techniques of ancient Korean martial artists was a yop pyeong su targeted just below their opponents' ribs. These fighters made a circular scooping action, using the outer, lower edge part of their palm to strike the rib cage.

Today, all three types of palm techniques are practiced the same way they were in ancient Korea. The basic practice curriculum is comprised of concentration, angle, absorption, meditation, and internal power.

Concentration allows Kuk Sool practitioners to place all of their focus and intention upon their target.

Adding to this a knowledge of striking angles enables palm stylists to determine from what direction to hit the target with maximum force.

Absorption of the palm technique is unique to palm strikes. What it means is that practitioners take some of the shock of their own palm strikes back into their own bodies, without being rigid as they deliver the blow. They literally move with the palm strike. As shock waves enter an opponent's body, they also cause a slight recoil back into the Kuk Sool stylist's body. Failure to absorb this force by moving with the strike can cause internal damage to the palm strike practitioner.

Body movement and generation of power for palm techniques come from the hips and waist, not the palm strike practitioner's arm. Power is then transmitted from the body, ground, and hips, bringing more body mass into the strike, which in turn creates more power and force.

Meditation and the internal power necessary for effective palm strikes are closely related. Without the right kind of meditation and breathing practice there can be no internal power, which is necessary to add maximum strength to the palm strike.

Palm strike practitioners are so powerful that they don't worry about finding a pressure point to hit. They can strike any part of an opponent's body with excellent results. No matter where they hit, their opponents first get dizzy from the shock of the blow, and then feel the full effects of the powerful strike.

This material originally appeared in the April 1998 issue of Inside Karate.

28

Buddha Hand
Wing Chun's Guiding Light

Santo Barbalace

Leung Chi Man was born in the town of Canton, China, in 1926. Coming from a wealthy family that donated large amounts of money to the local temple, Leung began his kung-fu training at a young age. The chief abbot of the temple was Leung's uncle and main instructor. It was said that his uncle's level of ability was so high he could strike a block of wood and disintegrate the center while leaving the outside unmarked. Leung's uncle was taught by a wandering monk named Leung Chang Sun, who was also a distant relative. The training included the complete *gu yee kuen* (ancient chivalrous fist or boxing) system plus another internal form of tai chi chuan (grand fighting/boxing), which gave the practitioner an immense energy level. Leung has said that the gu yee is for fighting, and the tai chi is for the energy; when combined, it is like having a sharp, swift knife.

In 1961, Leung moved to New York's Chinatown and began teaching the gu yee kuen system behind closed doors. He changed the name to *fut sao* (Buddha hand) *wing chun kuen* with the realization that the name gu yee kuen was no longer known. Also, Leung wanted to distinguish his family's method of wing chun kuen from the other branches of the Wing Chun styles. This was the reason for the addition of fut sao before wing chun kuen.

At 70, Leung remains one of the most skilled martial artists ever to reach these shores. He is well known among the closed-door schools for his internal abilities and his exceptional fighting prowess.

Fut Sao Forms

The fut sao family has preserved a unique curriculum with aspects not often found in some of the other Wing Chun styles. Training in fut sao Wing Chun begins with *siu lin tau* (small first practice) form. The

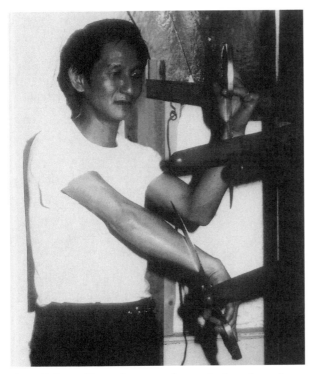

Grand Master Henry Leung performs the baat ham do (butterfly knives) on the mook yan jong (wooden dummy).

Henry Leung and Santo Barbalace practice sticky pole using a fingertip grip.

Grand Master Leung poses with top disciple, Santo Barbalace.

Santo Barbalace works the wooden dummy.

siu lin tau is the foundation form of the system. The entire form is done in the yee chi kim yeung ma (two fingers pinching the horse stance). All movements in the later forms are derived from the siu lin tau. Different motions found within this form would be *tun sao* (spreading hand), fut sao (buddha hand), and *sut sao* (shaving hand). When taught the siu lin tau, you are shown different breathing methods to perform when practicing the form for the basic chi development.

Cham kiu (sinking bridge) is the second stage and is taught for the development of the sinking energy. Different footwork such as the *pin ma* (side stance) and sei pihng ma (square level horse) are introduced to teach body unity and how to move the root. The techniques are introduced in the form and are incorporated with the hand movements and stepping. In the final section of the cham kiu, motions are done for the opening of points and releasing of energy.

Biu jee (darting fingers) is the third form and teaches students how to send their energy out and bring it back. Biu jee is mainly done in the sei piheng ma but also has *heun bo* (circle stepping) and *lin fa tso* (lotus flower drop). The form is rich with elbow techniques and short-power, finger-power techniques. Certain things are common in each stage of training; for example, each form has specific tendon-stretching exercises, power training sets, chi development exercises, joint grappling techniques, and vital-point strikes. Each form also has a short-power form for the further development of one's horse/root and internal. A person has to be proficient at each level and pass a specific energy-release test to move on to the next stage.

Hidden within the fut sao forms lie all the system's training. An example would be found in the biu jee form. There are movements that hide the *teet sao jeung* "iron palm set." Also, the *lop sao* set and chi gerk set are hidden in the cham kiu form. One way to look at techniques is to see every movement as having multiple purposes; *biu sao* could be used as a block, strike, joint manipulation, throw, or vital-point hit.

Sifu Santo Barbalace performing the baat ham do, or "butterfly knives," form.

Santo Barbalace demonstrates the six and one-half point pole using a fingertip grab.

Wing Chun Through Poetry

While training, the practitioner is required to learn the maxims and fundamental laws or physics of the system. All the maxims and physics are taught through the poetry. Leung says that when attacked, you only need to worry about what you do; if you stick to the laws and physics of the system, everything will happen correctly. Also, in the old days of training after each stage was complete, the practitioner would be required to drink a certain herbal medicine to strengthen the internal for the subsequent training.

Once the practitioner has completed biu jee and its requirements, he proceeds to the fourth form, *siu baat qwa*. The siu baat qwa, or the "small eight trigrams" set, contains a great variety of advancing and retreating footwork. A close-range boxing method, its emphasis is placed on speed, accuracy, and balance. It is relentless, using the force of the whole body while paying strict attention to the postures and their various angles. These are separated into roundness, flatness, and slightness.

The uniqueness of the fut sao Wing Chun lies in the siu baat qwa form. The form prepares the pupil for the footwork done on the wooden dummy form and with the weapons. Before learning the form, one is taught the eight-character stepping patterns that are the foundation of the footwork. Some of these stepping patterns are box stepping, cross-stepping, balance stepping, and snake walking.

Patterns are both linear and circular. The siu baat qwa training also helps the practitioner elude an incoming attack and be in a position to neutralize that attack and counterattack with maximum efficiency. While the siu baat qwa form may sound similar to other styles, such as baguazhang or the siu baat qwa form of Choy Li Fut, it should be noted the fut sao siu baat qwa set is a distinct and uniquely Wing Chun form that has been part of the system since its inception.

The *jook jong* (bamboo dummy) is also taught at this stage. Different from the *miu fa jong* (plum flower dummy), the jook jong is used for the different gliding footwork of the siu baat qwa. The miu fa jong, however, is used for the stances, footwork, and kicking and counterkicking of the first three forms of training.

Buddha Hand Dummy

The *mook yan jong* (wooden man dummy) is the next stage of Buddha hand training. Although a specific dummy form is taught, the Buddha hand student begins training with the wooden dummy from day one. Each form in the system is not only done as an empty-hand form, but is also performed on the dummy. The pupil also practices different sequences and principles on the dummy, such as the snake in the bamboo theory, iron palm, and vital-point striking.

The major difference is that this system's dummy is movable. The dummy is not locked or pinned in the center of the cross-beams (during the form and in some drills, motions slide the dummy to the left or right). Another difference is that the two top arms are not at different heights; their tips are level. If you are doing a form that is equal on both sides, it is important that one side is not trained differently than the other. The dummy form is the culmination of the system's four empty-hand sets. It has 18 sections/216 moves (108 per side) and is the last stage of training before the *sup baat dim yeet boc kic*.

Sup baat dim yeet boc kic (eighteen-point strike fighting) is a short, quick two-person routine. Used for the development of proper attack and counterattack, sup baat dim yeet boc kic is a moving form that focuses not only on hand skills, but on all attributes of the complete fut sao fighter—hands, kicks, footwork, points or targets to strike, the gap, and more. After learning this set, the pupil moves on to weaponry.

Baat jham do (eight chopping knives) and *luk dim boon gwun* (six and one-half point staff) are the two major weapons of the system. Originally called the pig skinning knives, the baat jham do training and form is the close-quarters weapons training of the sys-

Sifu Santo Barbalace stops . . .

. . . his student's punch with a *fook sao* . . .

. . . then applies a *chin na* lock . . .

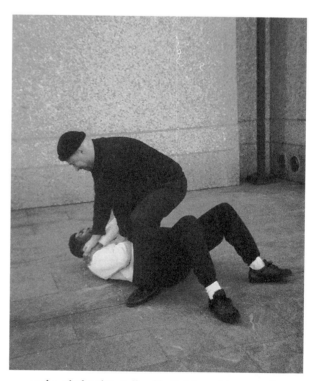

. . . and a vital-point strike. He finishes with a takedown hold.

Kenneth Delves redirects Kether Cooper's power from a sticky hands position.

tem. One noticeable difference with the knives is that each practitioner has to cut the knives to fit his proportions. This is the same as with the wooden dummy; each practitioner must set the dummy up according to his height. All movements done with the empty hand can be performed with the knives. For example, if you can use biu sao as a block, strike, joint manipulation, throw, or vital-point hit, *biu do* can provide the same results. Even though anything can be done with the knives, the main purpose is to finish your opponent by beheading him. Also, just like the empty-hand forms of the system, both the knives and staff are trained on the wooden dummy, and as the long pole is used for power training so are the knives. The extra weight of the knives provides a higher resistance for the different empty-hand exercises.

Long-Range Fighting

The staff is the long-range fighting weapon of the system, but at times it is used at close range. Unlike the long pole of the other Wing Chun families, this system's long pole is used for power training and a rattan staff is used for the form and fighting. During the previous stages of training the practitioner has spent considerable time cultivating his chi. Other than the obvious health benefits, chi development is needed for the proper execution of a strike with the staff. When striking with a staff you need to send your energy through the staff and into your opponent's to effectively disable him.

This also applies to dim mak with the empty hand and is why the dim mak application of a technique is taught last. Another part of training that is learned at this stage is called *chi gwun* (sticking staff), which is used for the same reasons as *chi sao* and *chi gerk*. Both the knife and the staff form are long-flowing movements that once mastered will only improve your knowledge and overall Wing Chun ability.

The Buddhist beads are considered a high-level weapon of the system. The beads are initially used for the training of techniques. Then one learns how to train the fingers with them, and finally to use them as a weapon. To the untrained eye, this apparatus would seem to give the same results as the rattan ring, but because of its flexibility, it provides a different result. When using the beads to fight, one can use them for whipping, entangling, and choking. The beads can be used either at full size or folded as if combining two smaller strings.

The iron fan is the last weapon of the system. Although rarely seen, this is the last implement the fut sao disciple is taught. The iron fan can be used open or closed. The bottom surface also has a function. Specific moves in the empty-hand forms relate to the use of the iron fan. Those who saw the movie *The Prodigal Son* witnessed Leung Yee Tai use the fan when he fought the young Leung Jan. Even though it is just a comical movie, one could see the butt of the fan being applied to the Stomach No. 9 point.

Forms and Sets and Drills

Before discussing the two-man sets of the system, it is important to mention the different energies or powers the forms and sets help bring out. Through constant practice of the forms and drills, those who study fut sao kuen develop four kinds of "thrusting powers" and eight "peerless actions" that are vicious movements.

The four thrusting powers are *tun* (swallowing), *tow* (spitting), *fao* (floating), and *cham* (sinking). The eight peerless actions are *bin* (whipping), *gan* (cutting), *wan* (seizing), *chong* (bumping), *tan* (rebounding), *so* (squeezing), *puan* (twisting and entangling), and *chung* (thrusting).

The students learn the "straight energy" and "rising energy," the study of which is more profound and abstract. The study of rising energy alone requires six or seven years of arduous training to understand its subtleties. Even an exceptionally bright pupil in arduous training must spend at least two or three years

Kether Cooper redirects Kenneth Delves's power from a sticky hands position.

before he can comprehend its various permutations and subtleties.

An integral part of the fut sao pupil's training is the development of his fighting skills through two-man sets. The first set is single-hand chi sao. The single-hand *chi sao* is done in two different patterns that help develop the use of *yum* and *yeung*. Next is the lop sao drill. Done in two patterns, lop sao aids in the student's joint grappling skills.

Next on the list are the six basic *heun chi sao* exercises. These circle hand drills teach you how to use small circular motions to dissolve hardness. They also further train your ability to stick to your opponent. Once ready, you can move on to chi sao. During chi sao, everything is applied in a controlled, free-form manner. This is where all your hits, joint locks, throws, and vital-point strikes are tested and further developed. In the earlier stages of chi sao, the student's main focus is on controlling and hitting.

Also, different exercises involve nonmoving and moving sequences. Some drills have the student attacking while the other is receiving or counterattacking. An example would be the *sup baat jeen kuen* (eighteen-arrow fist set). This set is not taught until the student has spent ample time with the nonmoving sequences. It is first taught without a partner.

Another two-man set would be the *san sao* (miscellaneous hands). The san sao are preset fighting sequences that further train one's fighting skills. Even though they are preset sequences, they are not locked in stone and can be adapted to any situation. All two-man sets and san sao sequences also are practiced on the mook yan jong. These drills are the stepping stones to actual street combat, and they provide the student with a step-by-step learning process. Though the student follows a definite progression, when it comes time to use the skills, there are no choppy movements or static positions (on-guard postures). This is why the style is often referred to as the "natural style." After years of training the forms, two-man sets, and other areas of the system, the student will have developed a smooth-flowing manner that he can carry over into everyday life. This level of development is called "intellectual fist" or "smart hands."

Other methods of development include doorway or wall training, candle hitting, iron rod sets, shifting shield sets, water jar sets, two-by-four sets, waist power sets, and phone book sets for strength, light skills, and internal work.

Fut sao Wing Chun strives for calm during motion; hides strength within suppleness; emphasizes poking and tearing; uses short, close strikes; prefers finesse over brute strength; and can be practiced in the space of a few feet.

It is a system that can be all things to all people.

Santo Barbalace is Grand Master Henry Leung's top disciple and currently teaches the senior members of the clan and select students in New York City. This material appeared in the July 1998 issue of Inside Kung-Fu.

Read the Future
in Your Pigua Palms

Adam Hsu

When we are provoked or find ourselves on the verge of a fight, nine times out of ten our immediate and automatic response will be to make a fist. As a matter of fact, even if hostile physical interaction is totally out of the question, when we are pushed to the point of real anger, how often do we instinctively clench our fingers into a fist? Consciously or unconsciously, this reaction is totally natural to all human beings.

In contrast, we touch with an open palm to soothe an upset. We wave our hands harmlessly in front of us to lighten a tense situation. Offering an open hand is an international signal that we mean no harm and wish to be friends.

There are also psychological reasons for making a fist. Tense and dangerous situations arouse strong emotions—especially different shades of fear and anger—in all of us. If we are forced to defend ourselves, we become nervous or scared. When people make us angry, we want to punish them by striking out physically or verbally. Anger may escalate to rage. Our minds and bodies become saturated with nervous tension. Clenching the hands and coiling the fingers tightly together is a natural, logical expression of this tension, which simultaneously provides us with a strong, solid weapon to launch at an enemy.

Gaining an Advantage

Generally, the fist gives us some measure of physical advantage when things get rough. It is stronger than an open palm and at the same time protects our

1. Raising.

2. Pushing backward.

3. Embracing inward.

4. Sinking.

5. Lifting.

6. Extending outward.

7. Folding inward.

8. Splitting up and down.

Qi shi (opening posture): The first movement of *pigua zhang*'s first form consists of eight movements, which must be linked together and performed nonstop. This educates the practitioner, from the beginning of the training, to focus on movement, not posture.

1. Opening.

2. Scooping.

3. Blocking.

4. Raising arm for the chop.

5. Striking the body.

6. Rebound to strike outward.

7. Final posture.

Pi (chopping): *chop* usually means a swift, downward cutting blow. Pigua's chop, however, also includes raising and flung-out motions made by the arms as they rebound from striking the body. Note that the movement never ends.

vulnerable fingers. It's no wonder, then, that of the two-hundred-plus martial arts styles that come from China, only a very few specialize in palm, or open-hand, techniques.

Fighting out of aggression is human nature. We don't need lessons to fight like this. A fighting *art*, however, takes a great deal of time to develop.

Kung fu took over one thousand years to reach its maturity. During the centuries of its evolution, the ancient masters noted that new students already had some physical power at the start of their training. There were several reasons for this. First, most people who qualified to begin martial arts were young and strong. Second, in those days just about everyone had to work. For the overwhelming majority, this meant physical labor. They chopped wood, hauled heavy water baskets, plowed the fields, and so on. To carry out their daily duties, people developed their own ways to use power. Third, fighting is a part of human nature. Those who have gentle dispositions may fight less; the restless and aggressive fight more. Only the volume is different. Kids fight all the time, though sometimes just for fun, like kittens or wolf cubs.

As we grow up, all of us accumulate some amount of natural fighting experience and develop different ways to issue power. These methods are not mature nor is their level high. So to study kung fu effectively, students must first eradicate their old habits and automatic responses. Their combat training must start again at the very beginning. They must relearn how to move, think, attack, and defend automatically and instinctively in the kung-fu way and issue the purest possible kung-fu power.

Soft Is Better

This is why masters always instructed new students—often at top volume—to relax. Their shouts would fill the practice area: "Relax, be totally relaxed! Don't use any power at all! Soft is better!"

The ability to relax is extremely important in the beginning stages of kung-fu training. The body becomes a clean slate ready to receive and absorb instruction. Imagine a teacher writing today's lesson on a blackboard that is still covered with notes from the previous day. Like the blackboard, a tight muscle is already in use and, preoccupied, perhaps is already tired out or expired.

When we make a fist, tightness easily spreads up the arm. This doesn't mean that fist strikes are no good or shouldn't be practiced. It is much more difficult to stay relaxed, however, while delivering a fist strike than while delivering a palm punch. Why? Because the tight, curled fist, of its very nature, contradicts relaxation to some degree.

Even a style like Bajiquan, known for impact training and explosions of power, emphasizes relaxation. From the very beginning of training, the Baji fist is held in a special, loose manner and tightened only at the moment of impact. Because this first position resembles the rakes that farmers used in their fields, the style's original name was *bazi quan*, or "rake fist."

Conversely, it's easier to keep the arm loose when delivering an open-fingered palm punch. Pigua zhang, a northern palm style, requires a great deal of relaxation to execute its powerful, whipping strikes.

Relaxation opens the door to more efficient and effective training and also to real kung-fu power. A good instructor encourages his students to relax and wipe away previous programming as much as possible, so that their bodies and minds will be clean and open to learning kung fu.

Kung-fu people need a different dictionary than do ordinary people. We don't call mountains, "trees," or black, "red." But we do have customized terms and also use some everyday words in special, technique-related ways. For instance, a kung-fu fist is not just a fist. In kung-fu terms, *fist* means the hand, forearm, and upper arm, wrist, elbow, and shoulder. The kung-fu *palm* is the open hand from fingertips to wrist, and then forearm to elbow, stretching out to the upper arm and shoulder. These definitions are not casual. They define and support the requirements of real kung-fu usage. If we use our arms solely to propel a hand to its target, then we are not practicing Chinese martial arts.

Lining Up the Attack

Martial arts practitioners from almost every discipline spend many hours in point practice. They punch and strike the air, then targets, and then each other. After a certain stage of improvement, kung-fu students must move ahead to line practice—whole-arm usage drills. A line is built from many points, linking each into a smooth, integrated unit. Line techniques are richer, deeper, and much more difficult to deliver than points. They contain many more possibilities for attack and defense, and action and reaction, than a simple fist attack. This is true even if the strike that finally impacts the target is delivered by the hand. Repetitive practice and effort alone are not sufficient to develop the special physical intelligence and reflexes needed to master this level of training. Moreover, to be successful, the mind must be able to adopt the new definitions of *punch* and *strike*. The muscles, nerves, and tendons must be available to cooperate in this not-so-natural training. Another way to put it: mind and body both must be relaxed.

When a football team scores a touchdown, the spotlight tends to shine on the one or two key players directly involved in the action. But even the most legendary football superstars know it is the cooperative effort of the team that ultimately makes touchdowns possible. Individual athletes spend many intense hours in training, not only to improve their own performances but also to work together with all their teammates as one unit. Their goal is a team that interacts in the smoothest, most coordinated, and most effec-

tive way, transforming strategy into powerful plays and exciting victories.

From the viewpoint of kung fu, our bodies work similarly to the scoring football team. The fist or palm impacting the target is only the servant that delivers the payload. The strategy, execution, and power are the result of a coordinated whole-arm—even whole-body—effort. High-level kung-fu techniques can only be performed through whole-body teamwork.

When we issue a kung-fu power punch, our legs—the body's foundation—start to create the twisting power from the ground up. The torso, of course, receives this energy from the legs, but very importantly, it also generates additional spiraling energy through its own powerful twist. This double payload is accepted by the upper body and arm, which through their own rotations add more energy to the attack-in-progress. Lower-, mid-, and upper-body power together are relayed through the arm and delivered to the target by the fist.

Throughout the entire process, all body parts cooperate so that the power is delivered through one continuous, unbroken motion. This is what whole-body kung-fu power generation, relay, and delivery are all about.

In kung fu, flexibility is an absolute necessity. Warm-ups and stretching are certainly very important. But there's another dimension to this; our muscles, joints, nervous systems, and minds must become flexible enough to perform several chores at the same time. For this to become possible, we must learn to be relaxed.

Punches are usually delivered in a straight line. Of course, there are different types of punches, such as the uppercut. But generally, or even naturally without any instruction, when people deliver a fist punch it usually travels in a straight path, with the shoulder or torso as its solid, almost unmoving base. This power is generated in the area between shoulder and fist. In other words, muscles and speed are normally used to create fighting power.

Pi (chopping). This entire sequence, filled with different techniques, comes from one long, continuous movement. The overhead attack is blocked . . .

. . . sliding and sticking with the enemy's arm to deflect the blow and control the elbow. A torso twist pulls the rear arm up to chop . . .

. . . while the left arm grabs and controls the enemy's arm. The blocking arm continues its motion, pulling the enemy in . . .

. . . as the right palm delivers a chop, but the enemy blocks the attack. The enemy's left arm is completely trapped as the chopping arm begins to rebound and right leg steps forward.

The right leg is now planted deep into the enemy's space and the right palm, backed by the entire body, continues to strike upward and outward . . .

. . . pushing the enemy off balance. The follow-through is complete and the enemy is defeated.

1. Opening.

2. Scooping.

3. Blocking.

4. Embracing (inward attack).

5. Striking the body.

6. Rebound to strike outward.

7. Final posture.

A Fighting Unit

Palm strikes, on the other hand, usually come from circular motions. An attack delivered with too much focus on the palm area tends to be small and the intensity of impact will be limited. For more strength, the action must involve a larger area. Chopping from the elbow is obviously an improvement, but raising the arm to begin the strike from the shoulder is much better. Notice that as the palm strike gets more correct, clear, and strong, more and more of the body, leading up toward the torso, becomes involved. Compared with fist techniques, palm usage encourages more body participation. The torso is no longer just the base from which the troops set out to fight, but more resembles a vital member of a cohesive fighting unit.

All this should alert us to the real value of kung fu's rare palm styles. Among them, pigua zhang is famous for its soft beginnings that ultimately lead to very powerful depths. The pigua style is a famous palm-strike style that originated in Hebei province, Cang county, China. Its name spread out into several different northern provinces, and then, of course, it migrated south. In addition to the original pigua are two famous branches. One is practiced with the *tong bei* style, mixed because of the two styles' similarity. Tong bei emphasizes arm training, but most of the time it uses the fist, though in a relaxed manner that is very close to pigua.

Another branch of pigua is very openly practiced with *Bajiquan*. Baji is famous for "fist," but as we mentioned earlier, the Baji fist is held in a very relaxed manner. Its flavor is quite different from pigua, and so they come together to balance each other out and harmonize the practice.

Blows transmitted by larger surfaces don't have the same intensity as those from smaller surfaces. Recognizing this, some styles change the fist's normal configuration to focus the power better. Sometimes Bajiquan strikes with the middle knuckle area pro-truding from the fist. Several other styles, such as *Hsing I Quan*, strike with the second finger. Six-harmony praying mantis advances the third finger. Palm strikes using the narrow edge of the hand, however, are natural. It doesn't take any extra effort to construct them. A powerful, whole-body-generated pigua palm strike can be devastating.

Remember to Focus

One reason pigua is fascinating and unique is that it is almost completely movement. In fact, this is one of the most valuable things it has to offer—pure movement. This very asset, however, makes pigua zhang extremely difficult to show, teach, or promote, especially through books, articles, and photos. Many people are first attracted to kung fu by its beautiful postures. Pigua, however, just keeps moving with only a few stops to create sections in its forms. There just aren't that many postures that can be captured beautifully in photographs or held for dramatic effect during performances. From basic training to its usage, it's impossible to transmit the art or even adequately convey its flavor without showing the movement.

Postures are important. Indeed, posture holding is an indispensable part of kung-fu training. But between postures is movement. Actual fighting is done not by posture but always by movement. Pigua's invaluable message to all practitioners is this: always pay careful attention that the movements are executed correctly. Movement is not a secondary factor. It's not just something that fills the time and space between beautiful postures.

In the early stages of pigua zhang training, students must relax and, very importantly, focus their attention on moving and executing techniques with the entire body. Students love to chase quickness and speed, but for beginners this invariably means overuse of the muscles. The arms are tightened, constricting,

Bao (embracing). Note that the entire palm is used: shoulder, elbow, and hand. The overhead attack is blocked . . .

. . . sliding and sticking with the enemy's arm to deflect the blow and control the elbow. The block continues by circling to trap the enemy's elbow.

The torso twists to deliver a lateral palm strike . . .

. . . as the left arm pulls the enemy into the blow. The right leg is now planted deep into the enemy's space . . .

. . . and the right palm, backed by the entire body, begins its rebound, starting with a shoulder strike. As the enemy is moved backward, the shoulder strike is followed by an elbow strike.

The follow-through is complete and the enemy is defeated.

Bao (embracing): Like the pi, the ending posture becomes the beginning of the next movement—another bao or different technique.

instead of opening up, the internal channels. It takes a long time to adapt the body and mind to this type of internal training. The body usually needs a period of slower practice to accustom itself step by step to a way of movement that awakens the internal energy pathways. Pigua also has special supplemental training to help with this.

The body's internal channels could be likened to bus routes. The bus stops (*xue dao*) are terminals for the energy flow. The routes (*Jingluo*) need to be kept in good working order, unblocked and clean. Pigua's internal training opens up the pathways, point to point, to create a structure. If all we do is wave our arms about as quickly as possible, then all we earn is external practice from the shoulder down to the fingertips.

The ideal pigua zhang training is complete. Pigua's internal focus enriches and deepens the purely external activity of ordinary athletic practice. It brings the body's internal systems into harmonious partnership with bone and muscle.

The rewards that come from correct training in this dynamic palm style are great: improved health and real power.

Adam Hsu is one of the world's most respected martial arts instructors. He is based in Cupertino, California. This material appeared in the February 1998 issue of Inside Kung-Fu.

30

The Many Faces of Shaolin Crane

Jane Hallander

Sometimes inhibited by his own physical stature and relative lack of physical strength, man looks toward certain animal species for the perfect martial techniques. Some animals were chosen for their fierceness, such as the aggressive praying mantis. Others became fighting models because of their speed, power, or soft internal energy. While most were known for one primary attribute, only one found a role in animal fighting techniques through its multiple benefits to hands, feet, and spirit.

This special animal was the crane, a creature who lent a new outlook on the use of both palm and fist techniques. It emphasized balance and tactical training for those who prefer to kick and delivered an invaluable mixture of both external and internal power and focus.

Aside from the Tibetan white crane kung-fu system, a product of Shaolin kung fu, China's most famous crane style is Buddhist in origin. It was one of the original Shaolin Temple five-animals training forms.

Monks to the Rescue

In ancient China, most Buddhist institutions were located in mountainous areas. The Shaolin Temple of Northern China's Songshan mountain region had gained a reputation for its outstanding martial artists. They were so good that they were called upon to help Li Shih-min, the first emperor of the Tang dynasty (A.D. 618–907), in his desperate battle against the vicious warlord Wang Shigang. Answering the call, thirteen monks of the Shaolin Temple went to Li Shih-min's aid, displaying such martial expertise that, after his victory, Emperor Li granted the Shaolin Temple extra land and gave it permission to openly practice martial arts.

A crane beak (he zui) strike to a pressure point inside the attacker's thigh.

A right crane beak strike and left crane neck block.

From the Shaolin Temple's mountainous location came the imitation of several fighting animal techniques, since many species of wild creatures inhabited China's rugged mountains. The monks, with their humanitarian natures, drew close to the many animals that inhabited the forests surrounding the Shaolin Temple. They began to notice the fighting tactics of each animal, such as those of the tiger, leopard, snake, and crane, along with the spiritual animal, the dragon. From that awareness were born the Shaolin five animal forms, the origin of much of Chinese martial arts' animal fighting tactics, including those of the Shaolin five animals.

Carol Ognibene, a kung-fu instructor in Bremerton, Washington, teaches the Shaolin five animal forms, with a special love for the crane fighting techniques.

"Crane techniques are perfect for women," she explains. "Since we are seldom as strong as our attackers, we need a fighting style that combines internal strength with what the Chinese call chou jing (wise force). Shaolin crane techniques are a combination of both qualities."

Carol Ognibene's husband, Vern Miller, is the head instructor at their Twin Dragons Kung-Fu school, where both he and his wife teach Choy Li Fut, Shaolin five animals, and Yang tai chi chuan. He is a direct student of San Francisco–based Doc Fai Wong, who is famous in kung-fu circles for his Shaolin five animal techniques, including the crane. Wong passed the knowledge on to his student Miller, who taught his wife Carol. Now specializing in crane techniques, Ognibene teaches her students the many sides of crane kung fu.

A Kinder, Gentler Art

Shaolin crane kung fu is known for its soft, relaxed power. Its principal striking tools are the crane beak (*he zui*), crane neck (*he jing*), and the crane top (*he*

A right crane strike aimed at the pressure point at the attacker's temple.

Ognibene uses her crane neck (he jing) block to both stop an attack and lock the opponent's shoulder joint.

ding), which are represented by specialized hand, wrist, and arm movements.

Crane top (he ding) strike.

Crane power is considered more soft than hard, unlike other animals, such as the leopard and tiger. Because the tiger uses its claws for ripping and gouging, it must put out a hard, forceful type of power. Likewise, the leopard form with its quick fist attacks, duplicates the strong, speedy strength of an actual leopard.

Crane power, however, relies upon perfect timing for its effectiveness. The crane beak can be a hard, forceful strike if sufficient speed is used, or with less momentum, it can be a penetrating pressure-point attack. A crane neck technique also uses timing for its characteristically relaxed, loose strikes to pressure points located in vulnerable areas.

The most popular crane strike is the crane beak (he zui). It is made by bringing together the first three fingers of the hand to a point and bracing them with the thumb and last finger. This hand technique is most often used as a reaching extension, making it longer than the ordinary fist. The wrist is kept straight when striking straight forward and bent when attacking to the side. Targets for the crane beak are soft, easily pen-

An example of a crane wing (he yi). Here the open-hand technique is defensive, and the kick is to the back of the assailant's knee.

etrated areas, such as the eyes, temples, throat, solar plexus, and armpit.

Training the Hands

External conditioning of the crane practitioner's fingers is necessary to project the sharp, penetrating power seen in crane beak strikes without damaging fingertips. This was done in ancient times by filling a leather bag with small metal balls and constantly striking it with crane beak hands. After each practice, the crane stylist's fingers were soaked in special herbal liquids to further strengthen the striking area and to prevent any damage to the sensitive nerves.

"Nowadays, we do push-ups on our fingertips, and strike bags, both hanging and wall-mounted," notes Ognibene. "The push-ups strengthen the entire finger, hand, and wrist muscles, while the bag toughens the fingertips."

A common crane-beak technique is to first block an oncoming punch by redirecting it with a crane neck block, and then strike directly to the eyes with a crane beak from the other hand.

Another popular crane hand is called crane top (he ding). It is formed by first joining the fingers into a crane beak and then bending the wrist. The bent wrist becomes the striking surface, or the crane top. Strictly an attacking hand, the crane top strike is used to hit large, easily penetrated areas, such as the bottom of the chin or jaw or below the rib cage. Crane top strikes are rapid, whiplike blows that serve to replace ordinary short-distance fist strikes.

A crane top becomes useful when an attacker punches to the midsection of the crane stylist, who stops the punch with a crane top technique that rapidly changes into a direct strike into the opponent's midsection. Another example of the crane top strike is to initially block toward the outside with the crane top, then continue with a high-striking crane top technique to the opposition's throat.

Ognibene strikes the attacker's chin with the top of her wrist in a crane top strike.

This Shaolin crane technique is called crane wings to the groin. It is both a kick to the groin and the offensive open-palm strike called he yi (crane wing).

By the Neck

The crane neck (he jing) involves the use of the entire forearm, including the wrist, with the hand in a crane beak position. When using a crane neck, it's important that the wrist stays loose and relaxed. This technique relies upon an almost sticky sensitivity to make it effective. A stiff, tense crane neck lacks effectiveness.

Mainly a defensive hand, the crane neck is used for both blocking and controlling an opponent's actions. For instance, a typical counter for a direct punch is to connect with the crane top, and while still sticking to the opponent's arm, redirect the punching arm toward the outside. Either a crane beak or crane top is then used as the counterattack. For close-in fighting, the crane neck is used as a hook to an opponent's neck or as a low-trapping hook to the ankle.

An open-palm strike called *he yi* (crane wing) represents the crane's wings. It is both an offensive and defensive technique. He yi is used defensively as an outward open-hand block. As an offensive technique he yi can be a slash across the opponent's eyes. Crane wing techniques can also be a double-handed horizontal strike to the throat, using the side of the hand as the striking area. Power for all crane hand techniques comes from strong, balanced stances and loose, supple wrists.

Since the nature of a crane is to stand on one leg, martial artists use this form to develop balance. The one-legged crane stance is also commonly used to evade an oncoming front kick by pulling one leg up and away from the opponent's kicking leg. Sometimes the raised knee becomes a blocking surface against front kicks. After the opponent's kick is blocked, a low side kick to the opposition's leg is a good counterattack. Another common use of crane footwork is lifting the foot out of the way of a leg sweep, then stepping down on the attacker's leg or knee.

The stoic crane also donates spirit to crane stylists. To correctly perform crane techniques, martial artists must be calm and alert—characteristics

Ognibene demonstrates a crane beak strike.

Ognibene blocks the attacker with a left crane neck technique, then strikes the opponent's midsection with her right crane beak strike.

of the crane. Concentration is essential to all martial artists. Crane techniques promote concentration through the balance required for one-legged stances and the perfect timing needed for the hand techniques.

For martial artists with backgrounds in internal training, crane techniques are even more effective because they require relaxation and smooth, unfaltering movements. Any hard or stiff actions defeat the spirit and purpose of crane strikes. Like the animal it imitates, crane kung fu is versatile and clever.

Jane Hallander is a former Inside Kung-Fu *"Writer of the Year." This material originally appeared in the June 1999 issue of* Inside Kung-Fu.

31

Kicking from Another Angle

Tang Soo Do's
Arsenal of Angular Kicks

Hector Vega and Jim Stroud

Two of today's most creative coaches and instructors on the open and AAU (Amateur Athletic Union) tournament circuits are Tang Soo Do and tae kwon do's Roger Haines and Steve Allen from Dayton, Ohio. Like mad scientists mixing a formula of kicking techniques within a laboratory, Haines and Allen have created champion after champion. Haines and Allen together have fifty-nine years of experience in Korean martial arts. Haines and Allen also have a teen fighting team called the SWAT (Southwest Association of Tournaments) National Karate Team.

SWAT is a group of young people from Dayton's west-side inner city who participate in martial arts tournaments in order to keep out of trouble, away from gangs and neighborhood crime. In a society that has a murder occurring every 27 minutes and one aggravated assault every 31 seconds, Haines and Allen

are trying to reduce the chances of today's teens becoming victims.

The angle kicking system for sparring put together nine years ago by Haines and Allen is one of the most effective fighting techniques and strategies. The goal of the angle kicking system is to attack your opponent with kicking techniques that travel on an angle so your opponent will have a problem blocking your offensive and defensive kicks. Basic techniques set up your angle kicks best. Your opponent may be looking for the basic side kick, round kick, and hook kick, so an angle technique will be a surprise.

Closing the Gap

The best way to attack an opponent is with combinations. It's best to move forward and try to control an attacker with a grocery list of kicking techniques that force your opponent to move backward. What often works best is to attack an opponent's body with a rear-leg side kick, then direct an angle lock-leg roundhouse kick to an opponent's head. If you attack low with something basic, follow up by attacking high with an angle kick. Other techniques are Pi-cha Gi (reverse roundhouse kick).

Pi-cha Gi

The Pi-cha Gi is used for close-in fighting. The reverse roundhouse kick can travel around your opponent's guards leaving open his lower body. Most people do not use the reverse roundhouse kick because they don't have good flexibility. To set up this kick, you bring your knee up high at a 45-degree angle, pointing the knee to the open area of your opponent's guards. Good flexibility is a must for this technique. The Pi-cha Gi is a good kick to set up other angle-kicking attacks.

Lock-Leg Roundhouse Kick

The lock-leg roundhouse kick may be the best kick in the tae kwon do and Tang Soo Do angle kicking system. It can be thrown with more speed by turning your hip over pointing in a 45-degree angle with the knee locked but not chambered. This roundhouse kick should be used if an opponent is advancing toward you; the kick will hit your opponent because of the circular motion of the technique.

Angle Hook Kick

The angle hook kick is a defense kicking technique used when an opponent is kicking at you off his front leg or back leg. As your opponent kicks, you execute an angle hook kick under his kicking leg. When using the angle hook kick, your knee points down at a 45-degree angle.

Angle Front Kick

The angle front kick can be used for offensive and defensive attacks in sport martial arts or street self-defense. On the defensive, as an opponent is kicking you off the front or back leg, you can block his kick by taking an off-angle step and countering with an angle front kick to your opponent's body. On the offensive, the angle front kick is very powerful for close-in, full-contact fighting. You can set up a lot of hand techniques with angle front kicks.

Angle Ax Kick

The angle ax kick is designed to go around the opponent's guard and strike him in a specific area. You adjust the angle to whatever you need to bring the leg around your opponent's guard. With the basic ax kick, you bring your knee straight up and down onto the opponent's head. The angle ax kick can be adjusted to hit on the side of the head or come down across the opponent's forehead. The angle ax kick works best when set up with a basic side kick to your opponent's body.

High Low Side Kick

Bring your knee up high on a 45-degree angle with a fake side kick to get the opponent's attention for a moment. Then, throw a power side kick to the body. This technique will open up your opponent for the lock-leg round and angle ax kick. The body attacks will bring your opponent's guard down a little, and that's all you need to make the angle kicks work.

Fake Side Kick, Lock-Leg Round Kick

Pick up your knee on a 45-degree angle aiming as if you are going to side kick a person next to you; off the fake, turn your hip over to a lock-leg round kick. This technique works well for opponents who like to punch.

This material originally appeared in the December 1998 issue of Inside Karate.

Kicking Okinawan Style

Dr. William Durbin

When karate was first introduced in the movies, the smashing ability of the art caught the interest of the directors, many times leading them to have scenes where the karateka smashed furniture in the process of fighting an opponent. Who can forget the scene of Bruce Lee smashing the furniture in the movie *Marlowe*?

But with the coming of the movie *Billy Jack*, a whole new and exciting aspect was introduced to the public: the skill of kicking. As Billy Jack fought his opponents, particularly in the park scene, his flashing kicks made people take notice. These kicks were choreographed and stunt doubled by the great master Bong Soo Han.

Bruce Lee himself added to the interest in kicks, performing some spectacular ones in the aforementioned *Marlowe*, as well as in his other movies. The series of kicks flashed against Chuck Norris in the col-

iseum scene of *Return of the Dragon* and in the multiple-attack scene in *Enter the Dragon* captured the imagination of the American public. Before videos were available for people to see these movies at home, flip-books were made showing Lee doing the kicks against his many opponents in *Enter the Dragon*.

As the years have passed, however, many have come to believe that karate specializes in punching skills and for kicking one must turn to the arts of tae kwon do or Northern Shaolin chuan fa.

This situation has not been helped by the fact that most scoring kicks of Japanese karate tend to be front kicks, and some Okinawan stylists have stated that Okinawan karate does not kick above the waist. But this only indicates what is emphasized in specific types of competition or by specific individuals.

One has but to look at the curriculum of most styles of Japanese and Okinawan martial arts to see that the complete range of kicks is taught. Both the arts of karate and kempo, whether they be Japanese or Okinawan, tend to have a full range of kicking, from stomps on an opponent's feet to kicks that strike the head.

Some people say that high kicks are only used for training to develop strength and flexibility; but one must ask, what would be the purpose of developing such superior dexterity if not to use it? Did the martial arts masters waste time developing skills they did not intend to use? One would think not.

Okinawan Background

By looking at some of the historical figures of Okinawa, it is possible to get a much better idea of what kind of kicking skills Okinawan masters possessed, and what are considered the actual fighting kicks of karate and kempo.

Bushi Takemura is one of the oldest known Okinawan masters famous for having great kicks. It is said that he was a tax collector, which was not an appreciated position among the common people. He, of course, was a member of the gentry, and as such would have had training in the martial art of the warrior class, which was originally called *Bushi Te*. Many times he entered a village to collect the tax and was attacked on the way out by irate citizens who resented the levy.

It is also said that he could use nothing but kicks and literally defeat multiple opponents. His most famous technique has been passed down as the scalping kick. Many have regarded it as a type of lead roundhouse kick, originally known as a side snap instep kick; but what allowed it to slice the scalp so strategically that the flap of skin and hair was cut loose is not known, though there are a couple of theories.

Shaolin martial arts relied on special nail-hardening substances to enhance the weapon ability of fingernails. It is believed that Takemura applied one of these substances to his toenails, creating an extremely hard surface. It is also believed that he trimmed each nail in such a way as to give an effective cutting angle to the nail when applied in a kick. Some say that any adult toenail trimmed correctly would have this capability even without any additional hardening. In sparring and tournaments, people have been accidentally cut by toenails in the past. In one of Bill "Superfoot" Wallace's title defenses, he cut an opponent's face with his toenail.

Another theory regarding Takemura's scalping kick is based on the use of a *nin-jutsu* device. Many of the Okinawan Bushi made close friends with the Satsuma warriors, and the Satsuma shared with the Bushi much of their martial arts training. This would be especially true of a tax collector, who would particularly benefit the Satsuma. The Satsuma were famous for their *ninpo* skills, which were a part of their Jigen-ryu. One of the devices nin-jutsu practitioners used was known as Tettsume, or iron claws, which would attach to fingernails or toenails like sharp metal sheaths. It is possible that Takemura acquired Tettsume and wore them on his feet to perform the scalping kick.

Whatever way Takemura cut an opponent, his kicking skill was phenomenal. Regardless of what caused the cut, it was the warrior's skill that snapped the kick into place exactly at the hairline of an opponent, an unbelievable ability were it not for the present-day kicking skill of Bill "Superfoot" Wallace. Anyone who has witnessed Wallace's skill and his ability to put his foot anywhere he wants, even when an opponent thinks he's ready to defend against it, gives credence to the legendary skill of Takemura.

The next great master kicker of Okinawa is the founder of the Shorin-ryu lineage, Chotoku Kyan. While many call Sokon "Bushi" Matsumura the founder of Shorin-ryu, this does not hold true in the light of history. According to records, the ryu of Okinawa were established sometime during the 1930s. Some say that the first system to be formally named was Goju-ryu, while others argue for Shorin-ryu. If Okinawan ryu were established in the 1930s, then considering that Matsumura lived from 1796 to 1893, it is impossible for him to have been the founder of the system.

What has led to much confusion in this regard is the use of the terms Shorin-ryu and *Shorei-ryu* by Gichin Funakoshi. When he moved to Japan, he ran into the Japanese attitudes of respect for ancient Chinese knowledge and for systems of martial skill. Thus he used the legend of two main temple martial arts that were supposed to have influenced Okinawa Te, used the term ryu to mean "style" rather than the typical Japanese meaning of "system," and coined the terms Shorin-ryu and Shorei-ryu. Some say that the Shorin refers to the northern Shaolin temple, while Shorei refers to the southern Shaolin temple. However, some Okinawans journeyed to China to find the Shorei temple, only it did not exist.

It is also believed that Choki Motobu actually founded the Shorei-ryu system, but since he and Funakoshi did not get along, Funakoshi continued to refer to the Shorei temple in his writings, not wanting to acknowledge Motobu's contributions to the Okinawan martial arts.

Regardless, Kyan is regarded as the founder of the main branch of Shorin-ryu, with Chosin Chibana and Shoshin Nagamine founders of other branches. On a historical note, people still argue over who first coined the term Shorin-ryu, Chibana or Kyan. But most consider the point moot, in that both did so during the 1930s.

Chotoku Kyan was extremely famous for his kicks, which included not only standing kicks, but aerial ones as well. It is said that he practiced leaping front snap kicks, striking the beams of the roof of his house, as well as jumping techniques up onto the guardrails of bridges.

But most of all, he is famous for a couple of incidents in his life where he took on multiple attackers with nothing but kicks. After a visit to a festival where he competed with two of his prizefighting roosters, he was attacked by a gang as he walked home carrying his fowl. For fear of dropping his roosters, he fought and drove off the entire gang with his kicks alone. Most impressively, he did not hurt his fowl by hugging them too tightly—a considerable feat because he was fighting a serious battle.

The second story revolves around a gang of bandits who were attacking and robbing people on a particular road. Kyan was asked to help stop the robbers. He took to walking the road each night carrying two chickens, so that he would look like a farmer out on business. After a few days, the bandits attacked him. They were armed with swords. He threw the chickens at them and then launched into a series of kicks that defeated the gang easily. Thus we can see how the founder of Okinawan Shorin-ryu truly was a great kicker.

Another great kicker of the Okinawan martial arts was Zenryo Shimabuku. Shimabuku was among the top ten students under Chotoku Kyan himself. When he first founded his system, he called it Shorinji-ryu, but this has since been changed to Chubu Shorin-ryu, to avoid confusion with Nakazato's Shorinji-ryu. Having learned to kick under the great kicking master Kyan himself, he wanted to expand his knowledge and so studied Northern Shaolin chuan fa, which had a very complete range of kicking. He then adapted the Shaolin kicks into his style and passed the ability on to his many students. Some say that Shimabuku was a better kicker than Kyan, though others say that Kyan's kicking skill was unsurpassable.

Unique Aspect of Okinawan Kicking

Okinawan kicking, which in modern times has been categorized very thoroughly according to type, originally had a very unique aspect to it. Instead of being regarded as just front kicks, side kicks, and such, the kicks were initially designated by the part of the foot used for striking.

Thus there were ball-of-foot kicks, foot sword kicks, and heel kicks. While the modern tendency today is to name the method of delivery, in the old days of Okinawa, the idea was to take each weapon of the foot and deliver it as many different ways as possible.

Based on the old method, vast arrays of kicks and many highly unusual angles of delivery can be developed. By telling students that in Okinawan karate one does not kick above the waist and limiting the kicks to the designations of front, side, and back, karate instructors limit the development of superior kicking skills in their students.

While kicks may not be everyone's forte, instructors have a responsibility to encourage their students to develop the widest range of ability possible. Many excellent martial artists who specialize in self-defense, or who have had the misfortune to use their skills in actual confrontations, can testify that kicks do work in reality.

Kicking Okinawan style focuses on one very important aspect. This is the snap, or the continuous movement out and back of a kick.

Many Japanese and Korean stylists lock their kicks for a moment at the extension of their kicks. This is not a healthy practice for the knee, and it gives a good opponent an opening to counterattack. But when a kick is quickly snapped back, as Choki Motobu advocated to his students and as seen in the kicks of Takemura, Kyan, and Shimabuku, then there is no

weakness to the kicking strategy and no damage done to the knee.

Most of all, Okinawan kicking follows the basic Okinawan premise, "In karate, there is no first attack." Many people who decry kicks say the leg can be grabbed when executed or the groin attacked when the leg is extended. Both these assertions are true, if a person is foolish enough to attack.

However, as a counterattack, which is the basic concept of Okinawan martial arts, kicks are excellent. It is possible to stay out of hand range and to intercept the assailant as he seeks to close the gap. This is the stop kick of Bruce Lee and a main kicking tenet of Okinawan martial arts.

Kicking Okinawan style thus uses a quick action in the execution of movement, focuses on using the specific weapon of the foot for striking, and develops full range of motion, meaning kicks are directed from the foot to the head. Kicks are used as counterattacks and follow the principles of defense typical to all Okinawan martial arts.

This material originally appeared in the June 1998 issue of Inside Karate.

The Ax Kick's Crushing Power

Art Michaels

You're frustrated with an opponent who lays back and then counters your offensive techniques. The score is tied, so you need only one more winning combination. You fire off a series of front-leg snap kicks with your right leg. As you expect, your opponent retreats, dropping his guard as he steps backward. Quick as lightning, before your opponent can counter, you arc your rear leg upward. As if you wielded an enormous ax, your heel crashes down on the opponent's chest. Your point and match.

"The ax kick is one of tae kwon do's most powerful kicks," says Harrisburg, Pennsylvania–based tae kwon do instructor Joe Fox. "You don't see this kick a lot in competition because it's hard to control. When you chop down powerfully, if you hold back, you become vulnerable to a counter. Still, it's a useful technique against an opponent who's more of a defensive fighter—someone who lays back and isn't especially aggressive."

That's why it worked in the opening example, Fox says, but to execute this kick effectively, you have to be very fast and flexible, especially in the hamstrings.

The ax kick is so named because, like wielding an ax, your leg rises high and chops down on the target. The most effective weapon is the heel, and sometimes the sole of the foot. Using the sole of the foot lets you achieve greater reach on an opponent who's retreating. Targets for this powerful kick include the top of the head, face, collarbone or top of the shoulder, chest, point of the hip, and top of the knee at the quadriceps.

Developing Speed and Power

"This kick requires even more speed and power than other techniques because you need that extension to raise the leg and you need strength to pull the kick down," Fox says. Fox uses focus pads to teach students how to chop down powerfully and accurately. "If you don't have the strength, it's difficult to pull the leg down, and just letting the leg drop doesn't generate power. If you're too slow, you're vulnerable to a counterattack, so you have to get the leg up and down quickly and powerfully."

Fox also encourages his students to train with weights. Leg curls help develop the hamstrings. Strengthening drills without weights can also be beneficial. Fox has students offer resistance on the heel as they curl the leg up, taxing the hamstrings. Lie flat on your stomach, bring one leg up at a time, and have a partner resist at your heel as you perform sets of repetitions. To work different parts of the hamstring, perform a set of repetitions with the leg in three positions—at 45 degrees from the floor, 90 degrees from the floor, and 45 degrees the other way from your back. Repeat these sets two or three times.

Stretching is also a large part of the training. In addition to the usual hamstring stretches, Fox suggests a two-person stretch against the wall with partners alternately pushing a leg up to stretch the hamstrings. Performing isometric exercises in three sets of 10 to 15 repetitions can also help increase strength and stretch in the hamstrings. Start with a mild stretch and perform the first set. Then stretch farther for the second set, and still farther for the third set. Repeat two or three times.

"The ax kick isn't as easy as it might look," Fox says. "It's introduced into most classes from day one by way of a straight high kick, or front-rising kick, during regular class kicking drills. These drills often aren't explained as the ax kick, but if you practice a straight high kick and pull it down quickly and forcefully, you're performing an ax kick motion."

Fox says this helps to strengthen and stretch the hamstrings. It also helps you develop the ability to keep your body straight as you pull the leg up. Later on, focus pad drills help increase the kicking height and develop the chopping motion.

Moving drills are also useful. You perform one ax kick after another, each with the rear leg. You could also perform this drill with shuffle ax kicks and alternate with the front leg.

Breaking is a good way to test the effectiveness of this kick and your overall focus—to see if you are powerful and accurate enough to break one, two, three, or more boards. Breaking also clearly demonstrates this kick's awesome power.

Basic Ax Kick

"To perform an ax kick correctly," Fox says, "the hips don't stay square, because you're reaching with the kick. The hip of the kicking leg rotates forward as the leg rises, and then you twist the hips back as the leg chops down. Arc the leg up each time as if you were performing an inside or outside crescent kick. With an opponent in close, you need that arcing movement to position the leg properly.

"A jump ax kick can be very powerful. Not only do you have the leg pulling down, but you're in the air and have the gravity and weight of your body pulling down, adding to that power," Fox says.

To perform a jump ax kick, Fox says, start as if you were performing a jump front-snap kick. Instead of chambering the kicking leg, however, bring the leg up in a circular motion and chop down.

Jumping straight up in the air and turning the hips to kick with the rear leg is less likely to telegraph the kick. Lifting the front leg and performing the kick with the other leg can be a decoy, but it draws attention to that front leg as if you were throwing a front snap kick, so your opponent will still prepare to counter your kick. This kind of jump ax kick isn't as effective or as explosive as jumping straight up and turning the hips into the kick.

Fox also notes that an ax kick can be chambered just like a crescent kick. "You get more of a whipping motion with a chamber," Fox says, "but when you chamber, you add a motion that takes away from the kick's chopping quality."

Fox notes that chambering also telegraphs the kick in a pronounced way. "If you do chamber this kick, you have to kick quickly. You have to land this kick when a person is pretty much in the same position as when you start the kick. If you add motions that telegraph or slow the kick, that person can more easily step back out of range or rush in and jam you—and having your leg high in the air is the most vulnerable position to be in. All in all, then, it's best not to chamber this kick, even though it can be done."

Jamming an Ax Kick

"Jamming is an excellent defense against an ax kick," Fox says. You move in underneath the kick, thereby dissipating its effectiveness, and counter with a reverse punch. Remember that this kick works best with less-aggressive, defensive fighters, who are less likely to jam you and who are more likely to retreat.

Another effective defense against an ax kick is simply to avoid it—step out of range and then counter immediately when the leg comes down.

Competition Factors

Fox says that if you have the flexibility and speed, an ax kick is more effective when performed with the front leg in a fighting stance—there is little telegraphing. You try to hit the target on the way down—but with the front leg, lifting the leg can be a front snap kick to the chin followed by the ax kick to the chest. This double kick is much like the common hook kick–roundhouse kick combination.

"To set up an ax kick, when you use an outside crescent motion with the leg, try to direct the opponent's attention in the opposite direction," Fox says. "Try jabs or kicks on one side, and then come back from the opposite side with an ax kick."

You could also set up an ax kick by jabbing with mid-level front snap kicks. Then come with the ax kick when the opponent lowers the guard to block what he thinks is another front snap kick. Remember, you have to be fast with this technique.

Self-Defense Applications

"If a defender hasn't developed the kick, then using it in a self-defense situation can be dangerous. If you're effective, it's just another self-defense tool, and someone on the street probably isn't going to expect this kick," Fox says. "The ax kick often becomes a person's favorite weapon—for those people who use it well. Of course, these people are more likely to use the kick on the street."

All in all, the ax kick is one of the most powerful kicks in the tae kwon do arsenal. But to be effective, its ingredients must include speed and power.

Art Michaels is a Harrisburg, Pennsylvania–based tae kwon do black belt and freelance writer-photographer. This material originally appeared in the January 1997 issue of Inside Karate.

Fantastic Flips and Kicks

The Double-Barreled Approach to Winning Wushu

Bruce Fontaine

Have you ever noticed that many of the martial artists who do well in forms competition are usually good kickers? Others who place well consistently might take to the air well, executing flips and such. But the guys who always seem to storm straight through to the winner's circle hit you with both barrels: flips and kicks.

Martial arts forms competition, like most everything, is subject to trends. If there is some sense of fashion to the martial arts, then to make it in the forms arena you must ride the crest. Forms competition is always evolving; if you're motivated to be a winner, then you can't afford to be a dinosaur.

Twenty years ago, the equation used to be quite simple—step, pivot, block, and strike. Do that better than anyone else and you were most likely to win the forms event. Nowadays, for better or worse, that equation simply doesn't work anymore.

Raising the Standards

So many variables can factor into the equation for success in forms competition. The lowest common denominators are the traditional tenets of power, speed, focus, technical execution, spirit, and form. However, as the competitive field broadens and the stakes get higher, standards are raised and new skills are introduced. As a result, other factors have to be taken into account. The winning-minded forms competitor should now also duly consider his competition routine's level of difficulty, originality, virtuosity, visual aesthetics, and presentation. To a traditional stylist that may not sound like what forms are supposed to be all about, but it's the reality of today's forms competition events.

Originally, forms and their practice served a multitude of purposes—from teaching a student the basic

The jump straddle kick, as demonstrated by author Bruce Fontaine, may not be a practical self-defense technique, but it is a high-level skill that requires explosive legs, full-range flexibility, and coordination.

skills of a style to passing down a specific system's traditional skills from one generation to the next. If that's the objective of one's forms training, then traditional forms will more than serve this purpose. If, however, it's your intention to compete among the upper echelons of today's top forms competitors, then perhaps revamping or modifying your existing forms, if not designing an entirely new routine, is in order. The inclusion of certain specific high-level skills such as flips and kicks is perhaps one of the most effective ways to bridge the gap between you and the current forms champions.

For showy skills like flips and kicks to be truly effective, they must tie in well to the form with which you intend to compete. This is particularly true with acrobatic moves. Oftentimes a competitor on the open circuit may compete with a karate kata (form). In the midst of his form he will stop, throw an acrobatic move like an aerial cartwheel or a back handspring, stop, hesitate, and then go on to the next

movement. While including such movements shows the competitor's ability to perform these skills, it also puts an uneven break in the flow of the form and leaves the movement looking somewhat out of place. Modern wushu stylists, the hype-meisters that they are, realize the importance of tastefully working in such skills, so the moves fit in and flow as part of a natural progression in a series of movements.

Tradition Comes of Age

Modern wushu proper, as it is contested in mainland China (and in many of the U.S. Chinese-style format tournaments currently becoming prevalent), is not all just hype and flash. Not only do wushu routines have strict regulations on the type and number of stances, kicks, strikes, etc., required in a routine, based on the style being performed, but they also have restrictions on the number of jumps and acrobatic elements.

Team Ultimatum member Don Lew shows there's virtually no limit to the heights one can achieve with martial arts acrobatics!

Author Bruce Fontaine demonstrates a classic Chinese acrobatic move—*hau pow fu*, or the "back pouncing tiger."

Jump kicks like jump roundhouse and jump spin heel kick, as demonstrated by Vancouver's Team Ultimatum member Don Lew, are always an exciting addition to any competitive form.

Kirk Caouette demonstrates the progression into a patented Team Ultimatum movement—back layout with a straddle kick.

Twisting and spiraling through the air with the legs lashing out in all directions is not only a big crowd-pleaser, but also a true skill, which is largely what martial arts are about.

The elaborate kicks of modern wushu as demonstrated by author Bruce Fontaine, always play well to judges and audience alike.

While modern wushu includes the full spectrum of traditional styles, the inclusion of acrobatics and high kicking is limited solely to specific suitable traditional styles. Throughout the evolution of the sport, modern wushu players have learned that the best ways to tie all the required basic elements of those specific traditional styles together is with the high kicks, jumps, and acrobatics that have gained them the notoriety they enjoy today.

Not only must you be good at the skills you wish to tie into your competition routine, but you must fit them in so that they all tie together into one cohesive assemblage. The skills you use should also suit the style you are performing; skills like flips and kicks are normally long and open, so the style should be one with big open movements. Extended high-kicking skills do not usually look good when performed with tight-knit, short-range hand techniques of a traditional Chinese style such as *Baahk Meih* or a classical karate style like *Uechi-ryu*. At the same time, dynamic acrobatic movements naturally do not pair well with a quiet, serene style such as *Yang tai chi*. Before making any drastic alterations to your routine, be sure the skills you plan to work in do not detract from the flavor or essence of the style.

If your style is suitable to the incorporation of high kicks and acrobatic maneuvers, it's only a matter of what skills you should use and how to use them—and that depends on individual talent. How you use those skills is really only limited by your experience and imagination. Just remember though, more important than the flash and hype you intend to put in your form are the actual basic skills of your style. Nothing looks worse than a guy who can fly through the air with the greatest of ease but can barely hold a basic horse stance.

If a forms competitor is not only good at his fundamental skills but also possesses exceptional abilities with kicks or flips, then it would certainly be in his favor to spotlight those skills within his routine. A form, particularly freestyle forms or ones of the individual's design, should reflect the capabilities of the athlete. Modern wushu stylists do this very effectively, designing a sequence of the skills they do best and then ending them dramatically, usually by landing in the full splits or a bold fighting posture (usually held momentarily). This not only leaves the judges and audience with a strong last impression of the sequence, but also gives them a moment to absorb what they have just seen.

Out of the Ordinary

A side aerial cartwheel is a typical acrobatic favorite of modern wushu players on both the open circuit and the Chinese tournament scene. While an impressive skill, the aerial cartwheel done solo is quite commonplace these days; however, do it coming out of a jump front kick, then finish off the cartwheel itself with a side body drop and you'll have a sequence that is sure to leave a lasting impression. Modern wushu players often appear like some sort of whirling dervish as they spin infinite circles tying together various kicks, leaps, and strikes. A sudden popping sound echoes through the arena as the wushu stylist's hand makes crisp contact with his foot during a full spinning inside crescent kick. He continues right through the spiral and leaps horizontally into the air, first into a circling butterfly kick, then right into a full twisting butterfly. As feet touch down, he converts back into a vertical spin again as he drops into a deep squat and executes a full circling front sweep. Suddenly the combination comes to a complete stop. The wushu stylist can be found frozen in a cross-legged resting position, arms held out and boldly beckoning his imaginary opponents forward.

Working it in all together to become more visually impressive is the key, and you needn't be a modern wushu stylist to do that. When designing that combination or sequence of moves, first choose the moves from your own personal catalog that you do well and would like to highlight. Then choose actions you feel help flow into and build toward that climactic movement. Try to choose actions that will almost give a subtle hint that you are building toward something big. Start off with a few slow, deliberate moves to allow the judges and audience to focus on what you are doing, then blast off through a combination of flips and kicks. End dramatically so all watching can catch their breath and take in what you just did. While the combination should make some kind of sense—combatively speaking—also think of your routine as being a story or movie. To build toward a climax, you must first grab the audience's attention and hold it with each consecutive movement, building anticipation, and finally astonishing them with a sensational concluding action. You should try working several different combinations of this nature into your routine.

Modern wushu players are not the only hype-meisters and purveyors of taste on the national forms circuit these days. Many American tae kwon do style forms competitors are also consummate masters of hype and flash, especially in the legwork department. Tae kwon do forms superstar of the eighties, George Chung, electrified audiences with his brilliant legwork. Using a similar climax-building formula, Chung and his signature routine, "Silver Bullet," would first build audience anticipation with several rounds of machine gun–like kicking combinations, followed by numerous gravity-defying jump kicks, and then finally astound all with his patented multiple-direction carousel kicking.

While a traditional stylist may have written off Chung's form as mere showboating, his individually

Weapon routines are made even more exciting with the addition of jumps and acrobatics.

tailored routine conveyed his superlative kicking abilities, bringing him countless trophies and awards. At the same time, Chung also proved himself time and again as a formidable tournament fighter. As with the wushu stylist, Chung made full use of his floor space and paid attention to the climactic progression of the techniques within his form. Like the routines of modern wushu, Chung's freestyle tae kwon do forms also tied together several various eye-catching techniques in such a way as to make them more impressive.

Look Like a Champion

It should be readily apparent that in forms competition, it really isn't enough to just be good at flips and kicks; your overall routine has to be impressive and well-conceived. When formatting sequences or combinations of techniques, look for the most visual ways to show off your skills and cover space. While designing kicking patterns, think of multiple levels and directions. Try using quick change-ups in your form. A recent but popular addition to the already vast array of wushu techniques is the "full back sweep into the jump spin heel kick (sometimes done into a fall) combination."

This combination is also effective because it goes from low to high—covering vertical space—another consideration when laying out the design of your combinations. Full use of space clearly goes over better in forms competition, particularly when making use of skills such as flips and kicks.

Certain traditional forms, while extremely effective at teaching a student the respective techniques of his style, are sometimes too one-directional or centralized for the purpose of forms competition, particularly on the open circuit. Although a competitor performing such a routine may demonstrate his style with the utmost proficiency, he will most likely lose to an opposing competitor of equal proficiency who simply covers more space, especially if that opposing competitor uses awe-inspiring high-level skills such as

flips and kicks. Though it may sound like sacrilege to a staunch traditional stylist, making the appropriate alterations to your traditional forms or creating a specific competition routine is something the aspiring forms competitor from a traditional background should take into consideration before deciding to throw his hat into the ring.

It doesn't necessarily mean you have to jump on some sort of cosmetic forms bandwagon, but you should keep in mind that in the higher levels of forms competition, the players are not only of a higher caliber but also know how to play to a crowd and the judges. In addition to displaying high-level martial arts skills, these athletes present a finely balanced package of flashy kicks, breathtaking acrobatics, and those bone-crunching falls that leave audiences cringing. Those extraneous additions might not seem to be legitimate martial arts or practical self-defense skills, but they are nevertheless an athletic spectacle to behold. Shooting out vertical side kicks requires extreme balance, control, and flexibility. Flipping over backward and curving gently to the chest requires the combined attributes of courage, explosive power, timing, and coordination. These aforementioned attributes are something any true martial artist would strive to attain.

If you should decide to dress up one of your favorite traditional or individual routines with the addition of space-consuming visual elements like flips and kicks, first try watching today's top champions to see what combinations they're winning with and what's going over big with the judges. Don't just copy them outright, though; unearth something new and more original that lets your own individual talents and abilities shine through. A true champion always looks to break new ground and blaze new trails.

This material originally appeared in the June 1998 issue of Inside Kung-Fu.

Kata
The Soul of Karate

John Van Weenen

To understand the meaning of kata, one must know something about their development through the ages. About five hundred years ago, karate reached a high level of development in Okinawa, an island of the Ryukyu Islands. Two schools emerged: *Shuri-te* and *Naha-te* (*te* means "hand"). Shuri-te, mainly practiced in the regions of Shuri and Tomari, was also called Shorin-ryu (*ryu* means "school"). Naha-te was popular around the port area of the city of Naha and was known also as Shorei-ryu. These karate styles, practiced solely in kata form, had been handed down from generation to generation among people in the warrior class as a secret military art. With the breaking up of the feudal system, these secret arts of combat became more widely known.

Each school has its own characteristics. Shorin-ryu is a fast school. Attacks are performed with tremendous speed as in *empi*, the "flying swallow" kata. In contrast, Shorei is slower but is done with far more power and definition. A good example is the *Hangetsu* kata. Shorin is divided into two sub-schools: *Goju-ryu* and Uechi-ryu. These four styles are the main styles in Okinawa today. Japan also has many schools of karate. The five largest are *Shotokan*, *Goju-ryu*, *Shito-ryu*, *Wado-ryu*, and *Kyokushinkai*.

Gichin Funakoshi, the man who introduced karate to Japan, studied both Shorei and Shorin. After mastering both styles, he combined the strong points of each to create his own style, which he called Shotokan. *Shoto* was Funakoshi's pen name, and *kan* means "hall."

The kata of karate are sequences of offensive and defensive movements applied against the simultaneous attack of several imaginary opponents. The movements are rationally and systematically combined. In the old days, students learned their basic techniques through the practice of kata. Through continual repetition of these forms, they gained insight into the true meaning of karate—both the spiritual state of perfect selflessness and the practical application of the techniques.

The Origin of Kata

The origin of many of the individual kata remains obscure. Some originated in China while others came from Okinawa. Many that began on the Chinese mainland were changed by the Okinawans at a later date. Today, none of the masters who created them are known with any certainty. In many cases, the purpose of the movements and even the method of their execution are uncertain or unknown. Why is this? The main reason, of course, is the method by which karate has been taught through the ages. Little has ever been written down with regard to karate. Knowledge was handed down from teacher to student by word of mouth and example. Secrecy surrounding the martial arts has also prevented the arts from being taught to "just anyone." Past masters, not wanting their knowledge to fall into the wrong hands, have chosen their successors with great care.

Shotokan Principles

In the early 1900s, when Funakoshi combined elements from both the Shorin and Shorei to form Shotokan, he changed many of the names of the kata,

too. Some dangerous techniques were removed to make the kata suitable for young people to learn in schools and colleges as a form of calisthenics, as opposed to a martial art.

In 1905, Sensei Yasutsune Itosu was most responsible for the *Heian* kata being taught to groups rather than behind closed doors. It is significant that all the Heian kata begin with *uke*, expressing humility. *Heiwa-antei* (peace and calmness) became Heian, or *Pinan*, katas.

The Japanese Karate Association, of which the late Nakayama Masatoshi was the chief instructor, follows the teaching of Funakoshi. The three principles that he laid down for his students to follow are (1) proper application of strength, (2) the most efficient expansion and contraction of the muscles, and (3) the correct speed.

Keep the principles constantly in mind when practicing any karate kata. Kata have been with us in a basic form for a long time, probably since the sixth century. It is remarkable that they have endured to this day. Although the techniques may have changed somewhat over the years, due to external pressures and influences from the great masters of the past, they are still practiced for the same reason today as they were then: for the perfection of character.

By continually striving to improve and perfect the techniques in kata, a person improves his attitude, mind, and character. A student training in a dojo today, in any country, could be training in the same techniques as his predecessors a thousand years before him. In these days of change and modernization, it is wonderful to be involved in an art that has truly withstood the test of time.

36

The Dos and Don'ts of Forms!

Chris Casamassa

Chris Casamassa has appeared in numerous television and film roles as an actor, stunt double, and fight choreographer. He currently plays "Scorpion" in the syndicated action series *Mortal Kombat: Conquest*. Other roles include Blade, "Scorpion" in *Mortal Kombat: The Movie* and "Red Dragon" on WMAC *Masters*. Casamassa is president of Red Dragon Karate's twenty-seven studios and was the number one rated competitor in open forms on the North American Sport Karate Association circuit four years in a row. Casamassa is known for the power, speed, and height of his jumps, spins, and kicks. "Developing speed, height, and power was not easy," he explains. "It took years of practice and concentration. But I knew if I was going to be among the best in the world, I had to work hard."

Regardless of how high, hard, or fast he went, you always knew Casamassa had a strong martial arts foundation. "If you can't do it right, it doesn't matter how good it looks," Casamassa explains. "Following the principles of the form should always be a martial artist's first priority." On the following pages, Casamassa shows you the right and wrong way to perform many martial arts performance takeoffs, jumps, spins, kicks, and landings. He also lets you know the best way to start and end your routine.

This material originally appeared in the September 1999 issue of Inside Kung-Fu.

Correct posture to start the form. Show a respectful attitude. The eyes are focused and the body is straight.

Incorrect intro. The subject is too relaxed. The eyes are looking away. This shows judges you are not confident.

Correct stance. The knees are bent and the hands are aligned with the body. The eyes should always follow the hands.

Incorrect stance. The legs are straight and stiff, the hands are open, and the eyes are not fixed.

Here is another example of a correct stance. The feet are planted, the hands and body are aligned and balanced. There is an air of strength and confidence.

Bad news all around. There's no balance, no focus, the wrist is bent and will break upon impact.

Correct posture for the round kick. The body is straight and the base leg is bent. The hands are close to the body for balance.

Here's how you should look at the end of a kick. The hips rotate for maximum leg extension. Don't forget to show intense facial expression.

This is the wrong start for a kick. The swinging will throw you off balance. You have to slow down the kick.

Incorrect form. Since the hands are too far away from the body, it destroys a competitor's balance. In the follow-up move, the kick is not fully extended. Poor form comes from body leaning.

A perfect jump kick. The height and hang time created here are generated by both knees being tucked. This allows the body to get the kick fully extended and then recoil in the air. The body is straight and the eyes are focused.

The head is forward and the hands are back. This provides perfect balance for the landing.

Perfect practice makes perfect technique. Form and balance are important when attempting a jumping technique. What your body practices, it remembers.

Here are examples of poor jumping techniques. Remember: It's not how many times you do something, it's how well you do things that count. In other words, quantity does not always equal quality.

Bad jump kick form. A straight non-kicking leg gives the performer less hang time. This forces a rushing of the kick.

Correct spinning hook kick. This is the correct start for a spinning hook kick.

On the spin, the knees stay bent as the body turns. The eyes search for a target. Note: The kicking leg remains on the ground.

As you chamber the knee, the kick shoots straight for the head. The tighter you chamber the leg, the faster and stronger the kick.

The kick completes the process. The base leg is bent but the body is straight. The eyes remain focused at all times.

Good form begins with intensity. And that often leads to consistent winning. A competitor must show the attitude of kata, "an imaginary fight between two or more opponents."

Incorrect spinning hook kick. The back leg is straight, which means it will be hard to balance.

The hands are down and the leg lifts off the ground too early.

This forces an early kick and that destroys balance. The kick itself is too wide and already extended.

This converts to zero power. Notice the poor lean of the body and the lack of eye focus. Trying to sacrifice form for height will lead to trouble. Balance is poor and the eyes are looking down.

PART THREE

Beyond the Fist

Exploring the Myths and Misconceptions of the Martial Arts

John Maberry

"We should not ask who is the most learned, but who is the best learned."
—MICHEL MONTAIGNE, FRENCH ESSAYIST

Myths and misconceptions run rampant in the martial arts. Most of them deal with a wide range of so-called death blows—mystical, imaginative techniques of awesome power that make for great fiction. They include plucking out the heart, the "stop the heart" punch, the "pierce the heart" kick, tearing out the eyeballs, the delayed death touch the poison hand, and driving the nose into the brain. Other misconceptions of less lethal proportions include "registering" your hands as deadly weapons, and the popular opinion that a first-degree black belt is an "expert." The amount of fantasy that obstinately clings to the martial arts is as staggering as it is embarrassing. The sad truth is that many people—practicing martial artists included—genuinely believe these myths. Here, John Maberry, a black belt and a leading martial arts journalist, explores the most glaring myths and misconceptions and, in a sane, sensible, hard-hitting style, shatters them one by one.

To research this piece, John Maberry surveyed 487 non-martial artists and 173 martial artists of various types, ages, ranks, and national origins. In addition he used various texts to back up his findings, most notably Gray's Anatomy, Asian Fighting Arts, *and* The Science of Man *(a comprehensive thirty-volume medical series). He also cross-checked with some twenty-five physicians, historians, and nineteen other scholars of various types. Maberry's notes alone number almost a hundred pages, and they're in shorthand! The following information is not simple opinion; it is well researched and thought-provoking, and it contains some very profound findings of interest to all martial artists, regardless of style or rank.*

The attacker whirled, his hands balled up into tight fists, his eyes afire with animal hatred. The slender karate master waited calmly as the hulking thug tensed to charge. With an almost subhuman growl, the attacker launched himself forward, his meaty legs working like pistons to drive his massive body toward the waiting master.

With little effort, the karate master batted aside the man's wild punches, using the rock-hard side of his forearm. The bones of his forearm, as in his hands and feet, had been carefully broken and reset so that they would heal stronger than normal. He felt no pain himself, but dealt it out in generous proportions.

He swatted the brutish thug's blows away effortlessly. After a moment the attacker staggered back, eyes wide with shock. "I must warn you that I am a living weapon," the master said softly, "and that my hands are registered with the police as deadly weapons." Snarling incoherently, the thug charged again, flailing wildly with his well-muscled arms.

"I warned you," the karate master said, ducking under a blow. "Now I must act!" With a powerful *kiai* the master sprang forward, his palm shooting out and catching the man's nose at the base. The master straightened his arm and the thug toppled back, a scream on his dying lips. He was dead in a second, his nose bone slammed up into his forehead, sending tiny shards of bone into his brain.

Sound familiar?

It's not an account of how one of the current reigning karate champions defeated an attacker. Nor is it a historical account of an actual battle. In one form or another, however, this type of story has been told and retold throughout the history of karate and kung fu, both here and in Asia.

Common Myths About the Martial Arts

It's really a pity, but quite a few people out there actually believe this kind of nonsensical fantasy. Many are themselves involved with the martial arts and should most certainly know better. The amount of myths and misconceptions that infest the truths of the martial arts is as staggering as it is embarrassing. In a business where much of the focus is on an understanding of the body and simple physical principles, there should be very little room for physical misconceptions. Nonetheless, misunderstanding and a general lack of information run rampant.

Take, for example, the short anecdote in the beginning of this article. In it are three myths and one common misconception. Can you find them? You might be surprised at the number of our colleagues who can't. The first and most glaring myth is the one that occurs at the end of the story, dealing with driving the nose bone up into the brain. Of all the myths involving the martial arts, this is one of the most common. Even extremely literate members of our society believe that this works. For example, in the national bestseller *Firestarter* by Stephen King, an assassin, John Rainbird, contemplates killing someone by this method. You'd think an assassin would know better.

The major fallacy of this technique is that there is no "nose bone" as such. The assembly of the nose consists, for the most part, of cartilage, and this is much too weak to penetrate the thick frontal bone of the skull. As far as penetrating through the nasal passages—as is suggested in many accounts of this technique in application—this is impossible due to the fact that these passages are acutely minute. There is absolutely no way in which shards of cartilage, or even splinters from the tiny lip of bone known as the nasal bone, could enter into the brain case. Understand, however, that any hard strike to the skull can theoretically result in death. Concussions, shock-induced internal hemorrhages, and injuries of this nature can result from a powerful head strike. But a strike to the base of the nose is certainly not a lethal technique.

A second popular falsehood is the old saw about "breaking the hand and foot bones to make them stronger." This one, though equally as ludicrous (in a practical sense) as the previous one, is harder to attack because it is partially based in fact. That is why this one has hung around for so long.

It is true that when a bone breaks it will heal in such a way that the fractured place will be stronger. This is partially due to the amount of raw calcium the body channels into the bone as it heals. Calcium is extremely strong, and when used as an internal cement, it forms a powerful bond. That's the fact. Strengthening the "entire" bone in this way, however, would require systematic breaking of the bone at intervals of about every eighth of an inch. When referring to even the small, two-inch hand bone (the blade of the hand), this still involves about sixteen precise breaks. Despite today's almost consummate medical science, this would be a difficult and tricky procedure. The average karateka, even one who is superbly trained, would not have the skill and knowledge to perform this feat.

Unfortunately, some individuals do break their bones in a vain effort to augment their strength and raw power. Perhaps they may acquire less vulnerability in some spots, but this certainly doesn't make them invincible. It does, however, expose them to an 80 percent higher risk of arthritis and other equally crippling joint and bone diseases. What a waste of time!

The third myth recounted in the story was the "registering with the police as a deadly weapon" bit. This practice, though briefly employed in Philadelphia and other cities in the mid-seventies, is no longer used in this country. Considering the number of black belts in the United States, it would be an almost impossible task to license them all. Considering also the number of "unregistered" karate and kung-fu schools, there is no accurate way of even determining just how many skilled martial artists are in this country. To be able to "qualify" as a living weapon, one must achieve a certain level of proficiency. But no one can positively determine who is and who isn't proficient. And simply licensing all of the black belts would exclude all kung-fu practitioners, as kung fu is not structured on the belt rank system.

Yet, surprisingly, many karate instructors perpetuate this myth among their students. Why is a good question. Those who were contacted during research for this piece were oddly reluctant to discuss the matter, usually fending off questions with vague and often pointless answers. It's sad to see this kind of thing in today's martial arts, but without more widespread education, it's going to continue.

Along these same lines, another popular misconception concerns street self-defense: that martial artists are forbidden by law to use their knowledge and abilities on the street. Of the several hundred people surveyed in conjunction with the research for this article, 85 percent thought that this was so. Eighty-five percent! Another 10 percent thought that martial artists were only allowed to use their hands to defend themselves. That makes a total of 95 percent who have a totally erroneous concept of what martial artists are and are not allowed to do. This may be, as was suggested by a local karate instructor, the reason more people do not seek out karate/kung-fu schools to join. They are afraid that the knowledge and usage of their skills might get them in trouble with the law.

The opening parable also involves a very popular misconception of what an attacker is. Most accounts of the martial arts, as applied in self-defense, describe the attacker(s) as huge, hulking, and impossibly strong. They also suggest that he swings wildly and charges at his opponent. Of the attacks reported by some 173 martial artists surveyed, only 2 percent of the attackers even vaguely fit that description. That is somewhat less than an overwhelming number.

The average opponent in a self-defense situation, or even in a simple fistfight or brawl, is just that—average. Larger persons are not especially prone to becoming footpads, muggers, and cutthroats. Most fights happen because of an argument that leads to a flaring of tempers and an eventual coming to blows. Muggings and street attacks of other sorts constitute about 1 percent of all self-defense situations, according to statistics supplied by the New York, Los Angeles, and Miami police departments. An argument can, and frequently does, break out between anyone—even friends.

In most fight situations, there is a brief exchange of blows, and from there the fight either evolves rapidly into a wrestling match (complete with kicking, kneeing, biting, poking, and so on) or is resolved by words. There is very little of one guy blindly charging at the other, although there is often some wild swinging of punches. The latter is a sign of an undisciplined fighter, the former is sheer idiocy, and few people are that stupid. Not to mention the fact that when a fight starts, the combatants are usually face to face, not twenty yards apart.

In other areas, too, a wealth of myths and misconceptions hang on to the coattails of the martial arts. Some are pretty gruesome: plucking the heart out, the "stop the heart" punch, the "pierce the heart" kick, tearing out the eyeballs, the "seven-year death blow," and so on. Let's address a few of these.

The myth about being able to pull someone's heart out is very old and very possibly was started by a martial artist of ancient China (since it appears most often in Chinese legends). There are two possible explanations for its creation. The first is the simple theory that it's an out-and-out lie, fabricated to scare off the uninformed and to build a mystique of deadly majesty and awesome power around the then-obscure martial arts. This is the most plausible.

The second consideration is one that grows out of *shinobi-jutsu*, or nin-jutsu (the "art of stealing"—espionage), as it is popularly known. In that art it is not uncommon for the ninja to wear special gloves that have blades affixed to them. Some, like the scaling gloves, bear the spikes in the palm. But one style has long, slender, and very sharp steel blades running along the backs of the fingers, attached to a steel wrist cuff at one end and pointed, thimble-like tips at the other. These metal vanes are especially flexible and painted black to blend in with the glove itself. When the ninja applied a knife-hand thrust, the spiked tips would help to penetrate the skin and the blades on the

glove would, in theory, enable the hand to pierce the abdomen.

In theory this sounds plausible, but in reality one encounters the problem of the actual density of the human body. Thrusting through skin tissue is difficult enough, but to penetrate to the point where one can reach the heart—let alone close the hand around it—one must force through tough abdominal muscles, internal organs, fat glands, and other matter. Superman, with a ninja glove, might have a rough go of it—but a man or woman? And without the ninja's custom-made glove, this technique is laughably impossible.

Another of these so-called death blows is the "stop the heart" punch and its variation, the "pierce the heart" kick. These techniques are purportedly effective for killing with a single blow. It is possible for a single blow to kill, and there are deadly strikes (the *shuto*-style chop to the throat, for instance). The claim here, however, is that the blow will shock the system so drastically that the beating of the heart will be arrested or, in the case of the kick, that the heart will be ruptured. This myth appears in the legends of karate, kung fu, and even atemi waza (vital-point techniques).

Like many myths, this one most likely grew out of an incident of pure chance. Perhaps one man struck another in the chest in a fight, and that other worthy opponent died. This is a great way for overblown legends to start. Unfortunately, most legends don't take into account elements like weak hearts, high blood pressure, heart murmurs, simple physical exhaustion, and other factors that could lead to a shock-induced malfunction of the heart. Furthermore, there is a chance that any hard strike to the chest cavity (and, no, actual hitting above the heart has little to do with it) can cause a disruption or a complete stoppage of the heart in the same way that a chest thump or fibrillation will possibly reactivate the beating of a stopped heart. But no technique can ensure this; and the odds are pretty slim. If they weren't, then there would be numerous heart-failure deaths in the karate tournament circuit each year. The blows there, though somewhat padded with gloves and boots, are nevertheless extremely powerful. It is possible, however, if one is tremendously powerful, to crush the chest and hope for a bone shard to pierce the heart. But this blow must be incredibly powerful and accurate, and few, if any, martial artists could accomplish this.

Tearing the eyeballs out or, as it is more prosaically known, "the twin dragons in search of pearls," is another unlikely technique. The actual ball of the eye is held in place with a very strong tendon and some small but powerful muscles; the flesh around the eyes is tremendously resilient. It is impossible for someone to thrust the fingers in, above, or below the eyes and scoop them out like olives from a martini. It simply doesn't work. To achieve this requires some surgery and a skilled hand.

The same goes for the myth of stabbing through the eyes and into the brain with the fingers. First off, popping the eyeball is less than easy, and beyond the eyes is not a gaping hole, but a wall of bone with a very small opening. That wall of bone is extremely strong. To pierce it with a finger strike would be similar to poking the fingers through quarter-inch sheet metal. That I'd like to see! Again, the survey shows that the majority of people responding believe this is possible. In fact the majority of the martial artists surveyed believe in these "deadly" techniques, reflecting the lack of education inherent in modern martial arts.

Another thing indicated by the surveys was the total lack of education about the history, development, and nature of the martial arts in the eyes and mind of the "man on the street." Two-thirds of those surveyed thought that karate, kung fu, and judo were all the same thing. A majority also thought that kung fu was part of karate and that all martial arts are Japanese. This may reflect a gross failure by the martial arts community to educate the general public through letters, articles, and public demonstrations. Such an education in the arts is sorely needed.

As a sorry side note I might add that 37 percent of the martial artists surveyed did not know the general origins of the arts. Many still believe that kung fu was something that grew out of karate. Even James Clavell, who wrote the magnificent novel *Shogun* and other works centered in the Orient, is unaware of much of the martial arts' history. He masterfully presented the samurai and their lifestyles, but in the novel he mentions that the old man tending Blackthorne had studied "judo and karate." Well, the problem here is that the story takes place in 1600—about two hundred fifty years before judo was developed. And karate, as such, was brought to Japan from Okinawa by Funakoshi early in the twentieth century. He most likely meant that the old man was skilled in some form of open-hand *jutsu* (atemi, aiki, jiu), but Clavell lacked the information to make the correct statement.

Also among the common misconceptions maintained by the general public and many members of the martial arts community is the belief that *shodan* (a first-degree black belt) is an expert in karate. It comes as a surprise to the average person on the street to learn that in the scheme of things, a *shodan* is himself a beginner. Black belt is the starting point, indicating that one has learned with precision the basic techniques, concepts, and history of the art, and has begun to gain control of his mind and an awareness of his body. This certainly doesn't qualify him as an expert (nor should any respectful or self-respecting shodan consider himself an expert).

Rank is always misunderstood as well. The process of issuing colored-belt ranks began in this century. It is a method of helping goal-oriented students, particularly Westerners, to maintain a steady interest in the art. In the Orient, the only belts used with any regularity are white, black (which used to be only a white belt worn so long and often that it had become black with age and grime—a symbol of long years of practice), and occasionally red, or red and white, for master (*shihan* and *kyoshi* grades). Those who claim a black belt in kung fu are certainly misleading. Kung-fu systems, for the most part, use no color ranking at all, with the exception of gold, which is sometimes used to indicate the rank of sifu (teacher). And the belt in kung fu is more of a sash than the thick, durable obi of the Japanese, Okinawan, and Korean arts.

Research indicates two major sources for these myths and misconceptions concerning the martial arts. One is a simple lack of knowledge or partial knowledge. The latter can often be more harmful than no knowledge at all. To recount something to another with only partial facts invariably leads to an attempt to draw conclusions through deduction. The intricacies and depth of the martial arts negate the validity of conclusions drawn in this manner. For example: A non-karateka sees a karate student breaking boards day after day for a week. The conclusion he almost inevitably will draw is that karate is primarily concerned with breaking boards. What he may not know, however, is that perhaps the karate student is preparing for a belt test in which he is required to break a single board, and he is practicing. Or he could be trying to perfect his penetration power but his heavy bag is out being recanvased. Whatever the reason, suddenly there is an inaccurate assumption about the nature of the martial arts that will almost certainly spread from one person to another. Hence, a general preconceived notion is created through lack of knowledge.

The other cause of the "martial arts" myths is one that martial artists should be ashamed of and should correct. Many of these falsehoods were deliberately fabricated by martial artists to hype the art or to scare off the unwanted general public. And sometimes self-inflicted ego-bloating was the motive. This is the motive least worthy of the martial arts codes of *bushido*, Hwarangdo, and Tao. To purposely stage a "demonstration" that presents a false image of the martial arts (and these are common) is a crime against the concepts and principles upon which the arts have been built. Unfortunately, some people shed their ethics with their street clothes and don self-importance with their *gi*. There are too many kyoshi ranks (a karate teacher of sixth or seventh *dan*) in "ego-jutsu."

The "veil of secrecy" is the motive behind many of the myths of the arts, because so many practitioners of karate, kung fu, and other martial disciplines do not want other people ("outsiders") to know what they are doing. One reason for this, which can be appreciated to a limited degree, is the fact that the less education there is about the arts, the more of an advantage the martial artist will have when involved in a fight.

This, although logical in one respect, ignores the fact that it doesn't matter how much the attacker knows about the nature of the martial arts. A martial artist who has practiced his movements and concepts carefully and extensively, and who is at peace with himself, can match just about anyone he may encounter on the street. That is the reason we, as martial artists, practice. Who cares if the average guy knows we can't do fifty-foot leaps or yank eyeballs out with the hook of our fingers? We still possess battle skills and knowledge of the principles and techniques of unarmed combat and have spent years learning how to apply them with grace, ease, and facility. It is more surprising to have an attacker find himself getting knocked flat with a single finger strike to a nerve center than with a flamboyant jumping kick or even a fifty-foot leap.

The martial arts are complete and dynamic enough in their purest unadorned form to be able to survive without these myths and facades. They deserve a chance to earn general credibility with the average man on the street. They won't acquire credibility if they are mired in lies, half-truths, and overblown accounts of what they are and can do. Now they have a chance to come out of the closet. It only takes a little truth to open the door.

The Death of Bruce Lee

No one has made a stronger, more lasting effect and impression on the martial arts than Bruce Lee. Even Robert Trias and Ed Parker, founders of the original karate schools in America, haven't had as much impact on as broad a scale. And, as with any superstar, his untimely death has been at the heart of many theories and wild speculations over the last several years.

Refusing to accept the fact that the man simply got sick and died was, and is, too much of a strain on the minds of the hero-worshiping public. Lee—the "Dragon"—was immortal, invincible. How could he just die? There had to be some form of insidious foul play.

His death, tragic though it is, has been perverted and twisted into fanciful, often farcical (in a grim sort of way), accounts of murder and terror. Dozens of unauthorized and unsubstantiated tales—unmindful of the medical truth—have sprung up in the last few years to fill the void of doubt concerning his death. These fables, fabricated by the mourning and the money-hungry, the grieving and the greedy, have circulated and now almost completely obscure, if not obliterate, the truth. A cross section of these myths might include some of the following gems, all of which have been drawn from movie plots, so-called fan magazines, and from data recorded by this survey:

- Lee was executed by members of the Shaolin Temple for betraying secrets. As Lee was not a Shaolin, nor was his parent art Wing Chun, a Shaolin discipline—not to mention his iconoclastic Jeet Kune Do (JKD)—this holds little water. This misconception may have come out of Lee's role as a monk in *Enter the Dragon*, in which he played a character with the same name as his own.
- Lee was executed by members of the Tong for various infractions, including
  a. having an American wife
  b. not forking over a healthy chunk of his earnings to the Tong
  c. killing some Tong members in a private duel
  d. killing the head (no less) of the San Francisco Tong in a grudge match
  e. busting up a Tong drug business
- He was killed by the ghost of his master, Yip Man, for "foresaking Wing Chun" and creating JKD.
- He was killed by "whomever" for betraying the jealously guarded secret of the one-inch punch.

- He was accidentally electrocuted while using his own muscle-building machinery. (Odd how they missed that during the autopsy. After all, electrocution does leave certain telltale signs.)

Want more? Bruce Lee

- died of an overdose of narcotics (Different stories suggest heroin, cocaine, quaaludes, acid, and so on. One magazine even stated that he died of a marijuana overdose. It has been discovered that he did ingest cannabis (pot) leaf, but I would hardly think—and medical science supports me—that anyone could die from it.)
- was beaten to death by narcotics officers during a drug bust (Even if Lee had been involved with some sort of drug bust—which he wasn't—I doubt a couple of cops could have knocked his lights out!)
- shot himself because he was tired of living (Not a dynamo like Lee. Even though he was under tremendous strain during his last days, with *The Game of Death* in the works, he was anything but the suicidal type. In fact after one collapse, prior to his death, he told his wife he was going to fight to live.)
- was killed by a renegade monk—with the "delayed death touch" or some other fanciful method of assassination—for various philosophical, materialistic, or political motivations (Whoever thought that one up has definitely overdosed on the pilot film for kung fu. Renegade monk indeed!)

Well, you get the basic idea. There are all manner of gruesome, unlikely, improbable, and outright ridiculous methods and reasons for his death. Consolidated, these concoctions would be excellent for the fertilization of a very large field. But neither electrocution, delayed death touch, nor a gunshot wound stole his life. In truth, he died of cerebral edema, a drastic swelling of the brain fluids, which caused intolerable pressure on the brain and cranium. The edema, which he had been treated for previously, was possibly triggered by a pain-killing narcotic, Equagesic, which he took to ease the terrible headaches that had plagued him for some time. Unfortunately, the Equagesic (his first usage of the medicine) contained the chemicals meprobamate and aspirin. He was probably allergic to one or the other, or both. In any case, the result was the same. The edema swelled and he died. Very simple, very straightforward. Incredibly tragic, yes, but his death was not, nor should it ever have been, the stuff of pulp fiction and wild speculation.

As an actor, Lee gave us four memorable movies, one of which, *Enter the Dragon*, became the standard against which all other martial arts films are measured. As a martial artist, his skill was consummate, and his grasp of the science of body conditioning and movement very rarely rivaled. He gave us much in the way of free thought and no-nonsense combat theory, and his own personal abilities were unquestioned. He was not, however, the superman of the movies. Death by natural causes does not take the life of a superman. Bruce Lee, the man, succumbed. It is time to allow him to rest in quiet, undisturbed peace.

The Problem with Demonstrations

The late Bruce Lee boosted the martial arts into the limelight. Though he did not accomplish this single-handedly (and most of his effect was posthumous), he was the guiding force and a major factor. Words like *kung fu* became household, if misunderstood, terms. During this heyday of the arts, roughly 1971–74, and lingering on into the current media revival, one of the most common elements of the "public" martial arts has been the demonstration. Demos, though exciting to watch, can often fill the viewing public with some incredibly off-the-point misconceptions about what the arts are and what they can do.

High soaring kicks; chopping cucumbers on someone's stomach; knife throwing; breaking enor-

mous stacks of boards, bricks, and ice; and other showstoppers can give the impression that this is what the martial arts are all about. And the public eats it up! What do they know? One has to actually study the martial arts to find out what they are really capable and not capable of. Many of the demo-oriented budoists unabashedly admit to hyping the art to create an air of "mystique" and "dynamic appeal." This presupposes that the martial arts, in and of themselves, are flat and unappealing. I beg to differ.

The bottom line of the martial arts is, and has always been, self-defense, with related emphasis on self-improvement, mind and body development awareness, harmony, and self-assurance. Fancy demonstrations do not serve to illustrate this point. They do, however, excellently pose the martial artist as a fame-hungry, attention-grabbing megalomaniac, with just a dash of masochism thrown in for good measure.

Advertising consultant H. Derrick Presser says, "Having arranged dozens of karate and kung-fu exhibitions over the last decade, I've seen what sells tickets and what does not. We experimented once with a New Jersey tournament by issuing two types of posters. The first type had a picture of two karate men sparring. The kicks were not high, but were well executed; the layout was very subtle, very tastefully done. The results: No sales, other than at local karate gyms. Then we issued a second poster, pulling the first one off the market. The second poster had a center shot of a man doing a ten-board break. Around the center shot were a bunch of hazy, almost out-of-focus shots of high kicking, flying kicks, throws, and so on. Ticket sales went through the roof. I thought to myself, 'We purposely made the poster look cheap, garish, and amateurish, and the thing sends sales sky-high.' It's a sad state."

Presser adds, "We polled the people who were buying the tickets with the second poster as initiative. Most were just average people off the street. Nothing fancy, no one actually involved with the martial arts. It shows, at least, that the public is fooled by flash, but that karate men and women are taken in more by the subtle and sophisticated approach." The poll and experiment conducted by Mr. Presser's firm was intended as a marketing research project, but the results do give us an insight into the misconceptions of what is important in the martial arts—as far as the average guy on the street is concerned. Flash earns cash.

Breaking

Perhaps it wouldn't be quite as bad if the techniques were honest and unembellished. But unfortunately, it is a common foible of the human creature to dramatize and cosmetize everything. The most common, inflated demo stunt is breaking.

The true break is a test of power (to some degree) and is often used in belt rank tests. It all started, of course, as a test of not only power, but the essential ability to penetrate a target. It was introduced to tourneys because the general public could not conceive of breaking something as firm as wood with the naked hand. It was something novel! True breaks do not rely on aids to make the break appear more difficult nor riggings to make the break itself easier. A common trick to make a difficult break easy to perform is the use of spacers. Spacers are small separating items placed between the layers of boards, bricks, or tiles. This makes the stack look higher, but it actually makes the break easier because the act of breaking the top board will force the arch created by the two broken halves through the layer below, until the whole stack is broken. This arch augments the power of the hand tremendously and makes breaking a stack of boards only a little more difficult than breaking a single board. The key here is the follow-up. As long as the power continues down through the stack, the succession of arches will work its way down to the ground. A difficult break would be to break the same amount of material with no spacers. A much more demanding break, this is a true test of breaking abilities.

The second and most common type of break is the showmanship break, done to excite and amaze spectators. Showmanship breaks are usually done with aids, like spacers, and something else to make the break look much more difficult than it actually is. A common prop is fire. Setting a stack of bricks or boards on fire prior to breaking them makes the stunt look incredibly dangerous and even more difficult. Well, it may have some extra element of danger, but it is not more difficult. Fire does not make anything stronger, only weaker. A fast strike will still penetrate the targets. The element of danger enters the picture only if the practitioner is too slow in his execution, or if he allows his arm or leg to linger after the break has been effected. During the actual break, there is little danger of being burnt. A limb moving swiftly enough to break the boards will move swiftly enough to go in and out of the fire before the heat raises the surface temperature of the skin or gi to the point of surface burning or immolation. Unless, of course, the arm or gi was doused previously with kerosene, which is unlikely.

You can prove this to yourself by lighting a match or candle and moving your finger through it at a moderate speed. Even at a speed that is not fast (though not too slow), your finger will pass through the heat before it can do any damage. And the faster the finger moves through the fire, the faster the danger will be over. So a fast movement through a small amount of flame will not result in damage or danger. Air-speed velocity will cause the wind to cool down the surface temperature, to say nothing of the fact that sweat and body oils will to some degree act as flame retardants.

Of course, there are examples of mistakes. Breaking expert showman Richie Barathy once set his arm on fire, on national TV no less, while performing a break. Obviously he had done something wrong, expert though he is. Most often, in demonstrations of this sort, the danger doesn't stem from not being able to perform the break, but rather from the wide margin for human error. Of course, this is never explained to the audience. They see a stack of boards and are told that it is the largest stack of boards ever broken by a single hand strike. "Wow!" they think, "I'm seeing something that has never been done before." What they don't know is that using spacers, a martial artist could shatter a stack of boards the height of the World Trade Center, if he could jump high enough.

The same goes for those oh-so-amazing ice breaks. A huge slab of ice looks quite formidable when stretched across two sawhorses. The average person would take a look at it and heavily doubt the karateka's ability to break it. And when the *karateka* does, the audience thinks the breaker must surely be the strongest man in the world. Poppycock.

Any object as inherently brittle as ice, when cut into a shallow rectangle (which is always the case), will be extremely fragile if struck in the center. There is nothing amazing here—even steel bends in the middle. With fewer supporting molecules, there is less innate density. Besides, the extreme ends provide a form of leverage, since they are braced firmly on supports. An ice break is certainly nothing worth writing to your *sensei* about. Now, if the breaker decided to exhibit a hammer blow break on an ice cube, that would be something worth watching. Smashing a simple little ice cube is a much more difficult feat than all of famed George Dillman's towers of ice.

Even simple board breaks have been dressed up to look more difficult than they are. By tossing the boards in the air, dangling them, setting them unsupported on one edge, and other variations, the breaker tries to show a new, more exciting break. First, it only takes somewhat greater speed and a greater snapping motion to break an unsupported board than it does to break one that is held firm. Second, the grain of the boards used in most breaking demos is usually so straight (and devoid of knots) that it could be used as a ruler. Any piece of wood with grain that straight will break with little more than a stern look.

But the public is easily fooled, and they often walk away from these demos amazed and in awe of the raw power of the martial arts "masters," having learned

nothing of the true essence of unarmed combat. To quote the character Lee in *Enter the Dragon*, "Boards don't hit back." Breaking is not a demonstration of martial arts techniques. Breaking is only a demonstration of breaking. Now, this is not meant to insult Mr. Barathy or Mr. Dillman, both of whom are excellent showmen and accomplished martial artists. Worthy of insult, however, are those so-called martial artists who employ outright trickery and deceit when performing breaking demonstrations. By this I refer to those who actually fake the break, deceiving the spectators into believing that they are watching a true "example of martial arts power."

The Trick Break

A once popular, now deceased, advocate of the trick break was John Keehan, known to the world as Count Dante, the "World's Deadliest Man." In his book on dim mak (death touch) he outlines a way to fake a brick break, ostensibly with a knife-hand chop. In this technique, he has the breaker hold the brick so that one end lies off the support surface. By chopping down and slamming the brick at the same time, the brick is broken. Well, of course the thing will break! Other faked breaks often misconstrued as the real thing by the public include breaking kiln-dried bricks (made brittle by intense heat), breaking boards that were baked in an oven for a couple of hours at about 300 degrees Fahrenheit (this dries up all the sap and makes the board very easy to snap), and the infamous fake ice break.

The Fake Ice Break

The fake ice break involves the clever process of sawing the slab of ice in half, coating the inner walls with a dusting of rock salt, and then pressing the two halves together again. The salt will melt the ice in spots, but the cold will shortly refreeze enough ice to hold the slab firmly together, but not enough to require great power. Of course, the martial artist makes the break look extremely difficult so no one else will want to try it (or if they do, he'll offer them a slab that has not been specially prepared). No liar ever wants to have his word doubted.

This kind of sham has three possible results. The first is that some people will be fooled, thus leading to a gross misunderstanding of the martial arts. It even leads to a misunderstanding of breaking, which can lead to a misunderstanding of the martial arts! Second, those who are fooled may want to try a break themselves, having seen how easy it is. This happens all too frequently, and usually with disastrous results. An incident recorded during the research for this article involved a young man who almost completely shattered his hand trying to break a three-quarter-inch-thick board, which unfortunately was plywood.

The third possible result is that those who discover the fake depart with the impression that the martial arts are all phony. Each martial artist, no matter what rank, art, or standing, represents the martial arts to the world. It takes only one to give the rest a bad name, and a bad name is harder to erase than a good one is to establish. This is not good public relations for something that needs all the positive exposure it can get.

On a similar note, an interesting statistic was uncovered during my research. It seems a large number of martial artists would like nothing better than to keep the general public in the dark about the true nature of the martial arts. At least 3 1 percent of the martial arts instructors surveyed said they would like the martial arts to remain obscure and shrouded in the same sort of confusion and vagueness it has had for so many centuries. The reason, on the average, seems to be that a clouded opinion of what martial artists are capable of gives them a distinct advantage in combat situations. It's called "mystique."

Psychiatrist Curtis Conners, Ph.D., suggests, "This is due largely to insecurity. Most of those cited on the survey do not have established schools, or train alone. It could be that they have convinced a circle of friends of their own proficiency, keep them in the dark all the time, and do not want the challenge of peers (produced by more available martial arts training) to disturb their ego-carved foothold."

Perhaps it is here that many of the enduring myths and misconceptions of the martial arts actually start. We know that some have been created by unscrupulous martial artists and some unethical representatives of the "yellow journalism" aspect of the martial arts media. But is it possible that some are created or maintained not to hype the art but diametrically to close it off? To make it elite? These possibilities have borne some careful study.

There are hundreds of myths and misconceptions about the martial arts, ranging from outlandish falsehoods to reasonable misunderstandings. None of them are good for the arts. Some may never be addressed and dispelled. Others may be flushed out into the light by the advent of the new renaissance (sparked by more mature, accurate media presentations, like *Shogun*, and the more practical approach to history, technique, and tradition in the dojo). As exponents of the martial arts, practitioners have the moral duty to try to show others the truth. The martial arts were meant for the protection of those who need protection, not for the personal use of the greedy, the secretive, and the fame-seekers. It is time honesty and openness bring back the soul and honor of the arts.

This material originally appeared in the February and March 1981 issues of Kick Illustrated.

Conquering Fear and Pain Through the Martial Arts

Dr. Tom Corizzi

Like all of us, I have faced fear and pain on many different levels. Having grown up smaller than most others my age, I was the target for bullies who fed on fear. Though I was strong for my size, I had been intimidated to the point of having very little self-confidence. This lack of confidence made it difficult for me to compete in team sports. So, I turned my attention to individual activities. First, weight lifting. Being small, I needed the extra size and strength that come from weight training. Before long, I could lift more than most of the other boys my age. I also turned to long-distance bicycling. I often covered twenty-five to fifty miles on a weekend afternoon. Once, when I was in the Boy Scouts, several of us needed to swim one mile for our swimming merit badge. A few of the older boys tried to convince me I wasn't big enough and would never make it. I almost

believed them and almost quit before I even started, but one of the counselors encouraged me to try. As it ended up, I was the first one to finish.

Participants in weight training and any marathon-type activity deal with a certain amount of pain. A person has to endure some pain in order to achieve a goal. Though weight lifting and bicycling do not necessarily deal with fear as far as a confrontation is concerned, they do change the person's perception of pain and help to build self-confidence. This brings me to the point of this article. Many physical activities deal with fear and many with pain, but few deal with fear, the fear of pain, and pain in the same way the martial arts do.

By training in the martial arts, we face our fears on many levels. We endure pain to certain degrees and, in the end, raise our levels of confidence. Let's look at these three topics individually and see how they interrelate and are affected by studying the martial arts.

Fear

Fear is the emotion dealt with most in studying the martial arts. Many people start training in the martial arts out of fear of being attacked. Through studying the martial arts, people can overcome many of their fears. Everyone is afraid of something. Some fears can keep a person from functioning. This type of fear is called a phobia. A phobia is an exaggerated and persistent fear, such as acrophobia, the fear of heights, or hydrophobia, the fear of water.

Odynophobia is the fear of pain and pantophobia, my favorite, is the fear of everything. We grow up with fear. We are born with certain primordial fears that help us survive, such as the fear of fire, water, and heights. As children, we are introduced to new fears.

It is hard to tell which fears are innate and which are learned as we grow. Out of my three children, two have seemed to be afraid of water from the very beginning, while my youngest son shows no fear of it at all. Therefore, to learn to swim, my other two children have had to overcome their fear of water.

We all have fears, but each in varying degrees. Many of us fear conflict, even in the form of an argument. If the individual involved is bigger than we are, this person can intimidate us and convince us to do something we might not want to do. This intimidation stems from the fear of conflict turning into a physical confrontation.

Many children experience this from bullies who may harass them with threats of violence if they don't do as they are told. Take for example the classic case of the bully who steals lunch money. First he will threaten another child with physical punishment if that child doesn't hand over the money. Then, to protect himself, he also threatens physical abuse if the victim reports it to an adult.

Fear also works in favor of muggers, rapists, and other criminals. Noncriminal acts of intimidation work just as well at work and home. Child bullies sometimes grow up to be adult bullies, and if you were intimidated as a child, you could easily be intimidated as an adult.

While learning martial art techniques, you start to lose the fear of physical confrontations. Your confidence begins to build not only for the possibility of being attacked in the streets, but for all situations. At work or at home, with family or a friend, you become more of your own person. You learn to say no to situations that you may have been intimidated into previously, because you no longer have the subconscious or conscious fear of physical confrontation.

The study of budo (martial way) or bu-jutsu (martial art) helps individuals overcome their fears. In Kamekan jujitsu, as in other arts, we start with the fear of falling. By learning to fall without being injured, students overcome the fear of falling. They progress by learning how to escape from different body grabs (being grabbed by the wrist or lapel, bear hugs, headlocks, and so on) without struggling.

A wrist or lapel grab is relatively unthreatening. Students can practice technique with very little fear. They then move to defenses against strikes and kicks. Some students may have an initial fear of being hit or kicked, but if done at a safe pace, students can practice comfortably, become proficient at the techniques, and soon lose that fear.

Eventually, the club and knife are introduced. These are all practiced in preplanned attacks to allow the students to feel comfortable with the techniques. Once students feel confident that they can handle a preplanned scenario, they move to spontaneous attacks. Again, there may be some initial fear that washes away with exposure to the exercise. Then come preplanned multiple attacks and, finally, spontaneous multiple attacks—first empty handed and then with weapons. Eventually, the fear of physical confrontation completely disappears. Along the way the students become more confident and less afraid.

This becomes reflected in daily life. Conflicts that arise are resolved more easily. The students are less afraid to stand up for themselves. As students learn to defend themselves, they become less afraid. They don't have to get angry; they have no reason to hate. They learn to avoid conflict rather than fight and to fight only when they have to, whether it is a physical fight or verbal confrontation.

Fear of Pain

Everyone is afraid of getting hurt, whether it's a fear of insects because you are afraid of getting stung or bit, fear of going to the doctor for a shot, fear of the dentist because of the drill, or, of course, the fear of fighting. Overcoming the fear of pain occurs in the martial arts. Through acceptance and a change in your perception of pain, you learn that pain is just another feeling. It's important to pay attention to pain if it is due to an injury, but it can be ignored when necessary.

As you learn more about pain and how much you can tolerate, your fear of pain and fear of attempting things that may cause pain will diminish. Fear of pain is just one of many fears. One of the reasons we may be afraid to stand up for ourselves, fight for something, or defend ourselves is our fear of being hurt by a threatening individual.

Through training in the martial arts, we become less afraid of someone being able to hurt us. By learning to tolerate pain and injuries, we become better able to stand up for ourselves and not be so afraid of getting hurt.

Pain

What is pain? Technically, pain is the transmission of certain impulses along nerves. The brain translates these impulses as pain. It is the body's way of letting us know that there is a problem or injury. Pain impulses can be created without actual damage having occurred.

In the application of pressure points or joint-locking techniques, we apply pain without injury. Pain impulses don't differ from one person to another. But how we perceive these impulses and our own individual thresholds for pain do differ.

Pain can be ignored. You can also learn how to accept pain and to differentiate between real pain from a problem or injury and pain that is applied without injury, reacting in a proper way to prevent injury. Your tolerance for pain can be increased.

Many professional athletes have been known to ignore minor injuries in order to continue competing. Through your martial arts training you, too, can learn the difference between real pain and warning pain. Think about the type of pain you might be exposed to during your martial arts class. If you study a style such as jujitsu, you may have to take falls that hurt until you learn to fall properly. You may also have to practice joint locking, pressure points, and chokes, techniques that, though they will not be applied to the point of injury, will be applied to the point of pain.

Some people find this type of punishment too much for them and quit the martial arts or look for an art that is either not as painful or painful in other ways. Striking styles such as karate and tae kwon do experience pain in different ways. Beginning training may involve learning stances that are painful because the muscles in the legs are not used to that motion. Getting punched and kicked through a protective pad will still cause pain but, again, without the injury that would be caused if the pad were not there. Training such as this better prepares the body for pain and allows it to tolerate pain better.

Through training in the martial arts, you will overcome fear and the fear of pain, develop more self-confidence, and have a more secure life.

Dr. Tom Corizzi is a chiropractor and instructor of Kamekan jujitsu. This material originally appeared in the April 1988 issue of Inside Karate.

You Can Win
the Game of Life

Robert Dreeben

Most martial arts have a philosophy or religion to which the system's roots are connected. On a basic level of applied practicality, it is not necessary to delve into the philosophical aspects of the art to implement the functional combative skills.

Yet, as most of us know, the martial arts have a deeper meaning that goes beyond striking, locking, and throwing. When you attain the higher levels of advancement, training, and understanding, the philosophical nucleus of your system not only takes on a new significance, but now reaches a level of applied dynamics. In other words, you can start to use some of these principles to better your daily life.

Conflict, movement, obstacles, and action are forces ubiquitous to the core of our reality and being. Not a day goes by where we don't have to deal with some type of conflict—be it mental, physical, financial, job related, or of an interpersonal nature. Then, at the end of the tumultuous day, when we kick back and watch television or go to a movie to relax and unwind, the principal element of the production's story line is . . . conflict. Hmm, haven't we had enough today?

It's very entertaining in a dramatic or action movie to watch characters encounter conflicts and overcome the obstacles to reaching their success. We can readily identify with the good guys and love to see them battle evil. This is close to our heart because we have all been victims at one time or another. If the hero in the story beats the bad guy with style, all the more exciting. If the show doesn't have conflict and obstacles in the story line, unless the subject matter is educational, it will be boring and uninteresting.

The following brief excerpts from *The Art of War*, *Tao Te Ching*, and *The Book of Five Rings* deal with achieving victory not only on the battlefield, but in life as well. Much of their philosophy can readily be applied to the conflict and obstacles we encounter in daily living. Many Japanese and Wall Street executives have also studied *The Art of War* and *The Book of Five Rings* because their military strategies, although hundreds of years old, still have timeless applications in today's society. A fundamental principle in *The Book of Five Rings* is, "Pen and sword are in accord." In *The Art of War*, the highest form of combat is to "Win without fighting." And in all three books, applying the concepts of change, adaptability, and strategic thinking to the situation at hand is paramount to achieving success.

One also begins to appreciate that being focused and having a planned strategy is important in life's daily movement from mundane tasks to significant decisions and choices. Individuals who use these concepts, have a proactive mind-set, and always "think ahead" are usually the ones who are not caught by surprise, don't have their guard down, nor are left unprepared.

By implementing the principles in these great literary works, you can achieve the ultimate form: "Victory without battle."

Of course, the excerpts taken from these works are but a small sampling of the great wealth of knowledge these books offer. Realize that the meanings of the passages are certainly not limited to the title headings I have provided. In the complete chapters, many passages are in context with other similar strategies that together form the complete theory delineated. Therefore it is necessary to read, study, and meditate on the entire set of books to gain a deeper understanding of the applied philosophy.

Perfection

Great completion seems incomplete;
Yet its usefulness is never exhausted.
Great fullness seems to be empty,
Yet its usefulness is never used up.

Great straightness seems to be bent.
Great skill seems to be clumsy.
Great eloquence seems to stammer.
Great surplus seems to be lacking.
Activity overcomes cold,
Tranquillity overcomes heat.
If you're quiet and tranquil you can become the
        ruler of the world.   *–Tao Te Ching*

In the case of those who are skilled in attack, their opponents do not know where to defend. In the case of those skilled in defense, their opponents do not know where to attack.

Be extremely subtle, even to the point of formlessness. Be extremely mysterious, even to the point of soundlessness. Thereby you can be the director of the opponent's fate.

–The Art of War

Knowing Yourself

To know you don't know is best.
Not to know you don't know is a flaw.
Therefore, the Sage's not being flawed
Stems from his recognizing a flaw as a flaw.
Therefore, he is flawless.   *–Tao Te Ching*

When you know others, then you are able to attack them. When you know yourself you are able to protect yourself. Attack is the time for defense, defense is a strategy of attack. If you know this, you will not be in danger even if you fight a hundred battles.

When you only know yourself, this means guarding your energy and waiting. This is why knowing defense but not offense means half-victory and half-defeat.

When you know neither the arts of defense nor the arts of attack, you will lose in battle.

–The Art of War

Proactive Strategy

Plan for the difficult while it is easy;
Act on the large while it's minute.
The most difficult things in the world begin as
    things that are easy;
The largest things in the world arise from the
    minute.
Therefore the Sage, to the end does not strive
    to do the great,
And as a result, he is able to accomplish the
    great;
Those who too lightly agree will necessarily be
    trusted by few;
And those who regard many things as easy will
    necessarily end up with many difficulties.
Therefore, even the Sage regards things as
    difficult,
And as a result, in the end he has no difficulty.

                              —Tao Te Ching

What is at rest is easy to hold;
What has not yet given a sign is easy to plan
    for;
The brittle is easily shattered;
The minute is easily scattered;
Act on it before it comes into being;
Order it before it turns into chaos.

A tree so big that it takes both arms to
    surround starts out as the tiniest shoot;
A nine-story terrace rises up from a basket of
    dirt.
A high place one hundred, one thousand feet
    high begins from under your feet.

                              —Tao Te Ching

Know whose armaments are more effective, and whose troops are carefully chosen and well-trained. As it is said, "If soldiers do not practice day to day, on the front lines they will be fearful and hesitant. If generals do not practice day to day, on the front lines they will not know how to adapt."

                              —The Art of War

Be invincible at all times, so as to be prepared for opponents. As Wu Qi said, "When you go out the door, be as if you were seeing an enemy." And Shi Li said, "Be prepared, and you will not be defeated."

                              —The Art of War

Therefore those who win every battle are not really skillful—those who render others' armies helpless without fighting are the best of all.

                              —The Art of War

In contests of strategy it is bad to be led about by the enemy. You must always be able to lead the enemy about. Obviously the enemy will also be thinking of doing this, but he cannot forestall you if you do not allow him to come out. In strategy, you must stop the enemy as he attempts to cut, you must push down his thrust, and throw off his hold when he tries to grapple. This is the meaning of "to hold down a pillow." When you have grasped this principle, whatever the enemy tries to bring about in the fight you will see in advance and suppress it. The spirit is to check his attack at the syllable "at . . . ," check his jump at the syllable "ju . . . ," and check his cut at "cu. . . ."

    The important thing in strategy is to suppress the enemy's useful actions but allow his useless actions. However, doing this alone is defensive. First, you must act according to the Way, suppress the enemy's techniques, foiling his plans, and thence command him directly. When you can do this, you will be a master of strategy.

                        —The Book of Five Rings

Just when the opponent is setting up a plan to mobilize its forces, if your army strikes and suppresses them, that is best. Therefore one of the great warrior-emperors said, "Those who are good at getting rid of trouble are those who take care of it before it arises; those who are good at overcoming opponents are those who win before there is form."   *—The Art of War*

Power of Softness

When people are born, they're supple and soft;
When they die, they end up stretched out firm
    and rigid;
When the ten thousand things and grasses and
    trees are alive, they're supple and pliant;
When they're dead, they're withered and dried
    out.
Therefore we say that the firm and rigid are
    companions of death,
While the supple, the soft, the weak, and the
    delicate are companions of life.
If a soldier is rigid, he won't win;
If a tree is rigid, it will come to its end.
Rigidity and power occupy the inferior position;
Suppleness, softness, weakness, and delicateness
    occupy the superior position.   *—Tao Te Ching*

In the whole world, nothing is softer and
weaker than water.
And yet for attacking the hard and strong,
    nothing can beat it,
Because there is nothing you can use to replace
    it.
That water can defeat the unyielding;
That the weak can defeat the strong.
                                   —Tao Te Ching

Changes

Military formation is like water—the form of water is to avoid the high and go to the low, the form of a military force is to avoid the full and attack the empty; the flow of water is determined by the earth, the victory of a military force is determined by the opponent.
                                      —The Art of War

So a military force has no constant formation, water has no constant shape: the ability to gain victory by changing and adapting according to the opponent is called genius.   *—The Art of War*

Therefore victory in war is not repetitious, but adapts its form endlessly.   *—The Art of War*

If you once make an attack and fail, there is little chance of success if you use the same approach again. If you attempt a technique that you have previously tried unsuccessfully and fail yet again, then you must change your attacking method.

    If the enemy thinks of the mountains, attack like the sea; and if he thinks of the sea, attack like the mountains. You must research this deeply.   *—The Book of Five Rings*

Focus

The primary consideration when you take a sword in your hands is your intention to cut the enemy, whatever the means. Whenever you parry, hit, spring, strike, or touch the enemy's cutting sword, you must cut the enemy in the same movement. It is essential to attain this. If you think only of hitting, springing, striking, or touching the enemy, you will not be able actually to cut him. More than anything, you must be thinking of carrying your movement through to cutting him. You must thoroughly research this.   *—The Book of Five Rings*

Strategic Thinking

A military operation involves deception. Even though you are competent, appear to be incom-

petent. Though effective, appear to be
ineffective.   *–The Art of War*

"Rat's head and ox's neck" means that, when we
are fighting with the enemy and both he and we
have become occupied with small points in an
entangled spirit, we must always think of the Way
of strategy as being both a rat's head and an ox's
neck. Whenever we have become preoccupied
with small details, we must suddenly change into
a large spirit, interchanging large with small.

This is one of the essences of strategy. It is
necessary that the warrior think in this spirit in
everyday life. You must not depart from this
spirit in large-scale strategy nor in single
combat.   *–The Book of Five Rings*

If the opposing army is angry, shame it; if the
army is strong, get it to relax. If the opposing
general is proud, humiliate him; if the general
is greedy, bait him; if the general is suspicious,
spy on him right back—therefore the manner
of victory is determined according to the
enemy.   *–The Art of War*

If you want to feign disorder so as to lead
opponents on, first you must have complete
order, for only then can you create artificial
disorder. If you want to feign cowardice to spy
on opponents, first you must be extremely
brave, for only then can you act artificially
timid. If you want to feign weakness to induce
haughtiness in opponents, first you must be
extremely strong, for only then can you
pretend to be weak.   *–The Art of War*

When the fight comes, always endeavor to chase
the enemy around to your left side. Chase him
toward awkward places, and try to keep him
with his back to awkward places. When the
enemy gets into an inconvenient position, do
not let him look around, but conscientiously
chase him around and pin him down. In houses,
chase the enemy into the thresholds, lintels,

doors, verandas, pillars, and so on, again not
letting him see his situation.

Always chase the enemy into bad footholds,
obstacles at the side, and so on, using the
virtues of the place to establish predominant
positions from which to fight. You must
research and train diligently in this.

–The Book of Five Rings

There are only five notes in the musical scale,
but their variations are so many that they
cannot all be heard. There are only five basic
colors, but their variations are so many that
they cannot all be seen. There are only five
basic flavors, but their variations are so many
that they cannot all be tasted. There are only
two kinds of charge in battle, the unorthodox
surprise attack and the orthodox direct attack,
but variations of the unorthodox and the
orthodox are endless. The unorthodox and the
orthodox give rise to each other, like a begin-
ningless circle—who could exhaust them?

–The Art of War

The rules of the military are five: measurement,
assessment, calculation, comparison, and victory.
The ground gives rise to measurements,
measurements give rise to assessments, assessments give rise to calculations, calculations give
rise to comparisons, comparisons give rise to
victories.   *–The Art of War*

When strong, appear weak. Brave, appear
fearful. Orderly, appear chaotic. Full, appear
empty. Wise, appear foolish. Many, appear to be
few. Advancing, appear to retreat. Moving
quickly, appear to be slow. Taking, appear to
leave. In one place, appear to be in another.

–The Art of War

When you are going to do battle, make it seem
as if you are retreating. When you are going to
hasten, make it seem as if you are relaxing.

–The Art of War

Attitude

To become the enemy means to think yourself into the enemy's position. In the world people tend to consider a robber trapped in a house a fortified enemy. However, if we think of "becoming the enemy," we feel that the whole world is against us and that there is no escape. He who is shut inside is a pheasant. He who enters to arrest is a hawk. You must appreciate this.

In large-scale strategy, people are always under the impression that the enemy is strong, and so tend to become cautious. But if you have good soldiers, and if you understand the princi-ples of strategy, and if you know how to beat the enemy, there is nothing to worry about.

In single combat also, you must put yourself in the enemy's position. If you think, "Here is a master of the Way, who knows the principles of strategy," then you will surely lose. You must consider this deeply.

–The Book of Five Rings

This material originally appeared in the August 1998 issue of Inside Kung-Fu.

Signposts on
the Road to Mastery

Tony Annesi

Instead of signifying a level of training, belt colors have become a rainbow array of "badges of courage." They mean more to students than certificates, years of training, or actual skill. Theoretically, one's skill should be at least suggested by one's rank level, so the first thing the student sets his sights on is, of course, the black belt. The novice feels that the black belt suggests a mastery over the materials of martial artistry, which he must learn in order to be devastating, awesome, and godlike. Well, maybe.

Traditionally, a black belt suggested nothing more than qualified beginner, not expert, not instructor, not master. If the student worked hard enough and stuck around long enough to earn a black belt, he may then have set his sights on higher goals. This definition is still common in many traditional or conservative martial arts schools.

But for many schools, those higher goals are attained by just doing more of the same. If you know one kata for each *kyu* or up (below black belt) level, you will need to know another one or two for each dan (black belt) level. If the lower ranks require one new kick, so will the upper ranks. If you have to memorize ten self-defense sets, figure on ten more for each black belt rank. Of course, nothing is wrong with accumulating a repertoire, but a repertoire alone does not a master make.

What Makes a Master?

Everyone seems to agree that a master should have skills high above the norm, but outside of that, no one agrees on the details.

During the summer of 1994, my training camp, with Bruce Juchnik and William deThouars, was entitled The Road to Mastery. We were attempting to discover a consistent set of steps that students pass through regardless of style or art, and illustrate these with techniques and practices from various martial cultures. During an evening session, the students and instructors met in a classroom to discuss the nature of mastery. Interestingly, specific physical traits, skill level, and achievements were played down and character was strongly emphasized. Students seemed to want their masters to be ideal icons, much like how Western fans view their sports heroes or movie stars. One visiting instructor said that "they want saints, not masters." Really, they wanted both.

Some martial practices put the label of master on an adherent when he or she earns a specific dan rank, often fourth or fifth dan. In other federations, the dan rank has nothing to do with the "master" title. But other titles do. In Japanese organizations, you have to be a certain rank to earn the shihan (master instructor) appointment, but just earning the rank does not automatically convey the title. Some versions of this hierarchy require instructors to produce other independent instructors before they can be called shihan. But is this sort of thing what we mean by mastery?

Two Roads up the Mountain

I have to posit that there are really two roads up the mountain of mastery, a physical road and a psycho-spiritual one. We all have known or known of martial artists whose physical mastery is unquestionable but whose personal dealings with people are less than desirable. Still other instructors carry the title and are the nicest guys on the planet, but have dubious physical abilities.

The problem is not one that can be investigated in a short essay. In fact, I spend an entire section of my privately published book The Road to Mastery: The Benefits of Budo on this topic. No matter what mastery means to someone, I suggest that the baseline of mastery is physical ability or skills backed up by technical know-how. But does this mean that natural athletes have a shortcut up the mountain? No, because a physical genius may lack the knowledge of technique, the ease of application, and the knowledge of precisely what to apply one's skill to. Each style or each art requires its master candidate to apply his or her skills to different techniques, so how can we possibly recognize a master unless we are at least well-versed in the specific style in question?

Every person in their development from novice through black belt to mastery needs to pass through a series of levels. I call them signposts on the road that spirals up the mountain to the peak of mastery. Each style may see the details encountered at that signpost differently—in fact, each may take a slightly different road up the mountain—but eventually each will encounter signposts like the following.

The Five Signposts
Basics

The first signpost is basics. No surprise here. One needs to start at the base of the mountain. During the 1994 summer camp, we discovered, however, that basics in Japanese karate, Japanese aiki-jutsu, kempo, and Silat Kuntao were not similar sets of blocks or punches, rolls and wrist releases. Karate developed foundational stances and blocks; Aiki developed falling ability and wrist releases; Kosho-ryu kempo gave quick stance and arm-movement basics and then got into concepts; Silat Kuntao emphasized awareness early on. One art's basics may be another art's intermediate or advanced teachings. But everyone in that art had to learn the basics in order to fully appreciate the next level.

Form and Technique

The second signpost is form and technique. Basics are used to develop either prearranged forms or pre-arranged techniques to begin application of one's art. These tend to be formal, memorized ways to apply one's art. They may take the shape of karate kata, aikijutsu waza, two-person sets, or prearranged sparring units. During the camp, we considered form and technique and their variations as one signpost, but later consideration prompted me to list variations as signpost number three.

Variations

Martial artists either learn variations or create their own, but at this level, students feel free to augment what they have learned to adjust both to their own bodies and to the simulated self-defense situations they may encounter in practice. Semi-free and free sparring, for example, cannot be memorized and cannot be dealt with by repeating a predetermined kata movement. The memorized learning has been valuable, but especially to set the stage for a more creative and freer approach to training. Some arts, like judo, move into free practice almost immediately. Other styles create a stronger formal base before allowing the student to make his own adjustments.

Most students stop at this third level. Many masters are just very knowledgeable about variations and can create them on the spot if needed. They have a huge repertoire of technique, so it is easy to mistake their breadth of knowledge for depth of understanding. But ten thousand variations will not edge a master above the third level.

Understanding of Principle

The fourth signpost is one that few aspiring masters actually pass. Having reached the third signpost on a high peak, they think they are on the top. The rest of the mountain looms above them, hidden in the clouds.

The concept of principle in the martial arts is a non-detailed, yet technically descriptive, explanation of why a technique works. The name of the principle becomes shorthand for the whole concept.

To understand principles is to conceptualize a myriad of concretes. It is much easier to keep fifty concepts in mind than ten thousand techniques. Try to sort through all those techniques when it is time to react. If you learn a few things that make all techniques work, the techniques you choose become much less important. As the specific techniques become less and less important, you appreciate other styles and other arts as simply different ways of expressing the same principle. Formalism becomes less important than functionality as you approach the fifth signpost.

Formlessness over Formalism

I have nicknamed this fifth signpost "Everything is the martial way." Because it is high up in the clouds and because the other four signposts are much more substantial and recognizable, people sometimes don't accept that signpost five exists. I feel assured it exists up there because I have seen and talked to a handful of masters who, although they do not use this type of categorization, possess various increments of the skills referred to by this signpost.

We all know that, at a more experienced stage, learned techniques should be so well ingrained that they "perform themselves," rather than having us choose to perform them. The fifth level extends this idea. It suggests that unlearned movements, the movements of everyday life, can be used as martial techniques once we have a grounding in basics, forms and techniques, variations, and principles. A simple reach becomes a block, strike, or throw. A seemingly unmartial shrug or twitch becomes an unexpected tool in self-defense. The non-martial and martial merge.

If this assumption is correct, mastery is marked not only by effortless but by nearly formless application of self-defense. Any action, of course, can be said to have a form. Formlessness, in this context, is the form that is not only intuitive but was never memorized, never practiced, and never learned as a martial technique. At this level, mastery seems to revert to informal, unprepossessed stylelessness. The upper-level black belt is very much like the white belt once again, but she, having climbed past the signposts on the road to mastery, is looking down the mountain, not up.

This material originally appeared in the June 1998 edition of Inside Karate.

41

The Tao of Yin and Yang in Taijiquan

Dr. John P. Painter

"OK, you punch me real hard, right here," the little man said, thumb pointing to his tiny nose. Knowing not to question a command, I launched a xingyiquan standing fist with all my might at the grinning face of my 79-year-old teacher.

I remember feeling a sensation like the brush of an eagle's feather near my elbow and a sudden jarring impact on my chest and finding myself sailing backward, totally out of control. I landed unceremoniously in a heap against the old mattress strapped to the fence. I stayed down for the inevitable lecture that was to follow.

Mr. Li, the former head of the formidable "Chinese Wagon Masters," a clan of bodyguards from Sichuan, China, now living in exile in the United States, sauntered the ten feet across the backyard, looked down, and said, "*Beng, lu, an*. This was the energy of the yin and yang, what we call *taijiquan*."

"How is that in English, Sifu?" I asked, slowly struggling to my feet and rubbing my sternum.

"It is from my family's taijiquan, you would say in English 'fistfighting method of supreme ultimate principle' or taijiquan. Beng, lu, and an are rebound energy, flowing back energy, and the pushing energy. Those were the three methods I used to help you fly a little. They are just part of the eight principle actions of our taijiquan method."

"Sifu, I hardly felt you guide my strike away, and at the same time I felt so much power from your palm!"

Beckoning mysteriously with his index finger he pointed to the back wall of his house. Pulling himself up to his full height and assuming an air of supreme importance, his bony finger traced a line around a circle painted on a weathered piece of plywood that hung from the wall. It was white on one side and black on

233

Taijiquan instructor Yang Zhenduo, the leading exponent of Yang family taijiquan, shows clearly the yin and yang of taiji posture. Here is brush knee twist step. Note the left supporting (yang) leg while the left palm is down (yin). The right palm pushes forward (yang) and the right braces (yin). The body is in perfect balance of taiji energy with yin and yang energies across from each other, and the center of the body is wuji.

I did not ask any more questions that day. I just listened as Li Longdao began my taijiquan and taiji instruction. I was only 16 then, and today at 54 I am still working on the multiple layers of the simple, yet very complex principles of taiji as they relate to life and the practice of taijiquan.

The Problem of Yin and Yang and Tao in Taijiquan

Today, with so many books and teachers sprouting up on every corner like convenience stores, many people have a confused view of what Chinese philosophy and the words *Tao* and *yin* and *yang* really are. This is especially true in the world of Chinese martial arts as taught in North America and Europe. Some think yin and yang are Taoist esoteric principles to be discussed in hushed tones; others think they are the essence of *taijiquan*'s healing powers. Still others feel yin and yang are philosophical concepts that have nothing to do with gong fu (kung fu) or combat methods.

As Mr. Li once said to me, "Too many people make things complex. You do not need to put legs on a snake. Simplify your mind and your life, then you can see the secrets."

A classic of misinformation came from taijiquan author Bruce Tegner in his *Book of Kung Fu and Tai Chi*: "In relation to the actual teaching of kung fu, the yin/yang principle seems nowhere evident; it appears as the symbol, but without meaning which can be connected to the teaching."

Sorry Mr. Tegner, but taijiquan as a health practice and martial art is totally derived from understanding the interaction of these two qualities of energy we call yin and yang. Taijiquan is an art that could not exist were it not for these principles. One must first come to know the taiji and the yin and yang of one's own body, then how to apply it to guide and control the actions of an opponent. Indeed, taijiquan employs the principle of yin and yang in every aspect of its practice.

the other. The two halves were divided by a reverse S-shaped line.

"That is the yin and yang, so what is the big deal?" I blurted out. The little man folded his arm in front of his body, placing his right palm against the inside of his forearm. He gently touched my shoulder, and suddenly I was flying once again, only this time sideways through the air.

"That was ji, or pressing form," he said, hands on hips staring down at me like a Chinese drill sergeant. "And this is not yin and yang. It is taiji, the foundation of all energy. When you understand this and how *wuji* creates taiji and taiji generates yin and yang, then you will know something. When you truly know taiji then I have no more to teach you. Right now I fear you know less than that, so let us start."

Taiji Principles Almost Extinct

While visiting with my close friend the late Master Jou Tsung Hwa in New York a few years ago, the discussion at supper turned as always to taijiquan.

"John, you were very lucky to have a teacher that showed you the old way of taijiquan and baguazhang," Jou explained. "I searched all over China for masters who knew the real martial ways, almost all lost now. People talk of it, but really no one knows the taiji or the paqua and how they are the master keys that make the taijiquan what it is."

He shook his head, looked down, and said, "In America even worse, all lost! We must work to preserve the real methods."

I was struck by the similarity between Master Jou's words and the 1897 Charles D. Warner editorial, in which he penned the now-famous saying, "Everyone talks about the weather, but nobody does anything about it." Warner could just as easily have been speaking about the principles of yin and yang as related to the practice of taijiquan and other so-called Chinese internal martial arts. Few people really understand or care anymore. They are too busy trying to perfect the outer appearance of a form so they can win a trophy or capture the will-o'-the-wisp of eternal health.

Knowing full well that this is a controversial and difficult subject, I will make a humble attempt to explain the world of taiji as related to the art of taijiquan from my point of view. I do not have all the answers and do not claim to have mastered the art. A thirty-year journey has turned up some interesting information that might be of interest to the reader. Let's start by trying to clear up some confusion about terminology so that we can come to know more about the subjects of Tao, yin and yang, and taiji.

The Tao

No matter which of the three main philosophies of China we look at, Buddhism, Confucianism, or Taoism, each has adopted the word *Tao*. The principles called wuji, yin and yang, and taiji, are part of concepts known as the Tao. For the Westerner, understanding the principles of Taoist thought is not an easy task. In the first place, Tao, like many other Chinese concepts, is mostly a construct of the intuitive, or right-brain, approach to life. Westerners tend to be predominantly analytical, or left-brained.

The late Master Jou Tsung Hwa explains his "mastery key" to taijiquan energy through the flow of yin and yang. Understanding this principle is the foundation of real taijiquan knowledge. Without it, the practitioner is just copying an empty form.

Street-combat applications of taijiquan. If the energy and principles of taiji, not the actual techniques, are understood, each technique can have many applications—from strikes to locks to throws. The author is shown using Li family single whip with a shoulder dislocation as a knife defense.

Master Lu Hung Bin in single-whip posture. Each posture must express the taiji concept in mind, body, and application to be correct taijiquan. Master Lu, even at eighty years of age, could easily neutralize almost any attack with a touch as light as a feather.

Taijiquan, when used as a martial art, has no form. Li Longdao said, "When hand and heart know taiji, techniques change as needed." This is one of the most powerful systems ever created. Unfortunately, most people only follow taijiquan, for the aesthetic beauty and health benefits without understanding the energy and power hidden inside.

Even the way we write in the West differs from the Eastern way. Calligraphy, the type of writing used in China, is not at all like the Western alphabet. Chinese characters are usually symbols that represent ideas and poetic feelings expressed as a sort of artistic shorthand that stimulates the right brain to feel a mood or energy about something.

Taoists seek to follow the principles of Tao; however, today Taoism is divided into two main branches. One has turned the simple philosophy of Lao-tzu into a complex religion, while the other Taoism is a simple approach to understanding nature.

Tao Means How

So what is the Tao? Tao is not a thing. A simple way of putting it is to say, Tao means "how." The how and why of things in the world both seen and unseen. In the classic of Taoist literature, the *Tao Te Ching*, the author, Lao-tzu, writes:

> The Tao that can be spoken of is not the eternal Tao.

> The name that can be named is not the true name.
> The nameless (wuji) is the origin of both heaven (yang) and earth (yin);
> That which we give name (taiji) is the mother of all existence,
> Darkness within darkness, the gate to all mystery.
> All who desire can see only the manifestation of it;
> All who renounce desire can see the mysteries.
> —*Lao-tzu, Tao Te Ching #1*

The Tao itself is a profound mystery; because it is so simple it appears complex. Lao-tzu also tells us that Tao, no matter how we talk about it, remains an enigma. It is not yin and yang or taiji but the progenitor of them.

Tao can be examined, but not touched; felt, but not seen. Its principles and laws of action expressed by yin and yang can be observed and used. We cannot use the Tao itself—it is a universal absolute. Tao is the beginning and end of all things; it is both ancient and new.

Lao-tzu says, "Something mysteriously formed the primal creator. I do not know its name; for lack of a better word I call it Tao."

Trying to find a literal definition for the word *Tao* is virtually impossible. The Chinese calligraphic characters for Tao are derived from two radicals meaning "foot" or "traveling" and the "crowned head of a wise man or sage." Together, they simply mean, the "path of life," or "the path a wise person walks." This is why I say, "Tao means how."

When we know how we should move with things, we are working in the flow of Tao. The original masters and martial artists looked at Tao or nature and found the yin and yang energies in it as a way to glean valuable information. By watching, listening, and learning how the flow of energy and cycles of life and death move through all natural things, one begins to see a pattern or way to the energy of things. Once you learn to see the ebb and flow of life's ever-changing currents, the better you can deal with the highs and lows thrown your way on a daily basis. Those who do not observe Tao or use its principles swim against the current and can expect a life of constant strife.

While Tao is the alpha and the omega, it is not the same as an anthropomorphic God. Tao is more like Einstein's idea of a "unified field" of energy that is the ground upon which everything that ever was, is, and will be is played out. The action and reaction, vibration and stillness, arising from it are the engine that drives it all. Let's take a closer look at the forces of Tao and their origins in China's prehistory.

Origins of Yin and Yang

The yin and yang concept is central to Taoist ideas. Derived from the philosophical principle of the *Yi Jing*

Tai.

Ji.

The first taiji symbol.

The taiji tu.

Wuji.

(Book of Changes), it is called *taiji*—not taijiquan as in the martial art, but taiji. Almost everyone who practices the martial art calls taijiquan (tai chi chuan) taiji, but they are using incorrect terminology when they do so.

This concept of polar opposites, yin and yang, and the word *Tao*, originated in China's prehistory long before even the Taoist, Confucian, or Buddhist sects arose. When the early Chinese felt the winter air grow cold and saw the trees become bare, they believed that life was over. No more warmth would come from the sun. But with the advent of another summer, followed by another winter, they noticed a developing cycle. They saw that things change and come back again. This realization helped the early Chinese to understand and bring order into the chaos of life.

The legendary First Emperor, Fuxi (around 2730 B.C.), in his writing on the *Yi Jing*, a book that began as an agrarian calendar, first discussed this idea of cycles and change. Here, for the first time, references to the cycles of nature, which became known as the twin polar energies of yin and yang, and the origins of taiji symbols were recorded. Later, over thousands of years of thought by the three main branches of Chinese philosophy, the concepts of the *Yi Jing*, yin and yang and taiji, were expanded to become the laws of nature governing all things.

Yin energy was considered gentle and receptive. Called the mother, it was drawn by Fuxi as a single broken line to represent the open nature. It represented all things that are expanding and flexible. The moon, water, and winter are all related to yin energy.

Yang energy was considered hard and strong. Called the father energy, it was drawn as a single unbroken line. It represented all things that were active and contracting or dense and very hard. The sun, man, and summer are all related to yang energy.

In time, these emblems as used in the *Yi Jing* were combined into four forms, then eight forms. The basic eight came to be known as the paqua (eight shapes) and could be mixed to create sixty-four combinations of the yin and yang energies.

The Taiji

Taiji is not the martial art—it is the name given to the principle through which Tao works in the universe. Taiji is the agency of Tao, but it is not Tao.

Tai in Chinese is the word for great or ultimate, expressing something that is very important or a big idea.

While ji (chi) originally meant "utmost point" or main principle, the Chinese character for ji derived from a representation in characters of a "ridgepole" that supports the center of a structure.

Combined, the two characters are *taiji* and mean "the one true principle" or the supporting idea of nature. This is a reference to the concept of universal law. The how and why of things can be broken down to stages of change as these principles flow one into the other.

The First Taiji Symbol

The circle on page 237 (top right) was used as the first graphic representation of taiji. It is composed of the *Yi Jing* trigram of gua (fire) and water wrapped around the empty circle symbol of wuji (void). The circle symbols shown on page 237 are attributed to a Neoconfucian, Chou Tun-I, who in 50 B.C. used them to show the interaction of yin and yang as described in the *Yi Jing* and the *Tao Te Ching*.

Chou Tun-I formed the theory of Tao evolution adopted by both Confucians and Taoists. In its most simplistic form, he said that everything began with wuji (void) and from wuji arose the energies of yin and yang. As the yin and yang interact, they are known as taiji—the ultimate principle. This theory, although thousands of years old, is strikingly similar to the way modern quantum physics explains the functions of molecules, atoms, and subatomic particles.

Wuji is the starting place of the taiji idea. It symbolizes the point beyond which we cannot go in mind or body and is a place of the unknown. A place where everything is about to happen, but there is no time, space, or activity. It is the same as the idea of the moment before the big bang. Chou Tun-I used an empty circle to represent this concept.

The character used for *wu* means "nothingness" and *ji* is "the main principle." So wuji can mean "the no-thing principle" or it can be called the still point, void, or origin.

Lao-tzu said, "The nameless is the origin of both heaven and earth. . . ." This is wuji, the no-thing origin of taiji.

The Taiji Tu

In time the common people of China and the Taoists adopted a second version of the symbol for taiji, which also was said to have been created by Master Chou Tun-I. It is the "double fish diagram" and is often mistakenly called the yin and yang. This icon is actually called *taiji tu*, or grand ultimate terminus principle.

The black and white curved figures fitting into each other express the Tao of eternal wholeness. The unbroken line surrounding the two symbolizes wuji. The reversed S-shaped curved line in the center simply divides the two. The two dots mean that nothing is ever absolutely one thing. Each thing contains just a little of the essence of the other.

Taiji tu also represents continuous interaction or movement. The meaning of the taiji symbol's white and black hemispheres evolved over time. They became symbolic of everything physical, spiritual, and emotional in the universe—male (yang), female (yin); sun (yang), moon (yin). For everything up there is a down. For every back there is a front.

There is no separate yin without yang or yang without yin. The two are part of one whole—the taiji—and the taiji is the creative principle of Tao. You can apply this idea to almost any situation and gain a deeper understanding of nature at work.

A more modern way of illustrating this symbol with an airbrush would be to have the two slowly dissolve into each other. The black into white would blend so imperceptibly that you can't tell where yin starts and yang ends. For in truth there is no clear separation of night and day. Day fades to dusk, to night, to dawn, and back to day. It is the way of *taiji* to move gently and smoothly.

Chapter 41 and 42 use Pinyin as well as Wade-Giles for Chinese terms. The Wade-Giles/Pinyin equivalents are shown below.

WADE-GILES	PINYIN
Tao	Dao
tai chi chuan	taijiquan
Lao-tzu	Lao Zi
Tao Te Ching	*Dao De Jing*
wu chi	wuji
I-Ching	*Yi Jing*
song	*sung*
ta lu	*da lu*
kung fu	gong fu

The Tao of Yin and Yang in Taijiquan

Part 2

Dr. John P. Painter

The Balance of Yin and Yang

In a correctly placed taiji tu the yang is on the left at the top and is associated with heaven, creative energy and heat, and yin is moving down the right side to the bottom representing earth, receptive and cooling energy. As one goes around the circle, a cycle of energy exchange appears. At the top, the yang is at its prime, then clockwise, the yin, or cold, begins to show. As it continues to fall toward the bottom of the circle all is yin, so cold dominates. Continue going clockwise, however, and the yang, or heat, will reappear. There are many different interpretations for what the lines symbolize.

In the *Yi Jing* winter (yin), a dormant period can be seen with three broken lines. Summer (yang) is the hottest time, with three solid lines. An agrarian calendar was created to chart the seasons. Over the cen-

turies Taoists and Confucians charted thousands of correspondences to these changes of yin to yang and back again.

If we study the diagram of the taiji tu placed inside the circular arrangement of the *Yi Jing* lines, it becomes apparent the three-line figures represent stages of change around the circle of the taiji tu. Knowing this helps us to understand what happens after a particular event.

The Tao of Taijiquan

Taiji is central to understanding the foundation of the martial art called taijiquan. The Tao of taijiquan would be to learn to apply the principles of yin and yang to every aspect of combat or fistfighting. It is really just that simple to say but very hard to do—so much has to be unlearned.

The author playing push-hands with the late Master Lu Hung Bin of Taiwan. His actions were so soft that it was very difficult to tell where he was going until it was too late. Then he would lightly push you off balance with no force at all. Few Western or even modern Chinese students ever attain this level of subtlety.

One-step practice helps taijiquan students understand the application of energy and power of individual techniques found in the forms. Here Dr. Painter's longtime student, Bertie Acker, shows Mr. Herrera the application of brush knee twist step from the Li family taijiquan style. Note the yin and yang of their postures caught by the photo. Mr. Acker is in a forward posture (yang) as Mr. Herrera falls back (yin).

Up or down,
Front or back,
Left or right are all the same
These are all yi (mind) and not external.

—*Zhang San Feng*

The yin and yang connection to taijiquan is through both the mind and body. A taijiquan student explores and discovers his body through the yin and yang principles. His goal is to move with effortless energy and, when necessary, to produce the highest level of force with the least amount of physical effort.

He explores his mind by learning to give up rigid ideas that produce tension. It's not so much memorizing a standard set of movements as understanding mentally and physically the principles relating to how much the mind controls the body that is inherent in the taijiquan forms.

Another famous taijiquan maxim says, "The mind commands, the body moves, and chi moves along." The key is to first get in touch with yourself. Where are you tense? How can you release that tension? Discover a way to move so the whole body shares in the motion. These things are essential to the study of taijiquan.

Yin and Yang of Physical Movement

Flexing and relaxing muscles generates every motion made by the body. In taijiquan terminology *flexing* is yang while *relaxing* is yin. For example, when you want to lift your arm to scratch your nose, you must

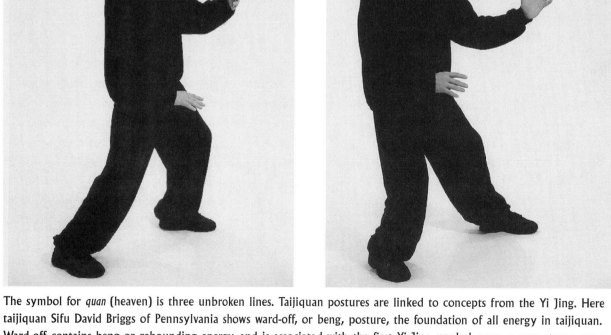

The symbol for *quan* (heaven) is three unbroken lines. Taijiquan postures are linked to concepts from the Yi Jing. Here taijiquan Sifu David Briggs of Pennsylvania shows ward-off, or beng, posture, the foundation of all energy in taijiquan. Ward-off contains beng or rebounding energy, and is associated with the first Yi Jing symbol quan, a very strong yang action that expands in all directions.

Students must be shown the proper way to express the taiji principles in their taijiquan practice. Senior instructor Andrew Garza, a nineteen-year student of Li-style taijiquan, shows a new student how to correct her front hand for single-whip posture at the Gompa Center in Arlington, Texas.

The yin aspect of taijiquan is shown by the *Yi Jing* trigram of *kun* (earth)—three broken lines. This receptive principle absorbs energy and is never harmed by it. It is associated in Li-style taijiquan with the move Lu, or rollback. Using these ideas and symbols helps create a strong understanding in the body and mind. Each of the principal taijiquan moves can be understood by studying their relationship to the *Yi Jing*.

flex, or contract, the biceps muscle to raise the arm. In contrast, the triceps muscle on the back of your arm will lengthen and relax. This is an example of yin and yang at work. Tense individuals often inhibit their own actions because one muscle is inhibiting another. The more smoothly you can release one muscle while flexing another, the less effort it takes to move. When you use less energy to move in this way, your actions become more mechanically efficient, and you can instantly generate more explosive power than if you are tensed.

Discovering Sung from Wuji

"The nameless (wuji) is the origin of both heaven (yang) and earth (yin)."

In taijiquan, learning to release tensions and be at ease or natural in movement is called being sung. Cor-

rect sung is often trained in the internal martial arts by standing meditation practice. Students learn to stand with no particular goal in mind other than simply observing themselves. As Lao-tzu said, "All who renounce desire can see the mysteries." The first posture is called wuji, or "the void." In this posture the entire body stands as if it were a tall tree with the spine straight, head lifting upward, hips sinking downward, and knees slightly bent.

The arms and shoulders relax downward. They should feel like a well-worn leather jacket hanging on a firm coat hanger. With patient practice, the student will learn how to release all unnecessary tension in his muscles and will be able to recognize an excess of stress not only in standing but also in motion.

Later, the student can take any posture found in his forms practice, hold it in a static position, and find the sung in that posture as well. Of course, the ultimate goal is to move from one position to another with complete sung energy so the body is ready to discharge power or strength in a fraction of a second.

Yin and Yang Principles of Combat

Just as the yin and yang apply to our own minds and bodies, so too do they apply to the methods of self-defense. Taijiquan martial practice as seen in the days before the Communist Revolution is all but extinct today. Now, thanks to the contemporary wushu,

health, sport, and entertainment forms abound, most of which are but pale shadows under the moon of the original methods of zhandou taijiquan (combat fist-fighting of the great ultimate principle).

In ancient times, taijiquan students learned forms to understand the principles of the taijiquan method. Forms such as choreographed dances were used in place of written books. They were sort of mnemonic systems designed to help the student remember principles in a stylized pantomime of combat with one or more opponents. The sequence progressed from simple to more difficult maneuvers and the student was required to learn each movement and its principles, to

The Wuji standing meditation posture. Using this method the taijiquan student finds his own inner stillness and peace. Wuji means ultimate quiet of nonaction. This is the moment that is pregnant with all possibilities. In physics it is the moment before the big bang—the ultimate still point or void.

Competition push-hands does not foster true understanding of taiji yin and yang principles. How can one "invest in loss" if one wants to win a trophy, adulation, and praise as the champion? The training method has sadly become a game of strength, cunning, and ego. The author considers the competition event as truly the antithesis of taijiquan principles.

find the yin and yang actions in the move, and to understand the use fully before going to the next move.

The Li family created its own style of *taijiquan* from Yang and Chen methods. It was designed first and foremost as a martial art method that very carefully observed the taiji principles in every posture and action. The style was called the willow principle of taijiquan, and the Li family's method of using postures was known as "Crossing the Great River." This was based on the *T'ai Chi Classics* that reminded the student to always have the body be like a taiji in all parts and to always have some power in reserve.

The "Crossing the Great River" concept requires the upper limb generating power to always be across from the lower limb that is the supporting leg. This creates a taiji of balanced yin and yang in the entire body, resulting in great stability and energy for all movements. Not all modern taijiquan forms use this principle, and as a result, they are at times not in line with the classic concepts of taiji theory.

The Key to Taijiquan Combat

In the Li family method of taijiquan, when the students understood the four principle actions of "ward off, roll back, press, and push," they would begin with simple push-hands training. Push-hands is a training exercise in which two people play a type of physical chess using the basic moves found in all taijiquan forms while touching arms in close proximity to each other.

The first objective is to learn how these basic moves neutralize incoming energy and then guide the energy back into your partner. The first stage, called *ding bu tui shou* (fixed-step joint hands), uses mostly prearranged form choreographed like a dance. Yin and yang are very evident here.

During the sequence ding bu tui shou, the student feels his partner's energy and tries to find yin and yang in his own body. The student learns that he must relax and receive (yin) a push from his partner as he simultaneously pushes (yang) his own technique into his partner's center of balance. In a perfect world the partner will sense this yang action and guide it harmlessly away from his center with a yin response. When done correctly, the two actions of deflect and push happen as one continuous flow without gaps or undue force presenting itself. Traditional push-hands practices involve no competition—only a learning experience for both players.

After the student understands the choreographed moves, push-hands can be done while standing facing each other with feet fixed in position, using a freestyle choice of tactics from the *taijiquan* form. This practice helps students understand the true nature of using very little energy to divert a great amount of force—that is, if they practice without ego or the need to win.

The Yin and Yang of Push-Hands

Traditional push-hands training slowly evolves from fixed-step practice, ding bu tui shou, to one where the practitioners walk with prescribed steps in the *huo bu tui shou*. Now they are not only feeling the yin and yang of the torso, arms, and shifting as in the fixed-stance version, but they are also learning to blend footwork. This long and tedious process has great rewards for those who put in the effort.

Finally comes the da lu method, incorporating the five stepping patterns and the eight entrances. Da lu is fixed at first, then is practiced with moving steps, and finally evolves into freestyle moving push-hands with a partner. Although the student does his best to unbalance or "get in" on his partner, his goal in all da lu is a smooth interchange of yin and yang energy, not to win or lose. Push-hands becomes a two-person learning experience and should be the first step toward free sparring and actual combat skills in taijiquan.

Competition Push-Hands

Unfortunately, tournament promoters today have made push-hands a sport. This sport method has moved far away from its original intent as a way of understanding the yin and yang of one's own and another's actions. Push-hands was designed as a training tool to teach the concept of yin and yang flow between two partners in preparation for combat. It should be an evolutionary step toward fighting, not a competition event.

Push-hands tournament champions seldom employ true taiji skills to defeat an opponent. These contests, which can only be described as a controlled shoving match, do nothing to foster an understanding of the true genius behind the real purpose of this training method.

In fact, these contests may be jeopardizing the survival of taijiquan as a unique martial art. The student who is out to win fame and honor cannot easily "invest in loss," as the *T'ai Chi Classics* say. With the "prize of gold" in mind, it is hard to be one "who renounces desire to see the mysteries."

Taijiquan Zhandouli

To further progress in taijiquan for actual self-defense, you must at some time practice a combat-effective "fistfighting method of supreme ultimate principle" (zhandouli taijiquan). This means you have to spar with or contest against an opponent.

This type of training often begins by one- and two-step prearranged drills in which a partner attempts to strike or grab you and you respond with a taijiquan tactic. Here the yin and yang begin to be classified as an exchange similar to that found in push-hands. The offending punch is yang. When you ward it off, you use less force to guide it; this is yin. This yin turns the punch aside, converting it to yin and opening the door for your energy to become yang with an offensive move such as a shoulder stroke or brush knee twist step. Now you are preparing to blend with a fast-moving partner. The mind must be clear and almost in wuji to allow the body to react spontaneously.

One-step practice leads to full sparring with a partner who is attempting to grab, throw, punch, or kick you. If your taijiquan principles have been completely absorbed and you have become conditioned by long training in freestyle da lu, application drills, and other peripheral training, you may just have a chance to blend with an attack and turn his yang to yin while you subtly adjust his Tao for him.

The material in Chapters 41 and 42 originally appeared in the January and February 1999 issues of Inside Kung-Fu.

43

The Secret to Middle-Aged Martial Arts

Lloyd Fridenburg

The reasons why men and women turn to the martial arts as a form of physical training are a topic of much discussion. One thing is certain: as people come to realize that age is merely a state of mind, martial arts training is no longer viewed as an activity just for the young.

It's not always easy to begin martial arts training after you have passed your so-called prime. Even those who have maintained a reasonable level of physical fitness may find martial arts training more challenging than they anticipated. Martial arts offer a symmetrical and all-encompassing form of conditioning that few have experienced. Add to this the psychological aspects that are not present in most other forms of physical fitness programs and it is easy to see why many older students find themselves overwhelmed when they first begin training.

Flexibility

Flexibility, or the lack of it, can present the greatest obstacle for the older student. It's unlikely that a strenuous stretching routine was a regular part of any previous activity. When was the last time you had to lift your leg above your chest during a squash game or stretch out your groin muscles before hopping on a treadmill?

There is no easy way to achieve your maximum range of motion; patience and perseverance are the only ways. Some younger students may be able to do full-center splits within a few months of starting but adult students, for a variety of reasons, may never do it. Don't get discouraged; just face reality and work within your own limitations. Increasing your flexibility is essential. It allows you to develop precise and

powerful techniques while at the same time greatly reducing the chance of serious injury along the way.

Partner stretching is an effective form of passive stretching. It allows you to assume the correct kicking positions for front, side, and back kicks, using a wall for support, while your partner slowly raises your leg and increases the stretch until you attain your personal maximum. Hold each stretch for a minimum of 30 seconds, and as the muscles begin to relax, ask your partner to take the stretch just a bit higher. With regular commitment to this type of stretching, you'll be amazed at how fast the tightness leaves your kicks.

Muscle tone is the first aspect of physical fitness to degrade from lack of use, followed by a loss of suppleness in the ligaments. You can overcome the first, but your ligaments may never regain their youthful elasticity. The old maxim "use it or lose it" certainly applies here.

According to Dr. Ted Gall, a Canadian chiropractor who also specializes in the treatment of sports-related injuries, "The older you are, the greater the chance that you have experienced some kind of physical trauma that has affected the joints, muscles, or ligaments." He is referring to strained lower back muscles, displacement of vertebrae, or sprains. Left untreated, they will have an effect on your performance as a martial artist.

According to Dr. Gall, the lower back should be the area of greatest concern to the beginner. "Picture the pelvic region as a ball," says Dr. Gall. "Attached to this ball are four large elastic bands. These elastic bands represent your lower back muscles, abdominal muscles, hamstring, and quadriceps. When these muscles are of equal strength and flexibility, the ball, or pelvis, functions smoothly." It doesn't take a mechanical engineer to recognize what will happen if even one of the elastics is tighter, weaker, or less flexible than the others.

Dr. Gall suggests that exercises used to strengthen or stretch the postural muscles (hamstring, quads, abs, and lower back muscles) are essential to help "balance the wheel."

Anaerobic Conditioning

Aerobic exercise, an important element of all physical training, is used to increase oxygen flow to stimulate heart and lung capacity and to increase endurance over a long period of time. Anaerobic conditioning helps the body perform at near-maximum levels of activity for short periods of time. Most encounters, either in a martial arts school or a street setting where your skills are called upon, last at the most for only a couple of minutes and usually for a few seconds. During that period you must be prepared to perform at your maximum, sometimes from a cold start. Adrenaline will take over, but you must still channel your increased energy properly while maintaining your composure under extreme circumstances.

Most martial arts styles incorporate a great deal of anaerobic training. If you do a lot of aerobic-style training, such as running or cycling, add some wind sprints to your routine. This will help you adapt more easily to martial arts training. Often, those who have played court games on a regular basis will find it easier to adjust, in the beginning, than runners and cyclists. Coping with this type of training will only come with practice and regular training.

Mental Attitude

Sifu Bob Schneider, owner and head instructor of the Waterloo Kung Fu Academy and disciple of Grand Master Pan Qing Fu, says, "The psychological aspect of martial arts training can be even more daunting to middle-aged practitioners than the physical aspects. It is very difficult for some individuals to accept the fact that they may not be progressing as fast as younger students. After all, our school combines ages from 15 to 50 in the same classes.

"Although more individualistic," adds Schneider, "many older students are intimidated by the speed and strength of those in their prime. In spite of this I expect just as much of my older students as I do from those in their prime. Sometimes even more. Older students may have more physical constraints than younger students, but it is the dedication and commitment of the individual that will allow them to succeed, not lesser demands from the instructor."

Believe me, I've looked over my shoulder from time to time at the young kid throwing head-height hook kicks with such ease that I felt I must be doing something wrong. My advice to students struggling with this situation is to progress at your own speed and don't compare your level of ability to anyone else's. You may never be able to kick like Bill Wallace, but with perseverance you will attain heights that you never dreamed of when you began your training.

Discipline is another aspect of training that is well-entrenched in almost all forms of martial arts. Self-discipline plays a role in most forms of physical activity, but martial arts training adds the element of imposed discipline. The level of discipline is as varied as the number of training facilities; nonetheless, it's there in some form. In our youth we rebelled against authority and insisted that respect is not unconditional—it must be earned. This is still true, but in a martial arts school respect for senior students and instructors is expected. It's part of the very fabric that holds the martial arts together. Many older beginners have trouble adjusting. Many leave without really giving martial arts a chance because they cannot adapt psychologically.

Common Injuries

The most common injuries, aside from the occasional cut or bruise incurred during sparring, are sprains and muscle pulls. Both are often caused by impatience or overexuberance on the part of the older student.

You're feeling on top of the world and know that today you can achieve those high kicks that have always eluded you. Then it happens. A sharp pain followed by a sinking feeling in the pit of your stomach. You have just overextended a hamstring or pulled a groin

muscle. What do you do now? If you're like most of us, you finish class, favoring the injured area, and limp home, sometimes wondering if it's all worth it. If you're not absolutely sure of the nature of your injury, seek professional medical attention as soon as you can.

Now is the time for RICE: rest, ice, compression, and elevation. Following these four simple steps will dramatically reduce the amount of training time missed. Applying ice immediately after incurring a pull or sprain can reduce the overall healing time by days or even weeks. If the injury is to one of the extremities, elevate the limb above the level of the heart as soon as possible. Elevation will reduce blood flow to the area and will limit the amount of swelling.

Compression, in the form of a brace or tensor bandage, will give added support to the injured area and should be used during workouts, even after you think the injury has healed. Make sure it's tight enough to give good support, but not so tight as to cut off the circulation. When you begin to leave it off for your workout, test the injury cautiously, and gradually increase use of the area. Be patient: injuries take longer to heal the second time.

Things to Avoid

The back, in particular the lower back, should be of prime concern to the older beginner. "Be particularly careful of any torquing movements such as spin kicks, turn kicks, or anything that involves sudden twisting of the upper torso," says Dr. Gall. Don't avoid them; after all, this is an essential part of your martial arts training and you didn't start training just to participate in easy and less risky moves. But proper technique is essential and must be learned before trying to use these types of kicks with full power.

"As age increases, spinal degradation increases," adds Dr. Gall. "The older a person is, the greater the risk of discal protrusion. Around age 30, blood ceases to flow directly into the disc and instead enters by infusion from the surrounding tissue. The disc becomes less pliable and is more susceptible to injury. Discal protrusion can be extremely painful and debilitating."

Strong abdominal muscles are essential to your martial arts training, but regimens that use straight-leg raises or straight-leg scissors put a great deal of strain on the lower back. An exercise that is less stressful to the lower back and provides a better overall abdominal workout is butterfly sit-ups. These work the upper, lower, and lateral abdominal muscles and put considerably less strain on the lower back. One leg is pulled into the chest as the other leg extends. The opposite elbow reaches over to touch the knee of the contracted leg, with the hands locked behind the head.

Refrain from any exercises that involve weight-loaded gravity, such as lifting weights while bent at the waist. Also avoid any type of ballistic ("bouncing")

stretching, such as the kind commonly practiced in gym classes a generation ago. This type of stretching can lead to pulled or torn muscles and ligaments.

Being aware of these issues and exercising a degree of caution and common sense will help you enjoy a safe and long involvement in the martial arts.

One final word of advice: "Don't set your goals too high in the beginning." A black sash in our particular discipline is five to seven years away even for students in their prime. Don't make the mistake of thinking you must progress at a certain rate to be considered successful. Liken the black sash or belt to the medal hanging around the neck of an Olympic champion. He or she is definitely the cream of the crop, but this is not to say that everyone else is a failure. Each level presents new and different challenges to overcome. Approach your training one step at a time. Remember: persevere and be patient.

This material originally appeared in the July 1999 issue of Inside Kung-Fu.

44

Train the External, Ask for Trouble!

Adam Wallace

The reasons for beginning a journey into the martial arts world are as diverse as the multitude of styles that coexist within it. Some people are motivated to learn purely for the sake of self-defense. Some long to build their self-confidence, while others aspire to compete in tournaments. Some desire to attain "Olympic-standard" fitness, and many stressed executives seek to release tension or aggression in a healthy way. Some begin as a spiritual quest or to achieve balance of body and mind. Some are drawn to the challenge of an art's acrobatics or attracted by the beautiful movements, while others care less about the aesthetics and merely want to develop practical techniques they can use on the street.

Sadly, some people hold a dim view of martial artists. These people tend to consider them "Neanderthal" types who can only communicate through brutal aggression, train their bare hands to be lethal weapons, and "talk with their fists." This is where any similarity between a fighter and a martial artist ends!

The Chinese word for martial art is *wushu*. It is made up of two characters: *wu*, which translated means "stop" and "fight"; and *shu*, which means "art." So the literal translation is "stop fighting technique." Therefore, a martial artist, in essence, is one who can resist the urge to fight. He has nothing to prove and is confident in his abilities. A fighter is someone who, when provoked (which in some cases may not take much) or attacked, will stand and fight until he has beaten down his opponent. A high-level martial artist, on the other hand, is one who will attempt the diplomatic approach first before fighting, which is the last resort. When all options are exhausted and he is engaged in combat, he controls the opponent either by redirection, using the opponent's force against him, or by *chin na* (joint seizing and locks), possibly without

252

Shaolin forms, such as "green dragon sword," are often thought of as external even though there is an emphasis on internal development.

Trees are used to train the external body because of the immense resources of chi, which is absorbed by the practitioner.

even having to strike him. Instead, he relies on his "stop fighting technique." Thus, a martial artist may be a skillful and indomitable fighter, but a fighter is just a fighter.

The Whole Being

The main difference between a fighter and a martial artist is that the former only concerns himself with developing his fighting skill, speed, timing, and punching power, and little else, while the latter simultaneously develops himself and refines his moral character. In other words, the fighter seeks to conquer and control others, while a martial artist seeks to conquer only himself, exercising discipline and control in every aspect of his life. The fighting skill in the martial arts is not the most important aspect. Fighting for its own

sake creates aggressiveness, which unbalances the mind and damages the individual's nature and eventually his health.

My *laoshi* (teacher), Michael Tse (an exponent of Wing Chun, Chen taiji, Shaolin, and internal training), always stresses that good martial arts teach the right attitude, respect for others, and morality. He maintains that when learning the martial arts it is important to achieve the health benefits first. How can one fight when in poor health? One's training should be practical but not at a cost to health. It is not advisable to repeatedly train taking blows. Some arts call this "conditioning." Most students who include this in their training are young and may not notice any damage. The body might hurt for a day or so, but as one grows older, it takes longer to heal and the pain lasts. Everything harmful done to the body now, one pays for later in life, with interest. It may take several years for the problem to emerge. Those who enter full-contact bouts do not contemplate the damage done internally. The body is covered with acupuncture points. Many of these points are sensitive, while some are acutely vulnerable and can cause the whole system to shut down temporarily, or even permanently, through the disruption of chi (vital energy) to the corresponding internal organ.

Many martial artists do not consider the internal body and miss the understanding of chi when they train. This is why, later in life, they may suffer conditions such as Parkinson's disease, rheumatoid arthritis, poor blood circulation, severe backaches, numbness of the limbs, or hypertension. Breaking techniques with tiles or blocks of ice, which rely on conditioning the hands only, will also lead to these complications.

Dying Young

Many famous and well-loved martial artists have died very young from heart attacks or strokes. External training alone exhausts the body and leads to weakness of the internal organs, which cannot support the body and the demands placed upon it from the training. Martial artists expend great amounts of energy, which need to be replaced. The external body becomes too strong and the internal body too weak. All kinds of problems can be prevented by balancing one's training with some soft and gentle movements and meditation. Old nagging injuries will also disappear with persistent internal training as balance is restored to the body.

Almost every martial artist has been injured at one time or another, so in addition to learning fighting skills, he should seek the knowledge of how to heal himself. Healing and fighting are two sides of the same coin. Internal training (chi kung) was developed over four thousand years ago to help with injuries. Chi kung, which includes meditation and movement, enables the "negative" chi to be released through the acupuncture points and the channel chi to flow

smoothly and naturally. In traditional Chinese medicine it is said, "Pain means the chi is not smooth. Smooth means there will be no pain."

Many martial artists train for stamina but overlook the importance of breathing. Even some practitioners of internal styles have difficulty mastering the principles of relaxing, breathing from the dan tian area (below the navel), and sinking the chi. Martial arts without internal training cause much biophysical energy to be wasted from accelerated breathing and heartbeat. This energy could otherwise be saved, enhancing the individual's natural ability and health.

The martial arts are commonly discussed from the perspective of "internal" or "external." Dynamic styles such as Hung Gar, Choy Li Fut, and Shaolin, among others, are considered external, while "softer" methods such as tai chi chuan, Hsing I Chuan, baguazhang, and Wu Dang arts are regarded as internal. No martial art can truly be labeled either. Only the different aspects of their training can be classified in this way. The training that develops the bones, muscles, and skin may be called external, while that which trains the *jing*, chi, and shen (or essence, vital energy, and spirit) is internal. Traditionally all Chinese martial arts contained both aspects, known as wai gong and nei gong, respectively. Unfortunately, in the case of the Chinese martial arts, internal training was largely omitted when the skills traveled to the West. There were a number of reasons for this, chiefly the traditional secrecy, modern lifestyle, and different cultural backgrounds of the East and West.

Incomplete Training

Many Western martial artists possess no knowledge of internal training themselves, so their training is incomplete. Other martial artists may only know some basic internal training and call themselves internal stylists, and they may even have contempt for the external martial arts because they too only know half the picture. Michael Tse claims, "They are like frogs

Martial arts with internal training can produce a body of "steel wrapped in silk."

"Horse stance" training works the legs to be strong and yang, and the upper body to be relaxed and yin.

looking up at the sky from the bottom of a well, who think that the sky is only as big as the mouth of the well."

There is an old saying in China, "All the martial arts come from the Shaolin Temple." Most other styles have in some way been influenced by it. The Shaolin system, which dates back to A.D. 495, is very extensive and encompasses many different methods of training the body, both internally and externally, often concurrently. "Horse stance" is a perfect example of this. A practitioner would be expected to stand for several hours; beginners find this difficult after only a few minutes. Horse stance, however, is not merely for developing leg strength. It trains the upper body to be very relaxed, or yin. The legs become strong, forming the root, and are yang. So with a strong root, or foundation, one can then develop a powerful body and concentrate on different parts, such as the head, chest, back, and fingers.

Many other Chinese martial arts have their foundation in standing. Chen tai chi chuan, for example, has *zhan zhuang* (standing pole), which along with developing internal strength and "rooting" also develops a calm mind so the chi will sink to the dan tian. If the chi is unable to sink, it remains either in the head,

resulting in insomnia and aggressiveness, or becomes lodged in the chest, causing feelings of oppression, anxiety, and shortage of breath.

Shaolin (Buddhist) training, for example, begins by simultaneously making the external body fit and strong and developing health. After a while, one learns to let go of the strength and any stiffness—the hard becomes soft. When softness is attained, the body feels light and one is able to jump very high, or even sit on a lotus leaf in a pond.

Internal Explosion

Other systems, such as the Wu Dang martial arts or Chen tai chi chuan, whose roots are in Taoism, begin soft and progress to become strong. They develop internal power daily until external power is developed, the channels become smooth, and the dan tian is strong. The object is to achieve "50 percent yang and 50 percent yin" where "Man and Universe become One." In the case of tai chi chuan masters, it is often said that their bodies are like "steel wrapped in silk." Taoist or Buddhist methods are merely different paths to the same destination.

The Shaolin fighting forms, many of which originate from animals, such as the dragon, crane, snake, tiger, and monkey, when performed seem very strong and powerful. Some, mistakenly, believe that this training is merely external. A good master should be able to execute these forms without any shortage of breath, because his movements are connected with internal training. Thus, when he reaches advanced years he should still be able to perform the techniques effortlessly yet with power. This is only possible because the internal body is strong. How can one be considered fit if he is not healthy first? Many Western martial artists and athletes are fit, but not necessarily healthy.

These forms must be performed correctly, however, otherwise the practitioner may seriously harm himself internally. In Chen tai chi chuan, for example, according to Ren Guang-Yi, without sufficient foundation from the first routine (which is more internal training), one may feel dizzy or vomit and, in a worst-case scenario, may even cough up blood after practicing the second empty-hand form (*Pao Chui*, or cannon fist), which is mostly external. This is because the internal body has not been developed first (the form is too strong for the body), and the chi becomes stuck in the chest and is unable to sink down. Tai chi chuan was created using highly effective martial arts techniques and combining them with internal training, the ancient exercises daoyin (concentrated exertion of inner force) and tuna (deep breathing exercises), together with knowledge of the Jingluo (meridians), and the philosophy of yin and yang.

There is no one superior martial art. But a complete system should cover internal training; otherwise it will be too yang, too strong. Following the laws of nature, Lao-tzu, the earliest Taoist philosopher, wrote in the *Tao Te Ching*,

> The softest in the world overcomes the strongest . . .
>
> Water and wind are the softest things in the world but when their force is concentrated it is enough to topple mountains and overturn the sea.
>
> Wind can erode copper and dripping water can bore through stone in the same way . . .
>
> The brittle shatters easily.
>
> *Lao-tzu,* Tao Te Ching

Tai chi chuan was created from many different skills, including some Shaolin fist.

Shaolin *damo* staff.

Tai chi chuan was created by combining martial arts techniques with internal training, knowledge of acupuncture channels, and the philosophy of yin and yang.

A martial artist develops not only fighting technique, but also health and morality. Chen Xiaowang (pictured here) is regarded as one of the world's greatest martial artists.

Master Ren Guang-Yi demonstrates *zhan zhuang* (standing pole) foundation training for Chen tai chi chuan, the emphasis of which is training the internal body, and developing a calm mind, thus sinking the chi.

Adam Wallace is an authorized instructor of wild goose chi kung and Chen-style tai chi chuan. He teaches in New York. This material appeared in the January 1998 issue of Inside Kung-Fu.

The Art of
Breathing Correctly

John P. Painter, Ph.D., with Dave Cater

Breathing. From the moment we are pulled from the womb to the moment we die, from the deepest of relaxing sleeps to the highest state of awareness, breathing is so natural, so effortless, so automatic, we often take it for granted. While it happens an average of over 20,000 times a day in our lives, while the only breath we notice is the one we have to catch, we seldom consider what it actually means to breathe. Or more accurately, what it means to breathe correctly.

The fact is, while we all breathe, most of us breathe incorrectly. This is not to say you're in danger of succumbing tomorrow if you don't learn how to breathe, but the way you inhale and exhale, the mode in which oxygen is deposited and eliminated from the lungs, can make a big difference in how you feel. Plain and simple, incorrect breathing techniques won't make you feel worse. You just can't hope to feel better.

There are two types of breathing most often used in internal arts practice: Buddhist, or postnatal, breath and Taoist, or prenatal, breath. Introduced and cultivated in taijiquan (tai chi chuan) practice, these methods work the diaphragm muscles downward and then upward during the breath cycle. This action also serves to increase abdominal and thoracic pressure during the breathing process.

The downward pressure during inhalation briskly forces blood occupying abdominal veins toward the heart, thereby strengthening the circulatory machinery. Muscular relaxation, combined with the actions of the foot pump associated with taijiquan practice, allows oxygen-carrying blood to quickly and easily reach its target.

Consider this: People are working on an assembly line. The factory has but one vent, located at a far end of the plant. Those workers standing nearest the air vent are refreshed. But the farther you travel down the line, the more stale and stagnant the air becomes. Pretty soon, workers feel the negative effect of fighting for the same musty air. Workers grow tired and listless, lacking the energy to complete their tasks. The assembly line, once a vibrant hub of activity, first slows down and finally grinds to a halt.

Consider your body's circulatory system an in-house assembly line. The better we breathe, the more life-giving oxygen gets to the workers. The better the workers feel, the harder they work. The worse they feel and the more starved for air, the less they're inclined to produce. Taijiquan breathing practice shows you how to deliver oxygen more quickly than you ever thought possible. It's almost as if the factory roof was removed and trees were planted at every station.

Benefits from Postnatal Breathing

While there are various schools of thought on breathing, the postnatal breathing method is easiest and creates the most profound sense of relaxation in the beginner. For best results, it is necessary to learn the correct breathing technique independent of the forms practice. Students learning breathing techniques should commit to a regimen of daily practice independent of forms practice. This can be done during standing chi kung or seated meditation work or while just sitting quietly in a chair. The formal breathing practice should be done with full attention on the process of breathing properly and repeated every day for no less than thirty days; a shorter period cannot guarantee the body will assume this breathing method on its own.

Postnatal Diaphragmatic Breathing

Stand in front of the mirror and stare at your chest. Now watch yourself breathe. Are your shoulders pulled back? Does your chest expand with every breath? Does your abdomen lie flat? If the answer to any of these queries is "yes," then you've discovered the "air" of your breathing ways. This is commonly known as thoracic, or chest, breathing. Thoracic breathing uses only the upper half of the lungs, which translates to about one-third of total capacity. If we took the same approach with our car, we'd be stopping for gas three times as often. Come to think of it, many of us get gassed three times as quickly because we don't know how to breathe.

Over time, the stale air in the lungs takes up space and decreases the amount of oxygen that could be taken in and used by the body. Cheating ourselves by not breathing deeply and correctly can cause a subtle, but cumbersome condition called oxygen deprivation. We may not notice it, but our lives are suffering with every wrong breath.

Results of Improper Breathing

Oxygen is the root upon which human life takes shape. You can go months without food, days without water, but try going more than a few minutes without air and you're asking for disaster. In fact, most of us can only go a few seconds without taking a breath. The results of improper breathing are quite simple and barely discernible. If the amount of oxygen can't keep up with the work of your cells, you'll first feel tired and run-down, then irritable and nervous. A loss of memory or a lack of concentration also are by-products of poor breathing habits.

But that's just the beginning. Oxygen depletion leads to tension and stress, which forces the body to work harder to fulfill its needs. You are now working too hard to accomplish too little. A breakdown of the body's systems and organs, such as the heart, brain, and individual muscles, is not only possible, but likely. You find yourself sleeping poorly and getting sick more often. Even digesting food is a chore. All because you're not getting enough air and the air you get falls far short of its goal.

Postnatal Breathing

Breathing properly involves naturally and completely inflating the lungs. The chest should be loose and relaxed, not pulled back as though you were standing at attention. The diaphragm should contract, pushing down on the organs. Coordinated with the abdominal (postnatal) breathing, the pressure of the diaphragm on the abdominal cavity will regulate the blood circulation to various organs and produce a rhythmic internal massage with every breath.

During this type of breathing, the abdomen and lower back near the kidneys should gently expand but the chest should move very little. The exception is at the sides near the lower part of the ribs where the diaphragm is located. Done properly, the lungs will completely fill with air. Reverse the process during exhalation by allowing the diaphragm to push up and empty the lungs. Now don't think because you've been breathing improperly all your life that the damage is irreversible. Nothing could be farther from the truth. In fact, once the new breathing procedure becomes natural, you'll feel the difference overnight. The cells get the oxygen they need to function correctly, which in turn helps the body function the way it was supposed to from the outset of life.

You'll notice less tension, better reaction time and concentration, improved memory, and clearer thinking. There is an increase in personal awareness, tactile sensitivity is enhanced, and you may even look younger because oxygen-rich blood is reaching your skin. Greater endurance replaces fatigue, sickness is replaced by health. You sleep better, look better, and feel better.

Practicing Postnatal Breathing

Chinese taijiquan masters developed a breathing skill they called chi kung by concentrating on what they were doing and focusing their thoughts into a spot three inches or about three fingers below the navel. This is called the dan tian. The first step to postnatal, or diaphragmatic, breathing success is to lie flat on your back, bend your knees, and place your feet flat on the floor.

Be careful to regulate your breath so every part of your body can relax. Cup your hands one over the other and place them on your abdomen about three inches below the navel. As you inhale, imagine the lungs and diaphragm pushing your hands toward your feet. Expect your hands to rise slightly as they ride your abdomen; however, they should feel like they are being pushed toward your feet. Do this for five to ten minutes each day.

Once you get comfortable with the first exercise, try it sitting, standing, and finally walking. Always pay close attention to the diaphragm and allow the lungs to fully fill with air. On every third breath, completely empty the lungs with a loud, forceful exhalation. This emptying of the lungs is great for clearing the head and oxygenating the blood, eliminating as much stale air as possible. Expect some dizziness at first, a positive sign indicating that more oxygen than normal is reaching your bloodstream. No need to worry; the dizziness will soon pass.

Proper postnatal breathing is a giant step toward a longer, healthier life. It is said an infant breathes from his belly, an adult from the chest, the elderly from their upper chest, the sick from the throat, and the dying from the mouth. Postnatal breathing is a key taijiquan quality because it increases awareness, endurance, mental capacity, and emotional stability. The breathing sets a rhythm for the training session and the deep, relaxed breath creates just the perfect atmosphere.

Taoist, or Prenatal, Breathing

Continuous breathing through the Taoist, or prenatal, method expands and contracts the diaphragm, which in turn compresses and releases organs in the abdomen. Consider this an internal massage thanks to the increase and decrease in pressure of the abdominal and chest cavities. A diet heavy on prenatal breathing has shown an increase in the function of the internal organs and stronger vascular circulation of the torso.

A secondary benefit of prenatal breathing is an increase in the circulation of blood and improved tonicity to the muscles in the urogenital area in both male and female taijiquan practitioners. Also benefiting from this type of breathing are the muscles and tissues of the lower torso, which support and hold internal organs in place, as well as stabilize the lower spine.

Currently under way are experiments where prenatal breathing is being used to help benefit males who suffer from prostate gland infections or enlarged prostate glands. Many taijiquan experts think that the continuous increase and decrease of pressure in the urogenital cavity may stimulate greater circulation, thereby improving the healing potential or preventing the onset of these diseases altogether.

Many taijiquan and breathing masters, however, are quick to point out the risks involved in prenatal, or reverse, breathing. Practicing incorrectly can lead to strain to the abdominal area and internal organs. A proper instructor is mandatory before incorporating this method into your practice. A safer bet is using postnatal breathing exercises. Not only is it a more relaxing way to develop health in beginners and casual *taijiquan* students, it is devoid of risks.

Prenatal Breathing and Martial Art

The original intention for matching breath and Taoist prenatal breathing with certain taijiquan postures was primarily for self-defense application. Many martial arts encourage their fighters to exhale when issuing strength. In fact, it is an accepted practice in many sports and physical pursuits (grunting in tennis, loud exhaling when throwing a punch in boxing) to let air out when reaching the peak of power. In taijiquan, where sinking the energy is popular at the time of issuing strength, prenatal, or reverse, breathing can be used to stabilize the lower back and "root" to the earth. Not only does it give you a feeling of firmness in the lower abdomen, it also preserves some air in your lungs. The martial result is a gain in stability and strength, projecting your opponent far away while maintaining sufficient energy for a smooth transition to your next move. The change from issuing force to

yielding and back again is a special characteristic of taijiquan.

During forms and function practice, no emphasis is placed on coordinating breath with movement. This prevents any interference with preestablished patterns. It is best to do the forms as they are taught and allow the body's natural rhythms to dictate speed of respiration while exercising. Recent scientific studies in sports medicine seem to discourage artificial regulation of breathing during physical exercise. Call it interfering with the body's own natural wisdom. According to the *Journal of the American Medical Association*, "The respiratory center of the brain, which receives chemical, reflex, somatic, and cerebral inputs, is a good computer in automatically regularizing the rate, depth, and pattern of respiration under various situations."

Because of numerous physical and mental factors, the beginning taijiquan student will consume much more oxygen than a longtime practitioner. A study in Taiwan showed that beginners consume four times the oxygen used by a veteran taijiquan student performing the same exercise.

Breathing properly can greatly enhance the health potential of taijiquan practice. Studies have shown that optimum results are obtained when a student works on breathing independent of forms practice and then allows his brain to make the necessary, natural adjustments in terms of how much or how little oxygen is needed. The more natural and smooth your breathing, the more natural and smooth your energy flow will be.

Let It Be

As explained by my teacher, Li Longdao of Emei mountain in Sichuan province, "The Taoist doctrine of *wuwei* is essentially the theory of 'letting it be.' As a philosophy of life this means that one should keep within the limit of one's nature and let the body functions take care of themselves."

Therefore, although manipulation of breathing during meditation is practiced by certain persons of the Taoist belief, it contradicts the fundamental Taoist philosophy of naturalness, which is a basic premise of taijiquan.

It is believed that people who want to use breathing for a different aspect of health benefits should practice separately from their taijiquan certain meditation or breathing exercises especially designed for this purpose, so that they may reap the benefits of each system fully instead of a compromise.

Breathing is important, but not to the extent that it requires conscious manipulation, an act that may sacrifice the quality of one's taijiquan practice. Learn to breathe and obtain the benefits from it, then carry on those aspects into the taijiquan practice. The taijiquan student who attains freedom from equating chi with atmospheric air or breathing will discover new understanding from the *T'ai Chi Classics*.

John Painter, Ph.D., N.D., is the director of The Gompa Center in Arlington, Texas. This material was excerpted from his new teacher's manual, Taijiquan and Health: A Western Medical Perspective on Taijiquan Practice. *This material originally appeared in the May 1998 issue of* Inside Kung-Fu.

Martial Arts and African Dance

The Hidden Connection

Earl White

"A man who loves music can make great progress in karate; a man who does not love music will never perform karate correctly."
—MAS OYAMA

The core of this article deals with African dance and how it can enhance one's art—in my case, kung fu. Any type of dance is beneficial, especially if you know what to look for and how to apply it to your particular system. Dances such as Spanish flamenco, Mexican hat dance, Irish jig, and tap dance develop tremendous foot speed, which complement systems that specialize in low kicks, foot stomps, sweeps, and leg checks. Ballet, jazz, and modern dance complement systems that require a wide range of kicking and agility. Also, the male folk dancing of the Russian and Ukrainian regions complement systems that require jump kicks and acrobatics, as well as grace (competition wushu).

The elegant hand gestures used to invoke certain spiritual and physical energy, which can be found in yoga and traditional religious Indian dance, are referred to as mudras. These have been said to

From the face-off position . . . the attacker throws a left hook to the body.

The defender (right) uses a single-arm wrap to lock the elbow and follows with a head butt or left elbow to the opponent's head.

He also could use a left knee strike to an open area.

influence ancient Chinese martial arts. In the Southern Philippines, music, dance, and fighting go hand in hand; the music gives the fighter (and/or dancer) his sense of rhythm or pace (his basic flow). If you wish to look more deeply into how dance relates to your martial art, look at the folk, tribal, and religious dances.

Moving History

Dancing and fighting are probably man's oldest forms of physical expression. The two art forms have tremendous similarities. Both require flexibility, grace, strength, endurance, coordination, explosiveness, speed, concentration, and focus. And both have the potential to be spiritually gratifying. Many martial arts instructors enthusiastically welcome dancers as students. Picture Mikhail Baryshnikov entering the doors of your training hall and wanting to study forms. You can safely assume you have a future forms champion.

Al Dacascos, a former fighting and forms champion in the late 1960s and early 1970s, was innovative with the use of contemporary music and traditional Chinese lion dance as a training aid within his schools. Dacascos's former wife, Malia Bernal, also a former fighting and kata champion of the same era, went on to create "Malia's Aerobic Defense."

Tayari Casel, known for his "kung fu versus karate" fight against Benny "The Jet" Urquidez, has done pioneering work in African dance and African martial arts, as has Kilindi Iyi, who is the author of two Unique Publications videotapes on African martial arts.

The full robe at right is called *agbada*. The robe is worn with sleeves rolled up or down to hide techniques or weapons. From the moment the opponent reaches . . .

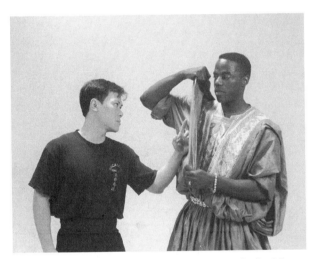

. . . the defender lifts his sleeve to block his foe's vision.

The defender then begins to cover his enemy's vision.

The sleeve is tightened to smother the opponent's face . . .

. . . followed by a choke.

The attacker fires a right punch.

The defender angles to his left with a left-hand parry . . .

. . . and begins a right-leg lift for a hinge kick. The hinge kick is executed to the knee or groin, causing the opponent to buckle over.

The defender then executes a flip kick to his enemy's face. He uses his right hand to guide the foe's face to the kick.

Other major contributors include Baba Ishangi, a pioneer of African dance in America. Bill Owens, a former fighting champion of the Northern California region and trainer of national and regional fighting champions, has done research on combative stick dances of Africa and the African diaspora. He also is the founder of Kusema Vijiti, a Swahili word meaning "talking sticks."

The World Kulingtang Institute, based in Reseda (Los Angeles), California, has done a wonderful job

The attacker goes for a shoulder-and-right-punch combination.

The defender uses his left hand to shield against the punch.

Shifting his weight, the defender shin kicks to his opponent's left leg. The defender's right arm slices through, striking his opponent's left arm . . .

. . . with a simultaneous left-hand eye strike.

of helping preserve the dances and martial arts of the indigenous people of the Southern Philippines. Billy Blanks, a number-one rated point fighter in the mid-1980s, has one of the most successful aerobic and martial arts studios in the Los Angeles area.

Ring of Honor

Some of the world's most famous boxers were known for their dancing ability in the ring. In 1892, heavyweight champion Jim Corbett was called a pioneer of "scientific" boxing because of his nonconventional style of footwork. Other fighters famous for their sweet moves were Sugar Ray Robinson, Jersey Joe Walcott, Sugar Ray Leonard, and—the most famous—Muhammad Ali.

Some Filipino martial artists believe the triangle foot pattern found in kali influenced the footwork of the Pinoy boxers of the 1930s through the 1950s. Also, the world's most famous martial artist, Bruce Lee, had his own training that required music. As a teenager he was a cha-cha champion and dance instructor in Hong Kong. Some traditionalists may find this connection strange, even disrespectful, but dance and music are not new to the martial arts world.

Ancient Greek writers chronicled the subject in relation to warfare of Ethiopians—not Ethiopians of the present-day country of Ethiopia, but people from the areas of Africa now called Libya, Egypt, Ethiopia, Sudan, and even present-day East India. Lucian Philopseudes, a Greek author, stated, "Even in raging war, the warriors did not shoot their arrows until they had first danced. The Ethiopians did not release their arrows, taken from the headbands, until they had first danced and terrified the enemy by their prancing." Heliodorus, a Greek author of *Aethiopica* (Ethiopian tales), stated that the Ethiopians would approach their enemies with twists and contortions. Their war dance involved abandoned vaults and styr-like leaps.

Dance and martial arts have an interesting, combined history that involves camouflage and assimilation. No discussion of the subject would be complete without a discussion of the Brazilian martial art, capoeira. Capoeira has some of the most sophisticated types of footwork and broken rhythm concepts in the martial arts community. Capoeira's dance influence allows for a tremendous amount of fighting creativity. Capoeira's deadly fighting techniques were hidden from the Portuguese by African slaves because of a law issued by the Portuguese banning all practices of religion and fighting arts. Instruments such as the drum and berimbau (musical bow) were banned as well—

the berimbau was considered the soul of capoeira. It calls the capoeiristas to the game (or fight) and tells them what rhythm to fight to and what style of fight to perform.

The indigenous people of the Philippines also camouflaged their sword- and knife-fighting with traditional dance; one of many involved the use of scarves in place of swords. As with the Portuguese of Brazil, the Spanish of the Philippines banned religious and fighting practices, as well as music, such as the kulingtang. Kulingtang was played during the warriors' practice in the fighting arts to set a rhythm and pace, as in capoeira. The ancient people of the British Isles adapted a stick-and-scarf dance from the African Muslims (Moors) who occupied parts of western and most of southern Europe from a.d. 711 to 1492. This dance can still be seen today in many European countries, known as the Moorish dance (England) and *Moorisco* (Spain).

It would be very difficult to define African dance, considering there are over fifty countries and at least 1,200 distinct languages. There are dances for war, healing, celebration, funerals, rites of passage, occupation, initiation, religion, and conflict resolution. There are specific dances that mimic water, wind, and fire, which represent forces in nature, similar to the forces of nature found in the Chinese internal arts of Hsing I and paqua.

Also, specific dances mimic animals and insects. The movements may be strong, angular, sharp, and acrobatic or soft, flowing, circular, and sensual. There are African dances to match the varied personalities of tai chi's fluidity to Shotokan's linear sharpness. There are also dances involving martial arts; some of these dances will never be seen by the general public because of their esoteric and religious natures.

So, the next time you watch one of those classic tap dance movies with Fred Astaire, Gene Kelly, and the Nicholos brothers—or, if you are fortunate enough to see Gregory Hines or Sevion Glover on Broadway—remember: there may be more in the dance than the tap.

From a fighting stance . . .

. . . a groin kick . . .

. . . causes the opponent to buckle over.

The defender angles slightly to the outside and begins a head grab.

The defender adds a slap kick to the enemy's face.

A side kick is evaded with a shift in body weight.

The defender counters with a combined elbow and knee smash to the enemy's ankle.

The attacker opens with a right-hand straight punch . . .

. . . which the defender shifts to avoid or absorb. The defender counters with a dropping elbow smash on his attacker's fist or forearm.

Selected Cultures with Martial-Related Dance

Location	Martial Art/Dance
Ancient Greece	pankration/Pyrrhic
Bali	*gabug/gabug*
Brazil	*capoeira/batuque, samba duro, maculele*
Burma	*bando/lai ka*
China	kung fu/ribbon dance, drum dance, lion dance
Cuba	*bombosa/mani*
Egypt	*tahteeb/tahteeb*
England	swordfighting/Moorish dance
Ethiopia	*dulla/dulla*
Hawaii	*lua/hula*
India	*kalari/nata*
Japan	karate, jujitsu/*gagaku*
Java	*pencak silat/silatbunga, baris*
Korea	*Tae Kyon*/folk dance
Madagascar	*morengey tambour/morengey*
Malaysia	*bersilat/pulut*
Martinique	*le ladjia/le ladjia*
Micronesia	*bwang*/folk dance
Northern Nigeria	*shakafa, kwambe/rawan gane*
Okinawa	Okinawa karate/folk dance, *hamachidori*

Location	Martial Art/Dance
Philippines	*escrima/sinulog, langka*
Senegal	*bure/doundoumba*
South Africa	Zulu stick-fighting/*geea*
South Western Nigeria	*gidigbo/gidigbo*
Sudan	*donga/donga*
Thailand	Muay Thai, *Krabi-Krabong*/folk dance, *Wai Khruu, Ram Muay*
Tonga	*luka luka/luka luka*
Trinidad	*kalinda/kalinda*

Earl White is a student and instructor of wun hop kuen do *(WHKD) kung fu under Al Dacascos and has appeared in three* WHKD *instructional videos. He also studies northern Shaolin kung fu under Jiang Hao Qwan and studied capoeira under Amen Santo. He has studied West African dance under Dele Adefemi, Malang Bayo, Nzinga Camara, and Keti. This material appeared in the May 1998 issue of* Inside Kung-Fu.

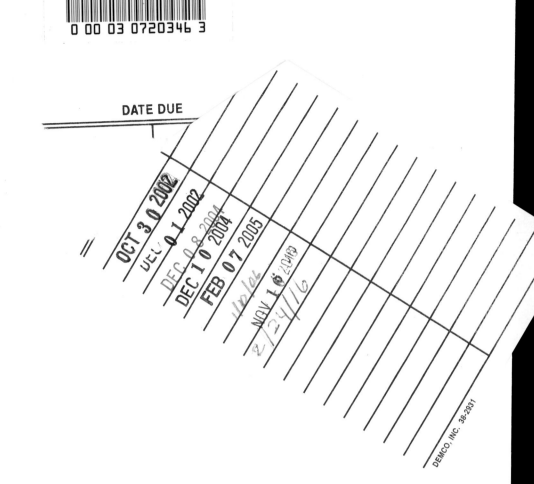